The Strange Transfiguration of Hannah Stubbs. [A novel.]

Florence Marryat

The Strange Transfiguration of Hannah Stubbs. [A novel.]
Marryat, Florence
British Library, Historical Print Editions
British Library
1896
339 p. ; 8°.
012627.h.5.

The BiblioLife Network

This project was made possible in part by the BiblioLife Network (BLN), a project aimed at addressing some of the huge challenges facing book preservationists around the world. The BLN includes libraries, library networks, archives, subject matter experts, online communities and library service providers. We believe every book ever published should be available as a high-quality print reproduction; printed on- demand anywhere in the world. This insures the ongoing accessibility of the content and helps generate sustainable revenue for the libraries and organizations that work to preserve these important materials.

The following book is in the "public domain" and represents an authentic reproduction of the text as printed by the original publisher. While we have attempted to accurately maintain the integrity of the original work, there are sometimes problems with the original book or micro-film from which the books were digitized. This can result in minor errors in reproduction. Possible imperfections include missing and blurred pages, poor pictures, markings and other reproduction issues beyond our control. Because this work is culturally important, we have made it available as part of our commitment to protecting, preserving, and promoting the world's literature.

GUIDE TO FOLD-OUTS, MAPS and OVERSIZED IMAGES

In an online database, page images do not need to conform to the size restrictions found in a printed book. When converting these images back into a printed bound book, the page sizes are standardized in ways that maintain the detail of the original. For large images, such as fold-out maps, the original page image is split into two or more pages.

Guidelines used to determine the split of oversize pages:

- Some images are split vertically; large images require vertical and horizontal splits.
- For horizontal splits, the content is split left to right.
- For vertical splits, the content is split from top to bottom.
- For both vertical and horizontal splits, the image is processed from top left to bottom right.

THE STRANGE TRANSFIGURATION

OF HANNAH STUBBS

NOVELS

BY

FLORENCE MARRYAT.

Each in cr. 8vo., cloth gilt and gilt top. 2/6.

MISS HARRINGTON'S HUSBAND.
MOUNT EDEN.
GERALD ESTCOURT.
LOVE'S CONFLICT.
TOO GOOD FOR HIM.
WOMAN AGAINST WOMAN.
FOR EVER AND EVER.
NELLIE BROOKE.
VERONIQUE.
HER LORD AND MASTER.
THE PREY OF THE GODS.
THE GIRLS OF FEVERSHAM.
MAD DUMARESQ.
NO INTENTIONS.
PETRONEL.

London:
HUTCHINSON & CO., 34, PATERNOSTER ROW.

THE STRANGE TRANSFIGURATION OF HANNAH STUBBS

BY

FLORENCE MARRYAT

AUTHOR OF

"*Love's Conflict,*" "*My Own Child,*"
"*My Sister the Actress,*"
etc., etc., etc.

"*There are more things in Heaven and Earth, Horatio,
Than are dreamt of in your philosophy.*"—HAMLET

LONDON
HUTCHINSON AND CO.
34, PATERNOSTER ROW
MDCCCXCVI.

PRINTED AT NIMEGUEN (HOLLAND)
BY H. C. A. THIEME OF NIMEGUEN (HOLLAND
AND
27 SHOE LANE, LONDON, E.C.

THE STRANGE TRANSFIGURATION OF HANNAH STUBBS

CHAPTER I.

"SIGNOR RICARDO, Prof. of the Italian Language!" That was the legend that was engraved on the small brass plate that surmounted the bell that admitted visitors to Mrs. Battleby's lodging-house in Soho. Signor Ricardo was everything that was estimable in Mrs. Battleby's eyes, only he was, as she observed to her next-door neighbour, Mrs. Blamey, "a Mystery". He was a tall, attenuated man, who stooped slightly in the shoulders—had dark-grey eyes, keen as those of a hawk, and shaded by bushy eyebrows—a perfect aquiline nose—and a grave, almost solemn mouth, which seldom smiled, and ended in a pointed beard, like that of Vandyke. He was very poor, being an Italian refugee, whose estates had been confiscated for some political error, but he was eminently a gentleman of the *ancienne noblesse*, and preserved the dignity of his birth, even whilst pursuing an occupation which is considered to place a man beyond the pale of Society.

"He's as good a lodger as ever I had," said Mrs. Battleby, on the occasion referred to, "as reglar as a clock, both in his 'abits and his payments—every Saturday mornin' he dislocates my little bill, though I believe he's sometimes sorely put-to to find the money, and every evenin' he's 'ome by eight o'clock and has his bit of supper and puts his light out by ten, but arter that—well! he's a Mystery!"

"Lor! Mrs. Battleby, ma'am, you don't go to think he's murdered anybody, do yer?"

"*Murdered anybody!*" repeated the other, with withering contempt, "why, he's the aimabeloust gentleman you ever come acrost. He wouldn't hurt a fly, the Sig-nor" (Mrs. Battleby pronounced the word Signor, with a decided accentuation on the letter *g*), not to save his own life! And got no temper in him. Never 'eard a 'arsh word, nor a hoath pass his lips. If you'd only seen him onst, you'd never arsk if he was a murderer, Mrs. Blamey!"

"Then 'ow is he a Mystery, which it's a word I never could abear."

"Well! it's this way. When the Sig-nor come to me, now three years ago, he hired three rooms at the top of the 'ouse. I had better rooms I could have let him 'ave, on the floor below, but no! nothing would suit him but my top rooms, hattics as I call 'em, and I had to turn Mary Ann—that gal as went off with the postman—out of her bedroom in order to accommodate him, and he's lived there ever since. One is his bedroom and the other his parlour, as you may suppose, but would you believe it, Mrs. Blamey, as I've never seen the inside of my own third room, ever since the Sig-nor has been with me!"

"My! what do he do with it?"

"'Ow can I tell? I tell you he's a Mystery! The first day I went up to clean his floor, I found the door locked, and when I arsked for the key, the Sig-nor he says to me, 'Excuge me,' he says, for he's the politest of gentlemen, 'but I will see after that room myself.' 'Lor! Sir,' I says, 'but if it's books or papers, I'll be as careful as careful,' I says, 'but you can't never struggle with the dust yourself.' But he was as firm as a rock, and that there door has never been unclosed to my knowledge since."

"Mrs. Battleby, ma'am, you gives me the cold creeps all down my back! Suppose he should be Jack the Ripper, and congeals the corpusses in your third room. Stranger things 'ave 'appened before now! I think it be'oves you as an 'ouseholder to break open the door!"

At this suggestion, Mrs. Battleby looked for a

moment confounded, but in a short time her confidence in the respectability of her lodger, not to say the remembrance of his regularity in paying his rent, restored her equanimity.

"No! Mrs. Blamey, no!" she replied, "wild 'orses shouldn't make me do it! I'll never believe no bad of the Sig-nor, though he *is* a foreigner, and many's the one as has warned me against him. And he has the respectablelest of friends. Doctor Steinberg is here five days out of the seven, and I've heard tell as the Sig-nor teaches Royalty to speak the I-talian langwidge. In course he is a foreigner, there's no denying that, but it ain't 'is fault, and I'd be the last to throw it in his teeth! But lor! here's the Doctor coming along as usual, and he and the Sig-nor will be closetted for hours together."

The conversation was here interrupted by the arrival of a young man of about thirty, who had fair hair, worn longer than is usual in this country, and whose short-sighted eyes appeared abnormally large through the powerful glasses he was compelled to wear. He was a German of the name of Steinberg, and the profession of medicine—a clever fellow who was rising fast, and knew how to make the best of his opportunities. He was interested in Signor Ricardo for several reasons, and was, as Mrs. Battleby had said, a frequent visitor there.

"Is the Signor in?" he demanded, as he came up with her.

"Yes, Sir! he came in half an hour ago. You might be sure of that! He is so regular that I calls him my clock."

"And alone?" continued Steinberg.

"Quite alone, Sir!"

"Very good! Don't disturb yourself, Mrs. Battleby. I will find my way up to his rooms."

And so saying, he passed her and ran lightly up the stairs.

"Anyways I must go," observed the landlady, as he disappeared, "for that gal of mine is so stupid I can't trust her to do a single thing alone. I don't know what my old friend Mary Stubbs was thinking of to arsk me to take her. She's no more good than the fifth wheel of a coach! I believe she's got a maggot in her brain. I found her making the kitchen table hop round the room yesterday, and when I told her not to be fooling like a child of five year old, she said she hadn't touched it. If I hadn't been a fool myself, I shouldn't never have consented to try a gal, as had never been to service before, and come fresh from the country, like a turnip out of a field. But her mother and me, we was brought up together, and she wanted to get Hannah into service away from Settlefield where they live--something to do with a lad as she wanted to marry, I believe—and I gave in. But she's likely to prove a plague to me, for she's always crying after her lad, and if I do hate one thing before another, it is a love-sick gal. You might as well have a basin of gruel to help you in the 'ouse!"

"She'll soon forget 'im in London," said Mrs. Blamey consolingly, "there are plenty of lads about! She'll 'ave another in a fortnight!"

"I dessay," returned Mrs. Battleby, "but meanwhile she'll do more damage than she's worth. She broke half a dozen bits of crockery this week, a rattling them about, and when I tell 'er to keep 'em quiet, she cries and says she can't 'elp it! Well, good evening, Mrs. Blamey! P'r'aps the Sig-nor will be wanting a little something extry for his supper, now that the Doctor's come to spend the evening with him."

And the neighbours parted until the next idle moment should arrive, in which they could relieve their minds by chattering like two magpies to each other.

Meanwhile Doctor Steinberg had run lightly up the staircase until he had reached the third story and tapped at his friend's door. The Signor gave the permission to enter, and his thin face lighted up with pleasure as he caught sight of Steinberg.

"Ah! the dear young man!" he exclaimed, in English, which was quite intelligible, though rather broken, "and have you come to cheer my solitude? That is very good! Now I shall have a pleasant evening! I want it, my good friend, for I have had a most fatiguing day."

"I can see that you are weary," said the young doctor, as he grasped his hand, "and more than that, Signor, you are weak. I am afraid that amidst your multifarious duties to others, you forget your duty to yourself! Your pulse is very feeble. You have neither eaten nor drunk enough to-day. I hope you have prepared a hearty supper for yourself!"

"I know nothing! My good Mrs. Battleby arranges all these little affairs for me! I had a good breakfast before I started this morning, but as for the mid-day meal—well, it is difficult for me to eat when I am tired, and even if I could, it would be still more difficult to digest. My stomach is feeble, Steinberg. If you could give me a new stomach, my kind friend, I know you would, but it is impossible. The machine will go on working a little longer, and for myself I care not how soon it may stop altogether!"

"No! no! you must not say that! Why! you are not fifty yet. You have a good thirty years before you in which to enjoy life and make your friends happy."

"Friends, Steinberg! with the exception of yourself, where are my friends?"

"O! you have more than you think for, Signor, and at all events one is enough to try and make you look after yourself. You are not so weak as you imagine. If you would rest by night, you would not feel the fatigue of the day so much. But these studies that you will pursue, are killing you! They would try the strength of the strongest man, repeated as they are with you, night after night, but added to the strain made upon your physical and mental faculties by day, they will end by landing you in your grave!"

"Then I shall have gained my desire," said the Professor, with a faint smile, "and the Great Secret will be solved!"

"Perhaps! but why, then, not wait for the Change which must inevitably come to all of us, to discover what lies beyond?"

"Ah! you do not know—you do not understand——" said the Professor, "my heart is being burnt up with longing and desire. I cannot rest! there is no peace for me unless I am striving to find out one thing—to solve one mystery—I feel as if I cannot die until I have found it out!"

"Found *what* out?" repeated Steinberg, "what is this secret you are so eager to discover the solution of? Will you not confide it to me?"

The Signor looked at the young scientist curiously, as though questioning whether he could trust him. Presently the gloom cleared off his brow and he murmured,

"Why not? You are my friend—my only friend. You would preserve it as I have done. But will you join me in trying to find the Secret out?

Will you also dip into the mysteries of Occultism, and hold converse with the Unseen World?"

"That I cannot promise you," replied the Doctor, "certainly not until I know what it is you are striving for. Remember, that I know but little of your doings, except that you shut yourself up in that little room for half the night and sit up poring over old books and manuscripts, long after you should be in bed and asleep. I conclude you study Witchcraft and Black Magic! Well! I am a Lutheran and have been reared to consider such studies wrong, and practised only by the children of the Devil, but I know nothing of them myself. What is your object in thus ruining your health? I cannot imagine any sane man who has duties in this world to fulfil, caring about such rubbish. True or false, leave it to those who have no more serious aim in life, and think only of your health and yourself!"

Ricardo leaned back in his chair and smiled furtively.

"Now, what is the use of it?" continued Steinberg, pertinaciously.

The Professor answered the question in a way that startled him.

"Have you ever loved?" he said.

"You must tell me first what you mean by the word."

"Have you ever loved a woman intensely—

passionately—loved her so much that your life was fused in her life—your soul in her soul?"

The Doctor sat up in his chair and stared at his friend. For a moment he thought he had gone mad.

"*Never!*" he said, emphatically. "As a rule, I have not cared for women. I look upon the sex as a necessary evil—something without which population cannot go on—without which, too, Nature could not exist—but as something also to be avoided as much as possible, and dealt with as little as may be!"

Ricardo sighed.

"Happy man!" he ejaculated at last, "you are to be envied, Steinberg. You have missed great happiness, and great pain."

"Happiness!" echoed Steinberg, "is it possible, Signor, that your grave demeanour and your mysterious studies have anything to do with a woman?"

"They have everything—everything, to do with it," exclaimed the elder man, excitedly. "Steinberg, I have never told you my history. You do not even know who I am! If I confide in you, will you hold my confidence sacred?"

The Doctor held out his hand.

"Most certainly ·I will. There is my hand on it. But do not stir up painful memories for my sake, Professor! If you are endeavouring to forget the Past, let it lie in it's grave!"

"I wish you to hear it," replied Ricardo, "I am old, I might go any day. You are my only friend. I should like you to know the truth before we part!"

"Why do you talk of yourself as an old man? What age are you?"

"I was forty-nine on my last birthday."

"Nonsense! You are in the prime of life. This intelligence still further confirms my belief that your appearance and weakness are due to your unnatural studies alone."

"But the pursuit of which holds the only consolation this world can afford me," replied Ricardo. "Wait till you have heard what I have to tell you, Steinberg, and you will acknowledge that I am right. First, then, as to my identity. My name is not Ricardo. I am Paolo, Marchese di Sorrento, the last member of one of the oldest families in Italy."

"A nobleman!" cried Steinberg, "and in this humble position? For what reason? What brought you down so low, as to be compelled to work for your daily bread?"

"A political offence, my friend, and not of my own doing! A plot against the Government, in which several nobles were concerned, and being the intimate friend and associate of most of them, my name became unfortunately mixed up with theirs, and I found my property and estates confiscated, and myself banished from Italy, before I hardly knew what it was all about. It was a great misfortune, but many have suffered in the same way. I came to England as the only land in which I could make a little money by teaching my native language, and I have managed to exist since and have found several pupils in noble families, as you well know. But my father's name—the title that had been handed down and honoured through so many generations—I could not retain that! It would have been an infamy—a degradation!"

"No wonder that you have aged before your time—that you are of so melancholy a temperament," observed Steinberg. "Your misfortunes have been sufficient to kill you."

"Ah! do not mistake me, my good friend! This reverse, however cruel, could not have had the power to sap my life-strings in this manner. There was worse behind it—so much worse that the blow of losing my name and money fell almost scatheless upon me! I had already lost my world."

Steinberg remained silent, waiting for him to proceed.

"I asked you just now if you had ever loved, and you told me, 'No'. You are right! Keep to your resolution. Never allow yourself to be entangled in a woman's wiles, for they are Death to those who trust in them. When I was only one-and-twenty and had just come into my father's estates and title, I fell a victim to the charms of

Leonora d'Asissi, a young lady my equal in rank and position, and after a brief courtship, we were married. Ah! Steinberg, how I loved—I adored—that woman! You, who confess to having never experienced the tender passion cannot enter into my feelings. We Italians are famous for our ardent love, and no Italian ever loved more ardently than I did. I lived only in her presence; I was never weary of contemplating her exquisite beauty; I waited on her as a slave; I made the day and night tremulous with the repetition of my love. Do not we often weary women by telling them too often that we love them, Steinberg? Are they fickle by nature, or is it only that they hate monotony? Any way Leonora, my adored wife, wearied of me and mine. She could not bear to remain in our beautiful villa in the country, where she saw no one but her enraptured lover, but pined to return to the palazzo in Rome which has been in our family for generations. Here, she would collect around her all the young married women like herself, with their attendant *cavalieres serventes* and turn night into day with her balls and feasts and concerts. And yet I suspected nothing!"

"Was there anything to suspect?" demanded the Doctor.

The Professor started in his seat.

"Ah! now you touch the root of the matter! Was there? *Was* there? The question haunts me night and day. But I was jealous, Steinberg, all my nation are! Where Love is so warm, doubts will intrude themselves. Perhaps we expect too much from women. Their natures are not so passionate as ours. We tax them too much—we look for a flame as ardent as our own—and when we do not find it, we begin to suspect it is bestowed upon another man. When I had my Leonora all to myself—when in the silence of night, her beautiful head lay in peaceful sleep upon my breast, I believed nothing but good of her—but when I watched her whirling round the ball room in the arms of some one of my acquaintance, or found her sitting in the conservatory with another, Suspicion would lay hold of my jealous temper, and I would question if after all, she were deceiving me, and everyone knew the bitter truth but myself."

The recollection of those days of anguish seemed to overcome the Signor even then, for he pulled out his handkerchief, and wiped the moisture from his brow.

"The relation distresses you," remarked Steinberg, "pray do not proceed."

"No! no! I shall not stop now until you have heard all. I have gone too far already. Amongst Leonora's acquaintances was a young man, a mere lad called Lorenzo Centi. Some one made a joke about her and this boy before me and aroused my suspicions concerning them. I found Leonora on more than one occasion sitting apart on a couch with young Centi—once, with their hands clasped together—and I forbad him the house in consequence. But a rumour reached my ears that, when I was away from home, my wife's woman was used to fetch Centi to her, and they spent the time of my absence together. I determined to watch. I professed to be going for a night into the country to see after my farm, but I returned at midnight, and found them supping together in Leonora's boudoir. I rushed in upon them furiously, and my wife turned and laughed in my face—knowing all my deep love for her, she laughed at my disappointment and she drove me mad. Before God, Steinberg, if she had only cried, or seemed frightened, or sorry, I should have spared her—I loved her so intensely—but her laugh raised all the Devil in me and before the smile had left her lips, she lay dead at my feet."

The stoical German sprang away from Ricardo's side. He had been prepared for much, but not for murder.

"No! no! you must be mistaken," he exclaimed; "you do not mean that you killed her!"

"*Killed her!* Of course I did, and would have killed her lover into the bargain, but that he escaped before I could lay hands on him. She laughed at my distress, and I stabbed her to the heart with my dagger. Better dead, a thousand times, I thought, than live a lie! But now—now——"

"You are sorry—you repent——" said Steinberg, sympathetically, "Yes! I can understand it perfectly! But it was done in a moment of anger—you were not master of yourself—you would act very differently were the time to come over again."

"Not if she were false," cried the Professor, "I would kill her over again this moment, if she deceived me! But did she—did she? That is the question that harasses me now."

"What! have you any doubts upon the subject?"

"I have every doubt—they torture me day and night. What proofs had I of her guilt? She was young and careless and very, very beautiful! Might she not have played with fire without considering the consequences—without being burnt? She laughed at me, it is true—but she did not know the depth of a man's love—the strength of a man's jealousy.

"She did not think, my poor Leonora, that my hand was on the fatal weapon I carried in my breast. Ah, Steinberg, it is better like you never to have known the rapture of possessing a woman, than to feel you have sent her out of the world, when perhaps she was innocent."

"It is terrible," said the Doctor, "but was it never cleared up?"

"*Never!* In my country, we think far less of such things than you do in yours. A husband who kills his wife through jealousy, and especially when he has found her with her lover, is too common an offender to provoke condign punishment. I was had up before the tribunal to afford an explanation of my wife's death, and the reasons I gave were considered sufficient. I left the country afterwards, more to escape from my maddening recollections than to avoid Society—I also had a burning desire to meet young Centi and give him his due, but he was so successfully concealed by his family, that I never gained my wish. Perhaps it was for the best. My hands might have been imbrued in a second unnecessary murder! When, after many years' wandering, I ventured to return to Rome, it was to find that my estates were no longer mine, and I was doomed to exile. Now, you have my history, Steinberg, and you may thank God that you have escaped so sad a one!"

Karl Steinberg was silent for awhile—so was his companion. This narrative had rather shocked the German's sensibilities, while it had excited great sympathy for the lonely man before him, who had been bereft of all he held dear, or that made life worth living for him.

The Doctor, with his want of faith in Women, had not much doubt in his own mind that the Signor's wife had merited her doom, but he declined to express an opinion on the subject either way. After a few minutes' pause, he said, with the view of turning a conversation which had become so painful to both of them,

"But what has all this to do, Professor, with your study of the Black Art?"

CHAPTER II.

RICARDO looked up dreamily, as if he had quite forgotten that part of the subject.

"Have I not told you?" he inquired; "do you not understand?"

"Indeed I do not! I am quite in the dark about it! You have related to me the painful story of your poor wife's death, with which I fully sympathise, but I do not trace any connection between that and your interest in Mysticism."

"How strange! How very strange!" replied Ricardo, shaking himself together. "Why! to me they are one. My one object in life now is to learn the truth—to hear if I were only the rightful agent to avenge a great wrong, or if my mad jealousy prompted me to commit a murder. It is for this reason alone that I have studied, as far as I am able, the Art of Magic, and pored over my books and my experiments half the nights through, in order to gain an answer."

"But how can that avail you, Signor? Do you

expect the Spirits of Evil to aid you in this matter?"

"No! no! Leonora herself! It is for Leonora only that I sit up night after night, listening for a sign, a whisper—straining my eyes for a glance, a shadow—but it seems all in vain. I must have help, and in this house, surrounded as I am by curious eyes, I know not how to obtain what I require."

"And do you really believe that your dead wife will be able by the aid of Magic to return to you in bodily shape and satisfy your curiosity on this subject?" questioned the Doctor, almost amused at the idea—so impossible did it appear to him.

"Why not? Why not?" inquired Ricardo, impatiently. "Others have come, and why not my beautiful Leonora? Surely, you do not disbelieve in the possibility of the spirit's return to earth? It has happened in all ages! Why not in this?"

"I know too little of the matter to be able to give you a sensible answer," said the Doctor, "but if possible, it seems most undesirable to me. These things will all be cleared up for us by and by, in the Hereafter, if there be an Hereafter. Meanwhile, cannot you persuade yourself to wait patiently until you join your wife in the Great Beyond? If you committed an unfortunate error and she was innocent, why disturb her in the rest she must have gained? —and if, on the contrary, she really deceived you, may you not be doing yourself an injury by drawing back to earth a malevolent spirit, who may still be harbouring thoughts of revenge against you?"

"No! no!" said the Professor, shaking his head, "you will not convince me I am doing wrong, or rob me of my one unceasing hope to see and speak with her again. It is the awful doubt, the suspense, that has turned my hair grey before its time, and made my voice quaver like that of an old man. If I could only raise her from the dead for one little moment—hear her say, 'I am innocent, and I forgive you!' I should ask no more—I should live contentedly and die happy!"

"And what means do you take to this end?" demanded Karl Steinberg, who could not help feeling a certain amount of interest in the matter, since his friend appeared so earnest over it.

Ricardo looked round the room as though to assure himself that he had no listeners—then rising, went to the door, and having locked it, turned to Steinberg, and said,

"Come with me and see my séance room!"

He stepped towards the door of the third room, which constituted him such a Mystery to his landlady, and which opened from the one in which they sat, and turned the key. Steinberg followed him curiously, but all he saw was, that the small apartment was hung round the walls and over the window and floor, with black stuff, and that it contained no furniture, unless a couple of cushions thrown on the ground can be called so.

"No air and no light!" exclaimed the Doctor. "And what do you do here?"

"When the household have gone to bed," said Ricardo, mysteriously, "and I am sure of not being disturbed, I shut myself in and burn the different incenses recommended in the books of Magic, and after a while the spirits come, and sit down on the floor beside me."

"Do you mean me to believe that?" exclaimed Steinberg, staring at Ricardo as though he were insane, as indeed, at that moment, he believed him to be.

"You can believe it, or not," replied the Professor, "but it is true."

"Impossible!" cried the Doctor, "you let your imagination run away with you. You work so hard all day and permit this morbid fancy to occupy your tired brain by night, until it has become in a measure, diseased. I know you think you see and feel these things, but it is a species of delirium or mental intoxication, bred of your intense longing to accomplish what is unaccomplishable."

"Very good," said Ricardo, quietly, "if you believe that, you must believe it! But what would convince you of the truth?"

"Nothing but the evidence of my own senses, whilst they were in the calm condition they are at present."

"If that is so, my friend, stay here and sit with me to-night. Then your own senses shall convince you."

This proposition took Steinberg by surprise. He was not entirely free from the universal dread of anything like communication with the Unseen World, although he had expressed his disbelief in the possibility, but his fear was mingled with curiosity, and the result was that he assented to Ricardo's proposal.

"I will, Professor," he said, "if only to try and show you that your supposed spirits are merely shadows cast upon the wall."

"A wall which has no light wherewith to cast shadows," remarked Ricardo, sarcastically.

"Well! well! that they are shadows thrown on the retina of your eye by reflections from your brain," replied the young Doctor, somewhat testily, for he did not like to be refuted on his own ground, "any way that the spirits of the dead have nothing to do with anything that you may see, or hear, whilst shut up in this little room."

"We are not arguing on what I may see or hear, Steinberg, but on what may strike your senses. Neither did I affirm that the living things that visit me, are spirits of the dead. My studies have taught me that there is a class of secondary spirits called Elementals, that have had nothing to do with this earth, but who yet can and do come to the aid of those mortals who solicit their assistance. The vapoury forms that appear to me may be only Elementals, but they come, all the same."

"If they come, they must be worth the trouble of investigation, if only in the interests of Science," remarked Steinberg, thoughtfully, "but after all, will it not resolve itself into the same old truth that we have been brought up to believe, *i.e.*, that we are surrounded by evil spirits always ready to whisper bad thoughts into our ears, and stimulate our worst inclinations?"

"But if evil spirits, then also good," interposed the Professor eagerly, "you surely would not deny the same power to all those departed this earth. If devils, then also my Leonora, to speak with whom I have been promised over and over again, and feel I only want more power to accomplish."

"Well! at all events I will sit with you this evening, Professor, and try to see as you do. But I hear footsteps on the stairs. Had you not better close the door of your sanctum, and turn the conversation to some lighter subject?"

Ricardo locked the door carefully, putting the key in his pocket, and by the time Mrs. Battleby appeared with the supper tray, the two friends were talking gaily of a new drama that had just created some sensation in the town.

"I wish you would come out with me sometimes, Professor," the Doctor was saying, "it would do you good to see some of these novelties and listen to the discussions over them."

"Ah! that it would, Sir," said Mrs. Battleby, who was never backward in joining in the conversation, "it would do the Sig-nor all the good in the world, instead of poring over them nasty, musty vollums of his, as must be enough to make any gentleman's 'ead ache."

"No! no! no!" exclaimed Ricardo, waving their suggestions away with his hand, "I cannot! It is impossible! I have other things to do."

"Or if you would 'ave your friends here more of an evening, Sir," continued the landlady, "nice, light-'arted young people, as could play the banjo to you and sing a bit, I'm sure it would cheer you up, and dissolve you from your studies."

"Nonsense! you don't know what you're talking about," exclaimed the Professor, impatiently. "Put down the tray, Mrs. Battleby, like a good creature, and leave the Doctor and me to ourselves. We have some important matters to discuss."

"Certainly, Sir," said Mrs. Battleby, as she bounced the tray down on the table with an energy that proved her wounded feelings, "and I 'ope as when you rings the bell, you won't mind my gal Hannah coming up to clear, as I've got a little marketing to do, and I knows you don't like the things lying about too long."

"O! dear no," said Ricardo, "let Hannah clear

the table by all means, and tell her to be quick about it, Mrs. Battleby, as my friend and I have business to attend to."

"Very good, Sir!" replied the landlady, as she left them to themselves.

Steinberg and Ricardo soon dispatched the simple meal set before them, and then the former, drawing out his watch, remarked that if he was to get home that night, he thought they had better set to work in their search after the Invisible World.

The Professor accordingly rang the bell, which was answered by a young woman whom he had never seen before, all the waiting in his room being usually performed by Mrs. Battleby. The stranger was about eighteen years of age, and looked as if she had just been transported from a stack-yard, or a cow-house, and set down in Soho. She was not at all attractive to the sight. She had a thick, ungainly figure, with a waist like a tar-barrel, and huge hands and feet. Her bosom was unusually developed for so young a girl—her face was broad and flat—her mouth wide—her nose short and turned-up, and her colour coarse and high. But to counteract all these failings, Hannah possessed a wonderful pair of grey eyes, set wide apart in a low forehead—eyes that looked you through and through, and yet had a far-away dreamy gaze that was very provoking to Mrs. Battleby who declared the girl was always more than half asleep. Hannah also rejoiced in a thick mass of light brown hair, which made her head seem much too large for her body. Taken altogether, she was uncouth, but there was an innocence and simplicity in her gaze which was very attractive when one had the time to discover it. As she stood silent on the threshold of the Professor's room, the men both thought she was one of the stupidest, most countrified lasses they had ever come across.

"Are you Hannah?" asked Ricardo, and on receiving an answer in the affirmative, he added,

"Well! your mistress said you were to clear away my supper tray, and when you have done that, you can bring me up a jug of hot water, and then you must not disturb us again to-night. Do you understand?"

For the girl was looking at him so stolidly, that it seemed doubtful if she had even heard what he said to her.

"Yes, Sir!" she answered, in a dull, low voice, as she piled all the plates and dishes on the top of one another, preparatory to making a grand smash if she should happen to slip going downstairs again.

"What a lout!" was Steinberg's observation, as Hannah disappeared.

"Just so," said Ricardo, "a simple piece of clay—a heifer newly driven from pasture—an animal with all her senses undeveloped—but not without a soul! Did you remark her eyes? They are unfathomable! I should be curious, had I the time, to find out what lies beneath them."

"Holloa!" cried Steinberg, with a laugh, "take care of yourself, Professor! Finding out what lies beneath women's eyes, is dangerous work! You might even animate this clod in your researches."

Ricardo regarded him reproachfully.

"Do you know me so little, as to jest on such a subject?" he said. "I, whose whole soul is bent on one object only. Steinberg, will you believe me when I say, that since Leonora died beneath my hand, I have never looked at another woman with even a semblance of the same feelings? I was only thirty when I drove her soul from me, but I have been widowed ever since, and shall remain so to my grave!"

"It's a mistake to take these things too seriously," replied his friend, "it is better to have lived as I have, caring for no one and regretting no one—for you see when a gap occurs I am able to fill it up without delay or compunction."

"Ah! I could not live like that!" said the Professor with a sigh. "With me it must be all, or nothing! Leonora was my All. I could kill her, but I could not replace her. Well! are you ready?"

"Certainly, when you are."

Ricardo rose, and (Hannah having re-appeared with the hot water) produced various pungent spices and gums, and with dried herbs and other mysterious preparations from a drawer, commenced to separate them into measured portions and to crumble them into a bowl.

"What is all this about?" demanded Steinberg, who having lit his pipe and got a tumbler of hot grog by his side, was disposed to view his friend's doings from a humorous point of view.

"It would take too long to explain a mixture to you, which it has taken me years to collect and assimilate," said Ricardo, "but it is the only potion that I have found really effectual—the only one that has brought the spirits round me. Some of these essences and oils came from India. An old friend of mine out there, took the trouble to collect and preserve them for me, and others I have paid far more than I can afford, for, but the result has been worth it all, as you shall judge for yourself!"

"But how, in the name of all that's wonderful, can a few scents, however potent, have the power to attract, or cause to be visible, spirits of air?" demanded the Doctor.

"You must tell me first what those spirits are composed of," replied the Professor. "You, as a medical man, know that our bodies are composed of chemicals—it stands to reason therefore, that our spiritual bodies are composed of the same, though varying from the earthly ones, as they themselves do. When you can give me a list of the chemicals, or essences, composing the spiritual part of ourselves, I may be able to find out why certain decoctions attract them hither and enable them to become visible to mortal sight. The fact is, Steinberg, it is all a great Mystery, which perhaps we are not intended to solve. But what is not a Mystery? Can you tell me that? What are Birth and Death, but unfathomable Mysteries, that we shall never know the meaning of, in this world? We accept them as ordinary things, because we see them happen every day, but we know no more about them—how they happen or how they are to be prevented—than you know of this mixture, which is now ready to be set alight to."

"Come on, old friend, then," replied the Doctor, as he led the way into the séance chamber.

Ricardo carried a lighted taper, and matches, which he was careful to secure in his pocket, for it was like a vault they entered. The sombre hangings which enveloped the apartment, shutting out both light and air, and the musty smell which came from them, mingled with the stale scent of the incense, made the place feel uncanny. Ricardo walked up to the cushions on the floor, and told Steinberg to seat himself on one of them. Having deposited himself beside him, and set alight to the incense, he blew out the candle, and the wreathing smoke which ascended from the bowl was the only illumination in the room.

Steinberg began to feel uneasy, notwithstanding

his vaunted incredulity. The German nation is famous for its many tales and legends of ghostly lore, and however our reason may seem to disprove their authenticity, our faith is prone to cling to the truths which have been instilled into our minds during childhood.

As he watched the smoke curling up towards the ceiling, Steinberg felt unusually cold—the little room seemed to fill with a chilly wind which blew upon his face and hands—and the silence which his companion maintained served to increase the gloom.

"May we not talk?" he whispered, presently, to Ricardo.

"Certainly, if you feel so inclined," returned the Professor, "but for myself, the occasion always seems so solemn, that I can only hold commune with my own thoughts and think of—her!"

"And you are not in the least alarmed?" inquired the Doctor, who had felt his companion leaning very hard against his shoulder, as if for confidence and support.

"Not in the slightest. I am awed—but not frightened," was the reply.

"Why, then, do you lean so hard against me?" said Steinberg.

"I am not touching you," replied Ricardo, "I am too far away! I am not seated on the cushion now, but in the centre of the room."

"Not seated on the cushion?" repeated Steinberg. "Then—in God's Name!—*who is?*"

"How can I tell? I have already said that I am not near you! Doubtless one of the spirits who visit me, is anxious to convince you of his identity. Speak to him, Steinberg! As yet, I have been unable to make them speak to me! You may be more successful."

But the Doctor had already rolled off the cushion towards the door.

"Let me out!" he cried, "I will not stay here a moment longer! I told you when you first made this infamous proposal to me, that it was diabolical! —that none but evil spirits could be induced to hold communication with men. And this must have been a devil, I am sure of it, else he would have had the decency to give me some warning, before sitting down beside me. Open the door, Professor! I have been brought up a Lutheran, and my Church forbids all such practices as these. I refuse to stay in this room any longer!"

"All right! It is all right!" said the Professor, as he drew the key from his pocket and unlocked the door, "you are frightened, that is all. I thought you would not be so brave when you came to see and feel them. But how about it's being all my imagination, eh, Doctor?"

Karl Steinberg, restored to the light, felt that he cut rather a sorry figure. His cheeks were blanched with terror, and his limbs shook from the same cause. But he tried to laugh it off.

"Now, confess, Professor, that you have been playing me a trick," he said, " it was you who came up and leant so hard against me, wasn't it? You thought you'd catch me tripping, you know, and put me in a blue funk. But you haven't succeeded, I'm as cool as a cucumber!"

Ricardo looked at him reproachfully.

"You are wrong," he replied, "and you know you are wrong! If it were I, and you knew it, why didn't you throw your arms round me? Why did you insist upon leaving the room? And why do you look so blue about the mouth and chin? Ah! no, my friend, you know it was not I, as well as I do! And such a pity too! They were coming so beautifully. They have never come so quickly before. You are just the man to help me. Come now, come back for a little, and I will promise to sit close to you all the while!"

And he laid his hand on that of the Doctor, as he spoke. But Steinberg pulled his vehemently away.

"No! no! not for all the world," he ejaculated, "I will not play with the Devil any longer! You must conduct your diabolical practices by yourself."

"But you will acknowledge they are not fraud then—that there is something to be frightened at?"

"I will acknowledge nothing! I am not in a fit state to argue the matter to-night. To-morrow, perhaps, I may be able to judge more calmly. All that I can say is, that I refuse to enter that room again."

"If I could only persuade you," continued the Professor, "if you had only waited a little while and watched the smoke from the bowl, you would have seen such beautiful forms shaping themselves amongst it! Women and little children like cherubs—sometimes I have sat up all night unable to tear myself away from so beautiful a sight!"

"All emissaries of the Evil One," replied Steinberg, who was still shaking from the scare he had received, "sent perhaps to lure you to your destruction. Take care what you are about, Ricardo! Some morning you may be found missing—dragged down to the Infernal Regions by these demons, who assume the appearance of Angels of Light in order to deceive you."

"*The Infernal Regions!*" exclaimed the other, excitedly, "and what would they signify to me, if I am never to see, nor speak, with my Leonora more. Ah! Steinberg, I forget! You know nothing but the name of this Love, which could turn Heaven into Hell without the presence of the Beloved One, and vice vêrsa. Had you loved and lost as I have, you would sit in that room, not a night, but every night, till you heard some news of her who made your world."

"Perhaps," replied Steinberg, stolidly, "but you see, I haven't."

"But you will try again, will you not? You will come when this first alarm has subsided, and see if you cannot stand it better? I, too, felt fear when first I sat alone and watched the spirits rise from the incense I had lighted, with my own hands. But that has all gone! I am as calm now as the dead themselves! And so will you be, if you will only try again!"

"*Never!* Not for all the wealth of the Indies would I enter that accursed room of my own free will, again. I am going, Ricardo! I don't feel well! I think the smell of the incense has upset me! Forgive me for leaving you so soon, but I shall be better at home. Good-night!"

He ran hastily down the stairs as he spoke, and the Professor, ruminating on the little trust there is to be put in one's friends in time of need, retired sadly to his bed.

CHAPTER III.

SIGNOR RICARDO passed a restless night. His disappointment preyed upon his mind and robbed him of sleep. He had so long wished to ask Steinberg to join him in his pursuit of Occultism—had so depended on his assistance—and prophesied their mutual success—that the Doctor's abject terror at his first experience, had thrown cold water on all his hopes.

Leonora seemed further off than ever, and he groaned in spirit to think she might be so near, and yet he was unable to communicate with her, and ascertain if he had been right or wrong in the indulgence of his revenge. Had his dead wife stood before him then, he would hardly have known what he most desired to hear her say. If she declared her innocence, his rash act had made him doubly guilty, yet if she confessed that he had been right, she was lost to him for ever.

But the Signor hardly thought of that—the burning truth was all he wished to discover. The real fact being, that Leonora had been all and much worse than he had ever believed her to be. She had been a heartless coquette of the worst dye—vain, deceitful, and self-seeking—caring nothing whom she wounded, so long as her insatiate vanity was gratified—with no thought, so long as she gained her cause, over whose dead bodies she trampled on her road to Victory. She had been guilty with Lorenzo Centi, and half-a-dozen other men, and the death-blow which her husband's dagger gave her, was the very smallest punishment which she deserved.

Yet Ricardo was not satisfied. With Leonora, whom he had so fondly worshipped, dead, his belief in her iniquity had died also, and all his fear was, lest he had slain a woman who loved him as much as he loved her. And he knew of no way by which his doubts could be laid to rest, except by bringing her back from the grave to tell him the truth with her own lips.

As he lay in his narrow bed that night, he conjured the Almighty by every petition he could think of, to permit her to return, if only for a moment, and allay his bitter fears by one means or the other. But no answer came to his prayer. No sound nor sight came out of the darkness to afford him the consolation of knowing that his prayer had reached the Throne. His Heavenly Father had deserted him; he was a child left out in the darkness and the cold; left to find his way home by himself. If he wandered from the beaten track, who could blame him? No helping hand was stretched out to guide him; no light appeared in the distance to show him the way; he must penetrate the Mysteries of Nature by himself, and as best he could. Once or twice during that long night, the Professor fancied he saw a faint, tremulous movement of the curtains that hung round his bed—thought he heard a whisper penetrate the air;—but he listened, and strained his eyes in vain—nothing more rewarded his rapt attention.

"Leonora! my beloved!" he said, in a low voice, as he sat up in bed, and tried to pierce the gloom with his mortal vision; "Leonora! come to me—speak to me! Tell me the truth! I will not be angry now! I know we all have sinned, and you were but mortal like myself—only solve these doubts. If you were innocent of wronging me—if that bitter blow was a foul injury to your faith to me, I will bear the purgatory it will bring me, thankfully, only to know that you are dwelling in the Light of God! And if it was only an act of justice—if, in the heat of your youth and carelessness, you were unfaithful to your marriage vow, I forgive you, my Beloved, —I forgive you from my heart, and will tell you so, as soon as we meet in another world. Only come to me, my wife—only look at me! whisper one word of affection, and I shall live and die, content!"

So the poor lover and husband raved, only to be

answered by silence and gloom. Leonora was there! He felt it, but he had not sufficient power by himself, to enable her to manifest her spiritual presence to him. If Steinberg would not sit with him, he must find some one else—for he could not stand the suspense and anxiety much longer.

He tossed and turned in his bed until daylight, and rose with the earliest dawn, worn and haggard, with the intention of walking in the Park before he took his breakfast. It was seven o'clock as the Professor turned out of the front door of his dingy lodgings—an unprecedented thing on his part, for he usually sat up so late, that he did not leave the house until his first lessons were due. As he reached the lower passage, he found the front door open and the girl Hannah cleaning the steps. Ricardo passed her with a bow, for he was a most courteous man in his dealings with women, but Hannah's head was bent upon her work, and she did not see him. As Ricardo gained the pavement he turned and looked at her. She was kneeling in the attitude in which such work is done, and her slip-shod shoes which had half fallen off, left her feet, encased in black worsted stockings, well exposed to view. They were large feet, as has been said before, and two holes in her stockings left the naked heels bare for the admiration of the passers-by. The Professor stopped for a moment and regarded those heels. They were not pretty perhaps, but they were rosy and firm, and undeniably youthful, and somehow they inspired him with a certain amount of compassion, to think that such young flesh should have to bear its burden of life so soon. He stood as though transfixed by the sight of those two rosy heels. No thought of lust, or even admiration, entered his mind, which was far too sensitive and refined for any feeling of the kind, but they excited his pity, and carried him back somehow to the days when he, too, was young and innocent. He felt as if he wanted to say something kind to the poor young girl who had begun so early to drudge for others. The rosy heels, though only seen through the ugly medium of a pair of ragged stockings, attracted him as a callow nestling with gaping beak, or a little pink apple hanging in an orchard might have done. He would have no desire to possess the callow bird, and the idea of eating the sour apple would have set his teeth on edge—yet they would have carried with them a memory of the days when he would have enjoyed them both—and in this light he felt drawn towards Hannah Stubbs as she scrubbed the front door steps. He had a shilling in his pocket, and he stepped back to give it to her. Perhaps a shilling might represent many things that would give pleasure to the little household drudge—but as the Professor drew near to her the second time, he perceived that Hannah was crying and the tears were dropping on the flags she knelt upon, and mingling with the hearth-stone. Tears in the eyes of a woman always excited the Signor's sympathy, and, forgetting the shilling, he inquired eagerly why Hannah wept.

The girl looked frightened at being detected in such an act of self-indulgence.

"It's nothing, Sir—nothing!" she exclaimed, as she hastily rubbed her eyes with her knuckles and smeared her face over with the hearth-stone.

"O! come, that cannot be quite true," replied Ricardo, "I'm sure you are not so foolish as to cry for nothing! Perhaps you have left your friends for the first time, and are new to service, and it seems hard to you. Is that so?"

The girl seemed grateful for the enquiry.

"It ain't that, Sir," she said, shaking her head, "In course I was sorry to leave mother and father and the rest, but 'tain't that as makes me cry. We've all got to arn our bread, and mother said it was time I was doing of something—and she will be so angry if I goes 'ome again so soon—that she will!" and Hannah commenced to sob anew.

"But why should you go, Hannah? Is not Mrs. Battleby satisfied with you?"

"No, Sir, I'm afeared not, though I does all I can, but she's angry with me a'cause of the plates and dishes which they keeps slipping about, but I'm as careful of them as I can be, Sir, and I can't 'elp the tables and chairs 'opping round the room—and whatever mother will think I don't know! She'll say it's such a disgrace, but it ain't my fault—Boo-hoo-hoo!" and here Hannah commenced to blubber afresh, till the Professor began to fear that she would attract the attention of the passers-by.

"Now, look here, my good girl," he said, "don't cry, or you will make Mrs. Battleby still more angry. The neighbours will think she has been beating you. Listen to me! Mrs. Battleby's a good soul, though rather strict perhaps, but I've known her a long time, and if you'll promise me to dry your eyes, and be as careful as you can of the china, I'll speak to her on your behalf when I come back from business this evening, and see if I cannot induce her to give you another trial."

"I'm sure you're mortal good, Sir," said the girl, as she dug her knuckles afresh into her eyes.

"Never mind the goodness! You do your work as well as ever you can, to-day, and I'll see what I can do for you on my return. What is your other name, Hannah?"

"Stubbs, Sir! I'm a Shropshire girl—was raised there, and never left the village I was born in till mother sent me to Lunnon. Lor! how I wish she 'adn't! Father is that hard on me, and what they'll say if I'm sent back in disgrace—Mother and Joe and all—I'm sure I don't know!"

"Who is Joe?" asked the Professor, kindly, "your brother?"

"No, Sir! My young man."

"Your young man! So you have a young man of your own already! And why did you come out to service, then, Hannah? Why did you not marry Joe instead?"

The girl gave a conscious grin as she replied:

"*We* was willing enough, Sir, but mother wouldn't hear on't. She said Joe hadn't enough to keep hisself, let alone me, and that a few years' service would do me all the good in the world. But it seems 'ard for to leave 'ome and all."

"Never mind, Hannah! I daresay your mother knows best, and the time will pass quicker than you imagine. Any way I shall not forget to speak for you to Mrs. Battleby, so good-morning!" And Ricardo went on his way, smiling slightly to himself.

Since the fatal night when his hand had sent the woman he loved best to her last account, Ricardo had felt very tenderly towards all women, for her sake. He was so dreadfully afraid of making another mistake about them. He thought more of this shapeless, ungainly girl as he took his walk in the Park, than he could have believed possible—not of her ugliness, nor awkwardness, nor little troubles—but of those mysterious wonderful eyes of which she did not seem conscious, but which looked as if they saw that which was invisible to every one else. How strange that such eyes—so the Professor thought—should be set in so rough a face and figure; eyes, which the greatest beauty in the land might have envied, combined with a shape which no decent housemaid would have cared to exhibit.

If Hannah's eyes had not been so mystical in appearance, would the Signor have borne her ordinary troubles so faithfully in mind, and spoken with Mrs. Battleby about their alleviation on the first opportunity? It is doubtful! Man, however supine, is apt to be led by his fancy. Any way, when his landlady made her appearance with his evening meal, he opened the subject at once.

"Mrs. Battleby, my good friend, I want to speak with you, on behalf of your little maid, Hannah! How has she offended you? Is she very stupid, very clumsy, very impertinent? Why do you propose to send her back to her good mother, who will doubtless be unpleasantly disappointed to see her again."

"Has Hannah presumed to complain of me to you, Sig-nor?" demanded the landlady, becoming instantly stiff and rigid with indignation.

"O! no, indeed, but I take interest in the troubles of the young. We have all been young, Mrs. Battleby, and all been ignorant and wilful and done silly things. I saw this young girl weeping this morning and stopped to ask her the reason, and all she said was, that you intended to send her home again and she feared her people would be very angry with her."

"If you'll excuse me taking a seat, for them stairs try my breath dreadful," said Mrs. Battleby, as she plumped herself down on one of the Professor's chairs, "I'll tell you all about it. Send 'er 'ome indeed! I should think I would, and it's the last kind act I'll do for Mary Stubbs as long as I live. We was neighbours-like, Sig-nor, this gal's mother and I, and so when she arsked me to take 'er gal and give 'er a trial, I said 'Yes', never thinking, may the Lord forgive 'er, as Mary Stubbs would 'ave put off a daft gal on me as trusted 'er."

"Is poor Hannah really daft, whatever that may mean?" asked Ricardo.

"And that she is, Sig-nor, and ought to be in the Hidiot Hasylum, if all had their doo. Why! she's done nothing since she come here, but 'op about after the tables and chairs."

"Hop about after the tables and chairs?" echoed the Professor, with open eyes.

"It's God's truth Sig-nor, and nothing else. I've seen the kitchen table, which it must weigh 'alf a ton, waltz after that gal all over the kitchen, and she'll set the cups and saucers and glasses spinning like tops. And then when I remonstrances with 'er, she'll cry like a ninny and say she's not done nothing. The way in which she's broke china since she's bin in this 'ouse is wicked. And I won't stand it no longer—that's flat, for if she don't do it, why, the Devil do, and 'ome she must go!"

"But, Mrs. Battleby, one moment! I do not quite understand you. If Hannah does not make the furniture dance, who does?"

"That is what I want to know, Sig-nor! But 'ow the gal moves a heavy table is beyond me. Nor 'ow she makes the glasses spin! But if I remonstrances with 'er, as I said before, she do nothing but cry and say 'tain't 'er fault, which is all nonsense. And so back she goes to Settlefield, as soon as I've got some one to take 'er place!"

"It is very curious," remarked the Professor, pensively, "and there must be some solution of the problem. Do you think that Hannah would make the table dance for me, Mrs. Battleby?"

"Lor, Sig-nor! don't you go a tempting of Providence! Let the gal and 'er tricks alone!"

"But I am interested in what you have told me, from a scientific point of view! There may be a reason for it all, and if so, I should like to find it out. Would you have any objection to my seeing Hannah by herself this evening, and questioning her on the subject?"

"Dear me, no, Sig-nor—not if you'll take the trouble! But you won't get nothing for your pains. She's just obstinate, that gal is, and cries if you hold up your little finger at her!"

"Does she suit you in other respects, Mrs. Battleby?"

"O! she ain't no better nor wuss than others. Them gals are all alike—a set of sloppy, dirty, careless 'ussies, as don't care if you go to gaol next week all along of their breakages and lies. In course you can interlude Hannah whenever you choose, Sig-nor. I'll send 'er up to clear as soon as you've 'ad your tea, and then you can 'ave a talk with 'er. But you won't make nothink out of it, them's my words! But that's the Doctor's knock, as sure as sure! Well! he is a good friend to you, Sig-nor, and no mistake!"

"Yes! I am glad he has come! I hardly expected him after last night," replied the Professor, who was quite excited at his new thoughts regarding Hannah Stubbs.

Karl Steinberg entered the room with an outstretched hand, as the landlady curtsied and disappeared.

"Forgive me, Ricardo!" he exclaimed; "I was a fool last night, and worse than that, too great a coward to confess it! I was horribly nervous and alarmed, but thinking the matter over has made me see the folly of which I was guilty. But I am convinced, that if you were, as you declared yourself to be (and I cannot doubt your word), in the centre of the floor, there was some force ulterior to my own in that little room last night, and I will not rest till I have found out the truth. Will you re-admit me to your séances? Will you forgive my first alarm, and let me pursue the study of the Occult with you?"

"My dear Karl!" exclaimed Ricardo, heartily shaking his proffered hand, "nothing would give me greater pleasure. But if we are to go in for these researches together, and in earnest, we must try and think of some plausible excuse for our spending our nights together, as I find my landlady, Mrs. Battleby, is much opposed to anything that she cannot understand. We have just been holding a conversation respecting her maid-of-all-work, Hannah Stubbs."

Ricardo then went into the subject of his talk with Mrs. Battleby at some length, and was pleased to see the interest which it excited in Doctor Steinberg.

"Have the girl up by all means," he said eagerly, "she may be what I have heard you call a physical medium, and we may evolve great things from her. She is countrified and stupid, you say! She probably in that case knows nothing of her own powers, and is frightened at the effects which she produces. I saw her last evening, did I not? She is just an animal, with grand vitality and perhaps magnetism —with any amount of bodily strength, and no brain. Have her up, Ricardo, by all means, and let us see something of these mysterious powers of hers."

"If she will display them," replied his friend, as he rang the bell.

Hannah appeared, looking as stolid as before, but with a faint smile for the gentleman who had promised to intercede for her.

"Shut the door, Hannah, and sit down. I want to have a little talk with you," commenced the Professor, gently, "I have been having a few words with Mrs. Battleby, and she says the only fault she has to find with you is that you can make the chairs and tables dance. Will you try and make them dance now, that my friend and I may see?"

The girl looked startled and edged towards the wall as if she wished to avoid contact with any of the furniture of the room.

"O! no, Sir, please don't arsk me," she said in a scared voice, as she glanced timidly in the direction of the tea-table, "'tain't my fault indeed, I've told the missus that over and over again. I don't know nothink about it, and I wish they wouldn't come after me—I do indeed!"

All this while, with her skirts gathered up tightly in her hand, Hannah was looking fearfully in the direction of the table, which now commenced slowly, but perceptibly, to move towards her.

"O! it's a'coming," she screamed. "O! stop it, Sir, do, for the Lord's sake! What do it want with me? I ain't got nothing to say to it! O my! O my!"

Meanwhile the table had advanced to her until its edge was against her body.

"Do you see that, Steinberg?" observed Ricardo, "The furniture has actually moved without contact. This is very marvellous!"

"Go away! go away!" cried Hannah, as she kicked at the legs of the table which was now pressing her against the wall. "O! Sir, please don't go to tell the missus, for it never was so bad as this before—never!"

"By Jove! look there!" exclaimed the Doctor, as a sound drew their attention in another direction, and they turned to see the Professor's rocking chair, quietly rocking by itself in the corner of the room.

"I never saw such a thing in my life before," said Ricardo. "Steinberg, this is a very wonderful girl. We must try to keep her to ourselves, at all events until we have solved the reason of her powers."

Then he turned to Hannah, who presented a ludicrous spectacle, squeezed up in a corner of the room by the table, and crying loudly without any means of drying her eyes.

"Stop that noise, my dear girl, do!" he said. "Don't be afraid! No one shall hurt you, and you cannot suppose that a table could! But my friend and I are very much interested in this strange power of yours, and would like to see some more of it. I shall ask Mrs. Battleby to let you come up here in the evenings when she does not require your services, and we will see that you are rewarded for your trouble. You are not afraid of Doctor Steinberg and me, are you?"

"O! no, Sir—only afeared of the tables and things as will foller me about whether I will or no! And it's not the fust time as the beastly things 'ave got me into trouble, neither!"

"O! it's not the first time, is it, Hannah?" inquired Steinberg, "and what harm did they do you before, my girl!"

"Harm enough," replied Hannah, blubbering, "they parted my Joe and me! His family was so nasty about it! They said they wouldn't 'ave their furniture broken for nothing, else maybe Joe and me could 'ave lived along of 'is mother, and I'd never gone to service at all!"

"Well! never mind, Hannah! If Joe is a wise young man, he will come after you and marry you, whether his tables dance or not. And, meanwhile, my friend and I would like to see all that you can do!"

"I can't do nothing, Sir!"

"Then who is it that does it?"

"Ah! that I can't tell you,—only that it's always been the same with me from a child! I've had many a beating for it! I often wish I'd been dead afore they've come after me!"

"What! the tables and chairs?"

"Yes, Sir! and other things as well—shadders and the like, as come round me of nights, and woices as talk to me. I 'ates them woices more than anythink, for Mrs. Brushwood (that's Joe's mother, please, Sir), it was all along of 'er 'earing one, one day, as made the rumpus between us. And then mother said I must go to service and shake it off. But they've been just as bad here as in Settlefield."

"Well, Hannah, will you take my advice?" said the Professor, "trust yourself to the Doctor and me and we'll cure you of this nonsense. It's all due to your health, you know!"

"Thank ye, Sir, but I can't take no pills, please! Mother, she's tried 'em with me scores of times but they always sticks in my throat till I retches 'em up again. Nor I can't swaller jalap. It goes against my stummick. But anything else, gentlemen——"

"Be easy, Hannah, we will not ask you to take either pills, or jalap. All we want is an hour or two of your time now and then! But I will arrange all that with Mrs. Battleby."

CHAPTER IV.

As the girl left the room, scrambling sideways, much after the manner of a crab, and glancing behind her the while, as if she feared the table might take a fancy to follow her downstairs, the two men looked to each other and smiled.

"I fancy you have lit on a gold mine there, Ricardo," said the Doctor, "there is something very marvellous about that girl. She must be a well of magnetism. I never saw such an effect produced upon inanimate objects before. Do you think there can be any trickery about it? These brainless creatures are sometimes uncommonly cunning."

The Professor was leaning back in his chair thoughtfully, supporting his chin on his hand.

"I don't know *what* to think about it," he said at length, "but I am determined to see more of her powers. Now, the question is, what excuse can we make to Mrs. Battleby for asking this girl to give us a few hours of her time, every now and then."

"The landlady has seen something of it already,

I think you told me, and does not approve of the proceedings."

"Very strongly disapproves of them! Declares that Hannah must go back to her people in the country—that she is a fool, or a cunning trickster, or the Devil is in the whole concern."

"And I am much of Mrs. Battleby's opinion," remarked Steinberg.

"What! that it is done by agency of the Devil? Nonsense! man, nonsense! If the Devil was all that was required to produce such marvels, we should all do the same. No! no! the girl is a medium—but of what kind, I am as yet unable to determine."

"I'll tell you what we can say," interposed the Doctor, "if the landlady is opposed to the girl's practices, she will not be sorry to have them cured. Tell her that I attribute the whole business to the state of Hannah's nerves—that she is a victim to what we call hysteria—and that if she will allow me to treat her for the complaint, I will undertake to cure her. And I say it with truth, Ricardo, for should she be shamming, I will soon find it out, and expose her; and should she be as you conclude, a medium, the exercise of her powers will be a drain upon her system, and prevent the exhibition of them elsewhere."

"I believe you are right, Steinberg, but where have you derived so much knowledge about media and their powers, considering that until this evening, you have refused to approach the subject of Spiritualism at all."

"I have declined to join in the pursuit of it, my friend, you mean. You cannot suppose that I have not heard, nor conceived some interest in, a matter which half the world is talking of to-day. But what I have read has predisposed me against it. I feel that it is fraught with more danger than good. For a sensitive man like yourself, I am sure it might, under certain circumstances, be *very* dangerous. That is one reason that I have determined to join you in your studies. If there is any fear of harm, I will share it with you. What you said last night concerning your desire to open out a communication with your late wife, set me thinking deeply. If you draw her spirit back to earth, how can you tell that it will be for her good, or yours—how can you tell, indeed, that it is her spirit or that of some wandering Elemental (as you called them yesterday) who may take her shape? This is the danger I would share with you! If, on the other hand, good and pure spirits can return to earth, I am anxious to have the privilege of speaking to them. Do you understand my motives now?"

"Perfectly," said the Professor, grasping his hand. "And now for Mrs. Battleby."

But they found the landlady rather hard of conviction. In the first place she did not believe the phenomena were due to anything but Hannah's "cussedness", and if the gentlemen only knew as much of gals as she did, they would think the same; "wants to shirk 'er work, that's what she do, and leave all the washin' up and dirty work to 'er missus"; and in the second, she did not see how she could afford to spare her for two or three evenings a week, when there was more work than they could get through together now.

"What should I want to 'ave 'er cured for?" she demanded, "it'll be better and cheaper for me to send the 'ussy 'ome to 'er mother, who ought to be ashamed for having sent 'er my way at all, than to keep 'er here, a'worritin' me day and night, and spending 'alf 'er time up with you gentlemen. Which I'm much obliged, I'm sure, and so Hannah ought to be, for your kind intentions, but in my opinion, she ain't worth curing!"

The Professor looked in despair at the Doctor, and Steinberg gallantly came to the rescue.

"You forget, my dear Mrs. Battleby," he commenced softly, "that I, as a medical man, take the greatest interest in a case like this. In fact, it is not too much to say that I would pay a good deal to keep Hannah Stubbs under my own eye for a few months. If you are determined to part with her, of course there is nothing more to be said about it, but I shall endeavour, in that case, to re-engage her for some of my brother professionals. But I thought I might manage to see her here and more conveniently, and benefit you a little into the bargain. Now—supposing you agree to let Hannah remain under your protection, what would be the cost of having in a woman to look after the house during your possible absence, and do her work, every evening for a couple of hours?"

"I don't know, I'm sure, Sir," replied the landlady with a sniff, for she did not like the interest being excited by "that 'ussy Hannah", "there's more things to be considered than the work. I may not care, nor more I don't, to 'ave a stranger a'messing over my property, and a'picking up everything as she can lay 'er 'ands on whilst I'm away."

"I see!" replied the Doctor, thoughtfully, "then name your own conditions, Mrs. Battleby, and I will see if I can agree to them."

"I don't know as I have any conditions to name, Sir," said the woman, still more ruffled, "the gal's my servant, and can't leave me any'ow under 'er month, and me without 'elp of any kind. But if you wants to 'ave 'er up here of an evening, and physic 'er and all that sort of thing, why I don't like to refuse a offer made in kindness, and p'r'aps you wouldn't consider as to pay 'er wages would be too much compensation for all the trouble and ill-convenience it'll put me to."

"Perhaps not!" replied Steinberg, who had taken upon himself to be spokesman on the occasion, "but what are her wages?"

"Ten poun' a year, and heverythink found!"

"Now, look here, Mrs. Battleby," continued the Doctor, "as this is a case which promises to afford me some interest and to be phenomenal——"

"Lor! is it raly?" exclaimed the landlady. "I didn't think the pore gal was as bad as that!"

"——I am willing to pay you ten shillings a week so long as we shall require her services—I mean, until I shall have cured her complaint, or pronounced it incurable! We doctors are always ready to pay for our little fads, you know!"

"And 'andsomely, too, I'm sure, Sir," exclaimed Mrs. Battleby, now wreathed in smiles at the prospect of getting her drudge for nothing, "and I gives my full permission for Hannah to attend on you here hevery evening, if so be you wishes it!"

"O! no! thank you! Three times a week will be quite sufficient, if you will give us the whole evening from after tea to supper. I am so often with my friend Signor Ricardo, that it will be more convenient for me to operate on her here, than at the hospital."

"O! lor, Sir, you're never a'going to cut up the pore gal, sure-ly!"

"No! no! indeed! Make your mind easy, Mrs. Battleby! I intend to treat her by an entirely new process which, if I am not mistaken, will have an almost immediate effect in preventing those nervous tremors which seem to assail her."

"O! Sir, if you'll cure 'er of them, I shall be thankful, for she must shake like an aspen leaf. I found 'er in the kitchen jest now, a'laying with 'er arms over the table trying to keep it down, and it was bumping under 'er as if it 'ad gone mad!"

"Ah! Electricity does wonders in these days, you know, Mrs. Battleby, and I promise Hannah shall be quite herself again in a short time."

"And now, my dear Professor," he said, as the landlady took her departure, "having settled Mrs. Battleby, what means shall we try by which to make the girl hold her tongue downstairs, about anything she may see or hear whilst with us?"

"These means," replied Ricardo, as he chinked the loose coins in his pocket.

"They do not always answer," said his friend, "and this seems a very simple and innocent sort of girl, who might be terrified out of her life if she guessed the real reason of our getting her to sit with us. I think it would be better to persuade her that she has a species of St. Vitus's dance, and that it will get worse and worse unless I cure it in time. I'll tell her, too, that she must be a little worse before she's better, and, between the dread of being sent home again and the dread of becoming incapacitated for work, I think we shall manage to make her hold her tongue."

"I shall leave that part of the business to you," said Ricardo. "You are more used to wheedle the ladies than I am. You doctors are terrible fellows! You keep a dozen weapons in your pocket for assuaging feminine fears, but I fancy you'll have to use them all upon poor Hannah."

The upshot proved that the Professor was right. The friends agreed to meet again upon the following evening, when Hannah was summoned as soon as she had cleared away their tea, and introduced to their designs.

At first the case seemed hopeless. Nothing would induce the girl to permit her powers to be used as a proof of what she could do. She declared that she was too much frightened of herself—that her one desire was to prevent such incomprehensible things occurring—and that she was sure, like Mrs. Battleby, that the Devil was in it, and prepared to drag her down to destruction.

Her tears and entreaties were pitiable to see and listen to, and for a while, the men thought their endeavours had been in vain. But when she was a little quieter, the Doctor took her in hand, and having commenced his practice by the administration of a composing draught, he explained to her, after his own fashion, that he and his friend only meant kindness by her, and wanted to cure the very things of which she complained. If she would place herself under their guidance, he said, he would guarantee to send her back to her family, quite cured of the annoyance she objected to.

Hannah opened her beautiful eyes wide, and listened. To be cured meant to be in favour again with Joe's people, and perhaps to become Joe's wife much sooner than she anticipated.

"But how can you cure me, Sir?" she asked, wonderingly. "It's summat in my fingers as makes the things dance! I don't do nothing, Sir, I assures you, and I 'ates it, I do, like cold pison."

"Then you'll be all the better pleased to get rid of it, Hannah," he replied, "but that is quite impossible unless you will give way to the feeling at first, and let me see just how it acts. Now! don't be frightened when you see the articles approach you! The Professor and I do not scream and run away. Stay by us, and let them do as they choose!"

"But I can't, Sir," cried the girl, breathlessly, as she attempted to evade the close attentions of an arm-chair, "they frightens me out of my wits. I wonder whatever I've done that dumb brutes won't leave me alone."

But though Hannah, with the assistance of her new friends, managed to set all the furniture in the room spinning, without being more alarmed than was evinced by her gasping and screaming and clutching either one or other of them by the arm, nothing would induce her to enter the séance room. As soon as the door was opened and she saw the black funereal hangings, she gave a shriek, and fell backwards into the Doctor's arms.

"In there?" she screamed, "but what for? I've never been in sich a dark 'ole in all my life! And what do you want to do with me there? Are you going to cut me up? O! Mrs. Battleby! Mrs. Battleby!"

Her yells alarmed the two scientists, who feared all their plans would be knocked on the head by an untimely irruption on the part of the landlady. So they slammed the door to, and pulled Hannah into the lighted room again, and tried to compose her by slapping her on the back and addressing her with soothing words.

The girl lay in the arm-chair in which they had placed her, seemingly more dead than alive. Fearing that the shock had really injured her, they were just about to call for help, when a gruff, manly voice spoke at a distance of two or three feet above her head.

"Don't be fools! Leave her alone! She'll go into the cabinet when I tell her to do so."

The Professor and the Doctor looked around them in amazement. Who had addressed them? The room was empty. Their faces now began to look scared at this new Mystery, until Steinberg whispered to his friend,

"She spoke to us last evening of 'Voices.' This must be one of them! I am certain it did not emanate from her own lips. Ricardo, this is better than I anticipated! Light is already breaking through the darkness. Depend upon it, this girl has been a medium for years, without knowing it, and we shall be the means of developing her occult faculties. Let us interrogate our unknown ally. Are you a friend?" he continued, addressing the invisible owner of the voice, "will you tell us your name? Are we doing right? Will you help us in our researches?"

But to these questions there came no reply. Hannah seemed to be sleeping in the chair, but presently she rose to her feet and with a deep sigh, as though she was doing something against her own inclination, staggered into the dark séance room, and seated herself upon the cushions.

"Shall we follow her?" demanded Steinberg of Ricardo.

"I suppose so! I do not know what to think. This is a totally new experience to me!"

Notwithstanding they did follow the girl, whom they found apparently sleeping on the floor, her figure being thrown across the cushions. Something awed them to that extent, that they did not dare close the door and shut out all the light, but left it slightly ajar, so that a ray from the gas lamp was thrown like a bar of pale gold into the gloomy room.

Then they crept up to Hannah's side, expecting they knew not what, and bent over her prostrate form.

"What will happen next?" said Steinberg.

"We must wait and see!" replied Ricardo.

"You won't have to wait long!" exclaimed the same voice which had addressed them before, "didn't I tell you that when I chose the medium would enter the séance room?"

"She *is* a medium, then?" said the Professor.

"Rather! One of the finest mediums this world has ever produced. But you must be careful how you use her! She will assimilate with any spirit that possesses her!"

"Are we doing right?" demanded the Doctor, "will our curiosity injure this girl?"

"I will take care that you do not injure her! That is what I am here for."

"Who are you?"

"The guiding control of this medium."

"I mean, who were you, when you lived upon this earth? Or did you ever live here?"

"Did I ever live here? How do you suppose I found my way back if I had never lived here? Of course I did. But as for your other question, I don't see that it is any concern of yours. I might deceive you so easily, that I had better begin by telling you the truth, and that is that I have no intention you shall know my real name. You can call me James."

"Will you tell us, then, why you come to us?"

"I did not come to you! I accompanied my medium. I led her to you. I have long wished to place her suitably, and I think you will treat her gently and use her well."

"I hope we may. We are both much interested in the Science of Spiritualism, and want to find out all about it. Do you think we shall succeed?"

"Everyone would succeed who put a great discovery for the good of mankind in the first place, and their own selfish interests in the second."

"Are our desires selfish?"

"I fear they will become so, if you do not put a check upon them."

"Teach us how to pursue our inquiries," said Steinberg.

"Show me my Leonora!" cried the Professor.

"There it begins, you see," replied the Voice. "The second speaker wants to see his wife again, never mind at what cost or risk to others. Was I not right in saying your desires would become selfish? It has not taken long either!"

"But, Spirit (if you are a Spirit)," exclaimed Ricardo, "you must read my thoughts and know what prompted my request. Surely nothing could be more innocent than the desire of a husband to see his wife again?"

"I am not sure of that!" replied the Voice, "however, if you persevere, I have no doubt that your wish will be gratified. It is impossible to credit what would occur, if people would only have the patience to wait for it."

"I could have the patience to wait for ages if necessary," said the poor Professor.

"You will not have to wait so long as that," said the Voice, "she is nearer to you than you think."

Whilst Ricardo remained silent under this unexpected joy, Steinberg put a few questions to the influence that was controlling the medium.

"Will you answer me a few questions, James?"

"Certainly! If I am able."

"Are you speaking to us in your own voice—I mean, have you a throat with gullet and larynx fully formed of your own?"

"No! I am talking now through the medium, that is, I am using her vocal organs—perhaps you perceive the difference in my voice. When I spoke to you in the other room, I had materialised a gullet and larynx of my own, but I could not sustain a lengthened conversation through them!"

"Will Hannah know what has happened to her, when she awakes?"

"No, and I beg you will not tell her. She is very ignorant and simple, and the effect might be harmful. Let her believe that she has merely been to sleep. And now I have used her long enough for the first time and had better go. Do not try to rouse her. Let her wake of herself. She will be hysterical, but the Doctor will know how to deal with that. Good evening!"

And here the Voice ceased. Though they addressed it several times, no sound or sign of any kind came through Hannah. She slept on like an infant, while the two men whispered to one another.

"Wonderful! Marvellous! I could not have believed such a thing, unless I had heard it myself! What a grand prospect lies before us! How glad I am, Ricardo, that I overcame my cowardly fears, and agreed to join you in searching out these mysteries!"

"The Voice said that Leonora was near me! I feel sure that before long I shall see her again, and all my cruel doubts will be set at rest," said Ricardo, with suppressed emotion.

"Yes! yes! never fear. We shall see all who have preceded us!" replied Steinberg, "and through the agency of this uncouth, barbaric girl. It is almost too wonderful for belief."

At this juncture, Hannah roused herself, and gave a shriek at feeling the darkness by which she was surrounded.

"O! lor! O! my! Where am I? O! wot is all this about? O! wot 'ave you bin a'doing of with me? O! please, Sirs, take me out of this 'ole, for if there is one thing which I can't a'bear, it is to be in the dark. It's 'orrible!"

She struggled to her feet and stumbling to the door, threw it wide open, admitting a full light into the séance chamber. Then she glanced round at the black hangings and with another violent shriek, rushed helter-skelter into the adjoining apartment, and fell into a chair, kicking her huge feet against the floor in a kind of Devil's tattoo.

"My dear girl! my dear Hannah! pray compose yourself! Nothing is wrong," exclaimed the Professor, as he patted her kindly on the head. "You've had a nice little sleep. The Doctor gave you some medicine for the purpose, because he thought it would do you good. You'd rather go to sleep for a little while than take bitter physic, wouldn't you, Hannah?"

"P'r'aps Sir, but I do feel so queer-like, as if my legs was all bruised. And my eyes seems weighted, as if I had lead on 'em. It's a rummy sorter sleep I've had, and I think I'll go downstairs and git into bed, for I've got no use of my legs at all."

"Good-night, Hannah! You won't mind the Doctor's medicine so much next time, will you?"

"I'm sure I don't know, Sir!" said the girl drowsily, as she passed the threshold, but the next minute she had started backwards with another scream.

"Why! what's the matter now?" cried the men simultaneously.

Hannah was standing near the door with her hand pressed against her heart.

"O! lawks! there's a lady standing on the landing a'waiting for me—sich a 'ansome lady, with a voil"—(so Hannah pronounced "veil")—"over her face.

O! lor! I shall never be able to git to bed to-night!"

"A lady!" exclaimed Ricardo, eagerly, "what was she like, Hannah?"

"O! I'm sure I don't know," replied the girl, testily, "I only wish she wouldn't come bothering me like that, jist when I was a'going to my bed. No! I don't know nuffin about her, Sir, nor don't want to either, a nasty black-eyed creetur, with a beastly voil. Here! let me go, please, Sir, or I'll never git downstairs to-night."

And so she left the mystified men to themselves.

CHAPTER V.

THE Professor and the Doctor sat up late that night, talking over the wonders they had experienced.

"Do you believe that the spirits of the dead can return to earth *now?*" demanded Ricardo of his friend.

"I am hardly prepared to answer you," replied Steinberg. "Certainly, the Voice we heard to-night was very marvellous. I am persuaded that, in normal circumstances, such a gruff, bass voice could not proceed from the chest of a woman. But there have been abnormal cases of the kind, therefore it is not impossible!"

"Good Heavens! Do you mean to suggest that this girl is tricking us?"

"Not exactly. We have had no proofs of it, still, in an investigation of this sort, one needs to be very careful. We must try and think of some test by which we should render it impossible for Hannah to speak whilst under trance."

"That will be difficult!" said Ricardo.

"But feasible," replied his companion, "if necessary, we must apply a gag whilst she is unconscious. Nothing short of that, or something equally efficacious, will make me give undoubted testimony to the honesty of her mediumship."

"My books tell me that such stringent tests are very apt to prevent all spiritual manifestations whatever," said the Professor, with a sigh.

"Then I should not believe in the manifestations, Ricardo! True spirit intercourse could not possibly be prevented by earthly means. Have we not heard of a heavy table with people seated on it, being lifted by invisible force, and transported to another part of the room? If spirits can accomplish that, they can speak through a gag. Did not 'James' tell us that, when we first heard him, he was speaking with a materialised gullet and thorax? If he will speak through them again if only a couple of words, whilst Hannah is gagged, I will not doubt her honesty. But in any circumstances, it is wonderful—wonderful!"

The two men were so anxious to pursue their researches, that they would have gladly asked for Hannah's services on the following day, but were afraid of raising Mrs. Battleby's suspicions by displaying too much eagerness to effect her cure. On the third evening, however, the landlady was all smiles and assurances that the girl was ready to wait upon them, but when the time came for her appearance Hannah Stubbs was nowhere to be found. Mrs. Battleby screamed her name from basement to attic, but neither sight nor sound rewarded her assiduity. The Professor and the Doctor had begun to fear lest their medium should have run away from them altogether, when Mrs. Battleby discovered her in her own bedroom, which was next the cellar, with her head wrapped up in the bedclothes, lest she should hear them calling for her.

"Well, of all the ungrateful, bad-natured 'ussies as ever I see, if you're not the wust," cried the landlady, as she seized hold of her arm and wrenched her from under the bedclothes. "Wot right 'ave you, I should like to know, to go to bed at this time of day, and not a single cup nor saucer washed up yet? Do you think I keep you to look at, you ugly, squab-faced creetur? Get up do, at once, and don't keep the gentlemen waiting a minute longer!"

But Hannah was sullen. She only shook herself free of Mrs. Battleby's grasp, and sat on the side of the bed, with her lips stuck out like those of a negress.

"Now then," exclaimed her mistress, "wot's this for, I'd like to know! If the Doctor is good enough to try and cure you (which I'm sure, I wonders he takes the trouble to do it), the least thing you can do in return, is to be grateful."

"Well! then, I ain't," replied the girl, "I'd rather wash up dishes or scrub floors a 'undred times over, than be physicked. I never could abear it! It give me a 'eadache last time, and I don't want no more of it."

But Mrs. Battleby had become reconciled to the arrangement, and had no intention of breaking it. She found that she got quite as much work out of Hannah as before, and she was not going to let the chance of keeping her at the Professor's expense, slip.

"Well! then," she commenced, "you'll do as you're told, Hannah Stubbs, or back you goes to Settlefield to-morrer, and with sich a character at your back as you won't easy get rid of! You'll please to remember that whilst you're here you're my servant, and bound to do my bidding, and I orders you to smooth your 'air, and go up to the gentlemen at onst, as they're ready and waiting for you."

Hannah burst into tears and muttered something about not having come out to service to be cut up, or pisened, just as the missus chose, but she crawled upstairs after a while, all the same, and presented herself at the door of the Professor's room, where she clung to the lintel as if she dared advance no further.

"Good evening, my dear," said the Professor, kindly, "you are rather late. Did not you remember that you were to see Doctor Steinberg again tonight?"

"I don't want to be doctored," said the girl, in

the same tone she had used downstairs, "it don't do me no good, it makes me wuss!"

"You have not tried it long enough to know if it will do you any good," replied Steinberg.

"And what do you mean by its making you worse?" interposed Ricardo, "how can it make you worse, Hannah?"

"Well, then, it do, a deal," said the girl. "I've been worritted out of my life since I been here, night afore last. That there lady as I met on the stairs has follered me like my shadder. She ain't no good, I know, and she gives me the creeps, and if that's wot the physic's going to do for me, I'd rayther leave it alone."

"No! no! no! it was not the medicine," said the Doctor, quickly. "You would have been much worse without it, Hannah! The lady and everybody who worries you will soon disappear, if you will go on with my cure."

"Come in and sit down, and tell us all about the lady," exclaimed Ricardo, eagerly. "There's plenty of nice hot tea left in the teapot, and here is some buttered cake! Sit down beside me, Hannah, and have some tea, and whilst you are taking it, we will hear all about this tiresome lady."

Hannah's eyes looked greedy, and her big mouth commenced to work in anticipation. She was thoroughly sensual, and the good things before her appealed to her senses much more than the honour of being asked to take a chair in the presence of gentlemen.

She sidled into a seat next the Professor, and having drunk a large cup of tea, found her tongue and her presence of mind, simultaneously.

"Well! Sir, it's this way," she commenced, "I've been in the 'abit, as I told you and this gennelman, of seeing shadders, and 'earing woices and sich-like ever since I was a kiddy, but I don't dare say nothing about them at 'ome, cos they do go on so dreadful about it, I'm quite afeared on 'em. But I haven't often seen 'em so distinct-like as since I've been 'ere, and they scare me mortal. The other evening I seen that lady I spoke of, on the landing, and blest if she ain't been to my bed each night since, and looking at me terrible with 'er big, black eyes through 'er voil."

"Big, black eyes," reiterated the Professor. "O! Hannah! do try to remember what she was like!"

"I ain't no cause to remember, Sir," replied the girl, "she's scared me too much for that! I only wishes as I could forget 'er. She is a tall lady, and foreign looking, summat like an Injun with a white skin. She's got big, black eyes as look you through and through, and a thin nose, pointed-like, and little white 'ands, O! so small, and long black 'air 'anging down 'er back, and plaited in a tail. There was a white voil over her face and 'ead, but I could see 'er quite plain under it."

"And what age—how old should you say she was, Hannah?" asked the Professor, breathlessly.

"Well, Sir, I ain't good at ages, but somwheres between twenty-five and thirty, I should say she was. She ain't old anyways, nor yet so very young, neither!"

"My God!" cried Ricardo, as he bent his face over his hands. "It is she—it is my Leonora!"

"I wish she'd come to you, Sir, then, instead of me!" said Hannah, stolidly, with her mouth full of buttered crumpet.

"Ricardo!" exclaimed Steinberg, laying his hand on the shoulder of his friend. "Calm yourself! Do not be too sanguine! This may be a wrong description, or if correct, that of another person. Remember, that any unusual anxiety to see any particular person, is more apt to mar than to promote your desire."

"Yes! yes! I know, but to think she may be so near me!"

"She has probably, if your own theories are correct, been always near you, though you have been unable to discern it. We must expect this girl to see a great deal more than we can ever hope to do."

"No doubt, but the description is so like! Those little white hands! how well I recall them, and the piercing, black eyes. Hannah! did this lady say nothing to you?"

"No! Sir, nuffin, she only stood there, pointing

up to 'eaven with 'er 'and. Leastways she might 'ave been a'pointing to the hattics, but it was uppards any 'ow. But I didn't see no more of 'er than I could 'elp, for I screamed so loud and 'id myself under the bedclothes, and the next time I looked, she was gone. 'Thank Goodness!' said I."

"Don't be afraid of her, she will not hurt you," said the Professor, earnestly, "she was a friend of mine, Hannah—a dear friend, and the next time you see her, if you will only speak to her and ask her name, I will give you half a sovereign."

"'Alf a suvvering," repeated Hannah, wonderingly, "well, I should like to 'ave that, I must say, but I can't do it, Sir,"—shaking her head—" not for a bag of gold, I couldn't. I don't mind a'coming up here to be physicked by the Doctor, for the missus says if I don't, she'll send me 'ome—but to talk to sperrits and sich-like I can't. I've never done it, a'cause I'm afeared they're the Devil, and I can't begin it now. I should think they would carry me away if I did!"

"Still the same old theory," said Steinberg to Ricardo, in French, "with rich and poor, wise and ignorant—that the Devil is at the bottom of everything that promises to let in a little light upon the other world. Ricardo, if nothing else prompted me to go on with this inquiry, it would be the hope of finding out if there is a Devil at all, or whether the evil in our own natures is not sufficient to do all the mischief in this world, that is attributed to him!"

During this short colloquy, Hannah Stubbs had displayed no curiosity by look or word, to learn what was going on, but as Steinberg concluded, she said,

"I suppose, Sir, as you've been putting some of your physic in my tea, for I feel uncommon sleepy, jest as I did the other night."

The Professor seized upon the opportunity.

"We thought it would be less unpleasant for you to take in that way, Hannah," he commenced, but he spoke to an unconscious hearer. The girl was already lying back in her chair, without sense or motion.

Steinberg hastened to lower the gas.

"How quickly she has gone off to-night," he remarked, "I wonder if this is Leonora's doing!"

"No! it is not Leonora's doing," echoed the Voice after him, "it is mine! And now as you want a test, Mr. Doctor, as to whether I speak through the medium's organs, or she speaks for me, please fill half a tumbler with water and pour it into her mouth."

"Pour it into her mouth!" exclaimed Steinberg, "but I may choke her!"

"Just do as you're told," said "James," "and leave the consequences to me! We're better doctors than you are, in the Spiritual world. We know what we're about and don't go by guessing. Now, where's the water?"

Thus adjured, Ricardo fetched a tumbler of water from the adjoining room and emptied half the contents into Hannah's mouth. She did not seem to resist the action. Her mouth was like a carved piece of marble. The fluid filled it, but did not attempt to pass down the throat.

As the operation was finished, she closed her lips again with a sigh.

"Well, that's a strong test," remarked Steinberg. "If any voice speaks now, it certainly cannot be that of the medium."

"O! you think that, do you?" almost immediately exclaimed the Voice, which they now called "James", "well, then, who am I?"

"That is just what we are trying to find out, James," replied Ricardo. "You are certainly not a mortal. Are you the spirit of a dead person, or an emissary of the Devil? Tell us the truth."

"I am certainly not an emissary of the Devil, who never existed except in your own bad thoughts," replied James. "When people do wrong, they say they were tempted of the Devil. That's only an excuse for not confessing that they tempted themselves. But I've never seen the Devil, nor seen anybody who has seen him, so I can't tell you anything about that. And I am not the spirit of a dead person, for the good reason that there are no dead persons. Everybody is alive for evermore, and the only 'dead 'uns' are the poor bigotted ignorant fools who are content to believe any fable that is told them, and never to find out the truth for themselves."

"Then you must not call us 'dead 'uns,' James, for we are only too anxious to find out everything about the next World, and are ready to believe all that you can teach us!"

"That's all very fine, but it's not my mission to teach you, even if I could! But I've had no opportunities yet of learning even as much as you have. You're educated gentlemen, as can read books for yourselves, but I was only a poor costermonger, as could neither read nor write whilst on earth, and had to begin at A.B.C. when I came over here."

"You speak better than most costermongers," observed Steinberg.

"Of course I do! Didn't I say I had everything to learn when I came to this world. If you took a costermonger in hand and taught him how to speak, he'd take after your pronunciation, wouldn't he? That's what I did. It was a gentleman bred that taught me. I guess he hadn't done as much as he might for his fellow-creatures when he was here, so they put him on to my little job."

"And why have you come to us then, James?"

"Didn't I tell you the other night, that I *hadn't* come for you. I came with this medium. I've been attached to her for several years past."

"Did you know her on earth?"

"No! I passed over years before she was born."

"Why did you attach yourself to her then?"

"Because I was told to do so. Things are very different here from what you earth-people expect. You do pretty much as you choose in this world, but you'll have to obey when you pass over. I was told off to control this girl I suppose, because she's likely to encounter the same sort of troubles as I did. Any way I'm here, and now I must go! Light the gas and turn the water out of her mouth, that you may be convinced she is not a fraud, and then lower it again and sit round the table in the dark, and I'll see if I can show you something."

The Voice ceased, and the men doing as they were desired, were astonished to receive back the half tumbler of water from Hannah's mouth, just as they had placed it there. Steinberg could not conceal his surprise. He sat gazing at the fluid as if it had been some sacred water brought from Jordan or Bethsaida, to cleanse him from his sins.

"Well! I couldn't have believed it possible unless I had seen it with my own eyes," he exclaimed. "Ricardo, this is the most wonderful, incomprehensible, astonishing——"

"Yes! my dear friend, but let us lower the light,

now, and talk of these things afterwards. James has promised we shall see something! Supposing it should be my Leonora!"

Steinberg turned off the gas altogether, and sat mute as a mouse, till something should arise from the darkness. Presently, the two friends perceived a bluish mist, like the smoke from a cigarette, rise from the other side of the table, and hover between the ceiling and the floor.

"It is my wife, I am sure of it!" said the Professor in an agitated whisper, to the Doctor, "can't you see the long white veil which Hannah described to us, and which she was so often in the habit of wearing. Wait a moment and we shall see her beautiful face peeping through the mist. How gracefully it rises—just like the swaying figure of a slender woman, such as she was! And now, cannot you see two eyes forming in the cloud—Leonora! my Beloved, speak to me, show yourself to me! O! I am as certain as I am of my own existence, that it is she!"

"I cannot say that I see any features," replied Steinberg, "but the form is certainly moving, and coming nearer to us! How cold the room seems to have suddenly become! My hands are like ice! What can be the reason of it? Surely, not the presence of a gentle woman spirit!"

"No!" returned the voice of James from out the darkness, "but perhaps the presence of a gentle spirit man!!! It is I, after all, whom you mistook for that which you are looking for. So do you mortals continually deceive yourselves and bring the science of Spiritualism into disrepute. It was *my* graceful figure which you saw floating in mid air, but don't be disheartened. Remember! if you can see a costermonger, you can also see a Queen! There is no difference here, of rank or sex! Good-night! The medium has had enough for this evening! I am off! Light up the gas and let her come to herself."

Hannah did not seem to be half so frightened this time as she had been on the first occasion, and, after a few yawns, said she was all right and felt much refreshed by the sleep the Doctor's physic had given her.

"'Tis ever so much better nor jalap," she said, grinning from ear to ear, "and so be it brings Joe and I together agin, why, I don't mind 'ow many evenin's I comes up 'ere, and goes to sleep."

"Have you and your young man quarrelled, then, Hannah?" demanded the Professor.

"Not exactly quarrelled, Sir, but we ain't as we was, not by no manner of means, and it has cut me up sorely. My mother, she wouldn't keep nothin' to 'erself, but kep' on tellin' the neighbours as I see wisions and things, and then Mrs. Brushwood, she cut up rough and says as she wouldn't have no ghosties nor sich-like about 'er 'ouse, and

Joe, he lives on 'is mother, so 'e can't but side with 'er!"

"Poor child! And so they turned you out of your home for a power which is no fault of yours," said Ricardo.

"Yes, Sir. Mother, she said I must go, an' p'r'aps they'd forget it arter a while. Mother was allays terrible angered if I said I had seen anythink. But 'twarn't my fault, for I 'ated it, and do so to this day, and all I 'opes is, as the Doctor's physic will cure me of seein' 'em, so that I may go 'ome to mother and Joe. Good-night, Sir, and thank ye kindly."

As the girl disappeared, Ricardo turned to Steinberg and said,

"I have half a mind to give it all up, my friend, at all events with this medium. I am afraid we are not doing right in deceiving her! She is so simple she takes our word for everything, and all the while instead of curing her, we are urging on the development of her magnificent powers."

"You may well say 'magnificent,'" replied the Doctor, "and if you give them up, I shall call you a fool. Supposing she does not wish to be developed, what of that, compared to the advancement of Science? She is like an ignorant person who shrinks from having an operation performed that will restore him to health and strength. Should I be justified, because the patient did not understand the value of what I was doing, in allowing him to have his own way and die? This young woman has a splendid future. She may be the means of regenerating mankind. Are we to let the interests of a Joe Brushwood, or her supposed passion for her bucolic lover stand in her way? Certainly not! For the sake of the world, you must not let her go. If you do, I venture to say you will never get such another medium—such an embodiment of animal health and vigour, combined with the psychic forces which make such demands upon them. With Hannah Stubbs under our own eyes, we may be the pioneers of a new Science. Without her we sink down where we were before, into a slough of uncertainty and disbelief. My dear friend, whatever you do, do not let your natural goodness of heart lead you to throw away a grand chance, which may never be renewed. Besides, do you not depend upon her offices, to restore your lost wife to you?"

"Yes! yes!" exclaimed Ricardo, "it is what I have been working and studying for, for the last ten years. I cannot give up that hope, whoever's happiness stands in the way. We must raise Hannah Stubbs above her low tastes, Steinberg! We must give her something better instead—a love of the Unseen—an ambition to benefit her fellow-creatures —a sense of the high duties to which she has been called."

"True!—if we can," replied the Doctor, thoughtfully; "but she is terribly ignorant and gross. Fancy! a maid-of-all-work being called to undertake a Mission—a creature without an idea beyond her breakfast and her dinner—without an ambition, higher than to become the wife of a farm labourer! It is enough to make one laugh, until one thinks with what it is coupled—the Power, denied to so many, to pierce the Infinite! She is as good and pure a girl as ever breathed, that I fully believe—and she seems very docile and good-tempered—but she is a hopeless clod!"

"No! no! not hopeless," exclaimed the Professor, quickly, "when once she is sufficiently developed for good and high spirits to control her, she must become refined and softened under their influence. If my Leonora, for example, who came of one of the noblest families in Italy, should speak through Hannah, the mere contact must intuitively teach her much that she never knew before."

"I expect that your Leonora could teach Hannah much in every way," thought Doctor Steinberg to himself, but he did not say so to his friend.

CHAPTER VI.

Two mornings after, Ricardo, whilst on his way to his professional duties, met Mrs. Battleby on the staircase, with a very stiff lip.

"May I make so bold as to ask, Sig-nor," she commenced, "'ow long the Doctor means to be a'curing Hannah Stubbs?"

Ricardo stopped short, looking much like a school boy detected in some forbidden pleasure.

"*How long?*" he stammered. "Really, Mrs. Battleby, that is a strange question to put to me! How should I know? I am not a medical man, and if I were, it is a thing on which I should find it impossible to speak with certainty. A long time, Doctor Steinberg anticipates, I suppose, since he offered to pay you for the investigation by the week. Surely, you are not tired of your agreement already."

"I didn't say so, Sig-nor," replied the landlady, with the same stiff manner, "but Hannah Stubbs, she is a very young girl, placed under my charge, as you may say, by 'er mother, and I think it is only proper as I should know what sort of physic it is, as Doctor Steinberg is a'treating 'er with!"

The Professor actually trembled. Had this woman obtained any knowledge of their proceedings, and was she about to draw back from her bargain, and forbid the girl visiting them any more?

"What a very strange lady you are!" he answered (Mrs. Battleby would have flown in his face, had he called her a "woman"). "I know nothing of medicines. How can I say if it be one thing or another? You must ask the Doctor! But it seems to have done Hannah good already. You should be satisfied with that!"

"Perhaps I should be, if I were sure of it," said Mrs. Battleby oracularly, "but I ain't sure. I was kep' up late last night, and she was sayin' some very queer things in 'er sleep, as I didn't quite like! You gentlemen must be keerful what you do with a young gal like Hannah, for she ain't too strong in 'er 'ead, as any one can see."

"Of course we will be—we are, very careful," replied Ricardo, as he shuffled down the stairs as quickly as he could.

This unexpected interview with his landlady kept haunting him all day.

Whilst he was attempting to instil the liquid Italian accents into the ear of the high-born, but dull Lady Alethea De Ruben, his thoughts were wandering back to Soho, and he was speculating what Mrs. Battleby meant by her sudden interest in Hannah Stubbs, and whether she intended to make a fuss about the girl visiting two men by herself, or to try and strike a higher bargain for her services.

Ricardo felt as if he were prepared to pay any price within his means, sooner than part with Hannah Stubbs, before she had fulfilled his dearest wishes, by bringing his dead wife back to him. Better a crust of dry bread and a glass of water, he thought, than to lose the knowledge which seemed just within his grasp. To know Leonora pure and good, and that after years of purgatory he might be reunited to a faithful wife—or to have the stain of innocent blood lifted from his brow—the mark of Cain wiped out for ever! One of these two things it must be, and he thirsted to ascertain which! He was so self-absorbed and *distrait*, that even Lady Alethea perceived the difference in her tutor and asked him kindly if he were ill.

"O! nothing! nothing! only a slight headache, dear Lady Alethea," he murmured, as he made a violent effort to collect his wandering thoughts, and fix them on the Italian grammar.

On his way home that evening, he called for Karl Steinberg, and asked him to walk back with him, whilst he confided his fears and asked what steps they should take, to prevent such a calamity as the loss of Hannah's services.

"It merely means," replied the Doctor, "more money. Mrs. Battleby has perceived the satisfaction we feel in Hannah's society, and judges wisely, that it does not all proceed from giving her medecine! My friend! these women are too sharp for us! Their brains are very light, but they make up for that deficiency by the cunning of the lower animals. After all, when you come to consider it, why should we interest ourselves because a maid-of-all-work is anæmic, hysterical? Had we not better make a clean breast of it at once, and tell the good woman what we do with Hannah during her evenings with us?"

"Not for the world," cried the Professor, hastily, "the more ignorant the mind, the more opposed it is to anything it cannot understand! We should not only lose Mrs. Battleby's patronage (if I may call her concession by such a name), but Hannah's also. For she would, of course, tell the girl everything, and she would refuse to sit with us any more."

"I see!" replied Steinberg, thoughtfully, "then my advice is to take no notice whatever of Mrs. Battleby's hints, which were probably only thrown out in order to make you betray yourself. She is curious, my dear friend—all women are—she fancies there must be something more going on than the curative process, and thought to bully you into telling her what it is. Keep your own counsel! She may suspect, but so long as the door of your inner chamber is kept locked, she cannot find out!"

"How I wish I was rich enough to hire this girl as my own servant," observed Ricardo, "and defy Mrs. Battleby, or leave her lodgings altogether! Then I would take a little house of my own, and people might say what they liked!"

"And what they liked would be, to spread a pretty tale of scandal about you and this country girl. I, too, wish that I were rich enough to settle her down in rooms of her own, where we could visit her at stated periods, and hold our séances, but it is impossible! I can only manage to support myself—much less another person. Attached to the Hospital as I am, I have my lodgings free, but I fear my salary as House surgeon would not go very far in an establishment of my own."

"Never mind, Steinberg! We will not anticipate evil, but do as well as we can with the means before us! This is our séance evening! From the progress we have already made, I anticipate great things to-night."

They hastened their steps as he spoke, and in a short time, they found themselves once more closetted with Hannah Stubbs.

Mrs. Battleby was evidently very curious on that occasion, and very unwilling to leave them alone. She brought up the tea-tray herself, and took it down again, and insisted upon conducting Hannah to their presence—a thing she had never done before.

"'Ere is Hannah, gentlemen," she commenced,

as she shouldered the red-cheeked maid into the room, "I've bin a'arsking 'er what the physic as the Doctor gives 'er tastes like, and she can't remember nothink about it, but says as 'ow it allays makes 'er go to sleep, which seems very cur'ous to me."

Steinberg having been in a measure prepared for an onslaught of this kind, had primed himself with a list of names, unintelligible to the landlady.

"Hannah is perfectly right, Mrs. Battleby," he said, gravely. "In order to cure the very unusual form of hysteria to which she is subject, I am compelled to treat her with Ilex aquifolium, Conium maculatum, and Æthusa cynapium, which drugs, though most valuable in themselves, always have the effect of producing a quiescent state in the patient, after which they are unable to recall what has passed. But I trust—more, I am sure—that my treatment will eventually dispel her symptoms. But 'Rome was not built in a day,' Mrs. Battleby, as doubtless you know well, and I warn you that to effect a complete cure in this case, will take some time. That is why I proposed to recoup you for the loss of her services."

"O! yes, Sir, I understand perfectly well," replied Mrs. Battleby, looking round the room the while, as though she would spy out the truth of the Doctor's specious argument. "But in course as I am sure neither of you gentlemen won't forget Hannah, she's but a child as you may say, and knows nothink of the world, and I 'opes you will be very careful of 'er!"

"Of course, of course! You could not trust her to better hands than those of my friend Doctor Steinberg," said the Professor, as the landlady was at last persuaded to leave them to themselves.

"By Jove!" exclaimed Steinberg in French, "I do believe the old woman imagines we intend to seduce this poor child! Heavens! what an idea! With all the beautiful women you see in Town, to fancy one ever bestowing a thought in that way upon this ungainly, uncouth girl! Your landlady is not so cute in this as in most things, Ricardo!"

"I only hope she may not prove to be *too* cute," replied his friend, "I fear she smells a rat, as the English say—that is, that she has a strong suspicion what we are about, and if that is so, she will put a stop to it."

Their colloquy was interrupted by seeing Hannah suddenly leave her seat and going to the séance chamber, pass in to the darkness beyond, without a word, closing the door after her.

"Why! what is she about, now? This is quite a new departure," exclaimed the Doctor, "shall we follow her, or remain here?"

"I think we had better remain here, and lower the gas," said Ricardo, "perhaps James will tell us what to do. Fancy! Hannah going into that dark room of her own accord! She has refused even to look into it before!"

"She did not go of her own accord," replied the Spirit Voice, "I sent her. Lower the gas more. Leave only a glimmer! That's right! Now open the séance room door a little, and take your seats at the further end of the room and wait! Some one is coming to see you to-night!"

The two men did as was desired of them, whilst the Professor was putting up an inward prayer that the "some one" who was coming, might prove to be Leonora.

"No! it isn't," answered the Voice, which now appeared to proceed from the dark chamber which they thenceforth called the "cabinet"—"don't you be in such a hurry to see Leonora, Professor! You'll have more than enough of her, when she does come. It is not any one whom you know, as far as I am aware, but it is not the medium. Mind that!"

And then the Voice ceased, and for half an hour all was silence. Then Steinberg, nudging the Professor, whispered,

"What is that?"

Ricardo glanced towards the cabinet, and perceived a faint filmy figure standing beside the half-opened door.

"Can it be James?" he whispered back again. They were too much awed to speak aloud.

The figure shook its head.

"Who are you? Cannot you come nearer to us? Cannot you give us your name?" urged Steinberg, and in his anxiety to learn more, he left his seat and approached the cabinet. The figure instantly disappeared.

"Forgive me!" he said, as he rejoined his friend, "I have stupidly been the means of that figure disappearing. I ought not to have left my chair, but my curiosity got the better of me. I hope it will come again."

A few minutes' patience was rewarded by the same apparition standing in the doorway, and holding out, as it seemed, its hand toward the Doctor.

Steinberg, not daring to move again, stared through his glasses at the outstretched arm, and then sinking suddenly towards the Professor, he leant heavily upon his shoulder, and exclaimed,

"My God! It is Mrs. Carlile!"

"And who is Mrs. Carlile?" asked Ricardo, who had never heard the name before.

"A patient and friend of mine! She had her hand amputated—I performed the operation under chloroform—and she never recovered from the anæsthetic. Look! don't you see her arm is without a hand! Good Heavens! I never thought I should feel a thing like this! Have you any brandy? Can you get it? I feel as though I should faint!"

The figure had retreated again by this time and Ricardo procured Steinberg what he asked for. As soon as he had drunk the stimulant, his courage returned.

"Come back!" he cried, "dear Mrs. Carlile, my poor friend, come back and assure me of your forgiveness! Tell me that you know it was an accident due to the chloroform. It made me so unhappy! I did not sleep for weeks afterwards, thinking you might attribute your untimely death to my negligence. Poor girl! It was a crushing blow to me at the time."

The figure appeared for the third time, and waved its left hand and nodded its head, and the Professor declared he distinctly saw it smile. As for the Doctor, he was too prostrate for the moment to see anything.

They waited for some time after that, in hopes that the spirit of Mrs. Carlile might return, but all was darkness. At last, just as they were thinking of breaking up the séance, a white-robed form again made its appearance on the threshold of the cabinet·

"Mrs. Carlile!" cried the Doctor, in a fervent voice, "speak to me! Convince me of Immortality, and your forgiveness at one and the same time."

But there was no response. The spirit, whoever it might be, could not speak, but the head was turned towards the Professor.

"Perhaps she could communicate better with you than with me!" said Steinberg. "Speak to her, Ricardo, ask her to give me some unmistakable token of her friendship and belief!"

"Do not be afraid of us!" commenced Ricardo, in his gentle voice. "If you are Mrs. Carlile, give my friend here some sign that you have forgiven the past!"

"That you are reconciled to your cruel fate," interposed the Doctor, "that you did not mourn too much at leaving your husband and your infant children—that you know now that all things are ordered for the best and by a Wiser Law than ours."

But the figure kept its head turned in the direction of the Professor. At last, as though with a violent effort, it pronounced the word "Paolo" and immediately disappeared. Ricardo sank on his knees in an attitude of prayer.

"Leonora!" he cried, "Leonora! I have found you at last."

Steinberg was about to address him, when they were startled by a sudden and violent knocking at the outer door.

"Who is that?" asked Steinberg, whilst he whispered to his friend, "Calm yourself, Ricardo. Some one is asking for admittance. What is to be done?"

The Professor started to his feet.

"They cannot—shall not—come in," he exclaimed. "It is an outrage! I gave strict orders that we were never to be disturbed. Tell them so, Steinberg! And at such a moment, too!" he added, as he wiped the beads of sweat from his brow.

"Who is it? What do you want?" demanded the Doctor, of the intruder.

"It's me, Sir," replied the voice of Mrs. Battleby, "which there's a lady downstairs as wants to see Hannah Stubbs most particular! Will you please to open the door, Sir?"

"No! Mrs. Battleby, I cannot! The lady must call another time! My patient is asleep from the effects of the medicine I have given her, and I cannot have her awakened. It might be dangerous!"

"I won't waken her, Sir, if you'll kindly let me have a look at her, so as I may tell the lady as I see her asleep with my own eyes!"

"You must tell her so on my authority," replied Steinberg, "I cannot have Hannah disturbed on any account!"

"What! not when I, as is her own mother's friend, ask to look at her for a moment as she is asleep. Well! all I can say, Sir, is that I never 'eard tell of sich a thing—not in my borned days—and I can't believe as any gentleman as calls 'isself sich, would keep a pore gal from 'er friends, when they arsks to see 'er."

"If the lady is a lady, she will not wish the girl to run the risk of danger from being roused, as your loud talking is likely to do now," replied Steinberg, angrily, "and if you do not go away, or hold your tongue, Mrs. Battleby, and any harm comes to my patient from your intrusion, I shall report your behaviour to the Hospital authorities. How do you suppose I can administer such drugs as Colium maculatum and Æthusa cynapium, if the patient is to be disturbed whilst under their influence. If Hannah Stubbs dies from your violence I will have you indicted for man-slaughter."

"Lawk-a-me!" exclaimed the landlady, as she stumbled down the stairs again, "that would be a pretty thing to bring against Martha Battleby, as never hurted a wurrum in 'er life! But I believe as you're capable of that, or any other villainy," she continued, as she reached the kitchen again.

Needless to say that the lady, who was so desirous of interviewing Hannah Stubbs, existed in her brain only, and that her sudden irruption upon the "foreign gents" as she sometimes designated Ricardo and his friend, had been induced solely from her intense curiosity to find out what these nightly visitations on the part of her "slavey" meant.

"Which I don't believe, Mrs. Blamey," she confided to her crony, "as it's for the purpuss of curing that gal of her highstrikes, not if you was to tell me ever so! They've got some designs on the pore gal, mark my words! I never did think much of foreigners, for they're a wicious, immoral lot, as 'ow could you expect anythink else from a nation as lives on frogs and sour wine. Not but what I 'olds the Sig-nor to be a quiet, and respectable gentleman,—least-ways 'e 'ave been so 'itherto, but that there German doctor with 'is long 'air, and his glasses, is enough to demoralise the best man living. We hadn't nothink of these evenin's alone with gals on pertence of curin' their illnesses, before 'e came. The Sig-nor, 'e allays was a Mystery, and I've said as much before,—but a gentleman as is a Mystery with 'is books and 'is larning, is a very different thing from a gentleman as is a Mystery with gals. Hannah Stubbs, she's hignorant and hidle, but she ain't no more hill than you or me! We all 'ave our crosses in this life, Mrs. Blamey, but we don't go and sit alone with gents to cure 'em, and I don't like it, and that's the fact!"

"And I don't blame you for one, Mrs. Battleby, ma'am," replied her friend, "I never did like secret ways and never shall. Where there's secrets and mysteries, I says, there's summat wrong. And how you could have stood being locked out of your own room for so long, beats me! It's a puffect insult to a lady of your position, the mistress of her own 'ouse, and left a widder with an independency, and though I'm only an 'umble and down-trodden wife,

I wouldn't have stood it, not if I entered under their very eyes!"

"But it was a sort of agreement-like, Mrs. Blamey, as the Sig-nor was to 'ave them three rooms to 'isself, and open or shut, they're 'is. And 'ow could I enter when he keeps the key in 'is pocket, night and day."

"And ain't there no other keys in the 'ouse as would fit that room, Mrs. Battleby, ma'am?" insinuated Mrs. Blamey. "Couldn't you try anyways, or get another key fitted whilst the gentleman is hout, and so look into it without his knowing nothink about it."

"Well, so I could, to be sure!" exclaimed the other, "but I never thought of trying yet. But it seems to me a plain duty, Mrs. Blamey, to find out what they're going to do with that there pore gal! Why! 'oo knows? that Doctor might be Jack the Ripper—which many said 'e was a doctor—and going to cut up Hannah into bits. And whatever should I say to 'er mother, which was my friend when we was little gals together, if her daughter disappeared under my roof and wasn't never 'eard of again?"

"It is your dooty, Mrs. Battleby, there's no doubt of that, and if so be you're afeared to enter the room by yourself, why, I'll go with you as soon as look at you."

"Bless you, Mrs. Blamey, I ain't afeared, no more than of a black beadle, but now you've put it straight afore me, I will find out what them two is a'doing with that gal, as sure as my name's Martha Battleby! You never know what men are, till you find them out, and though these look so respectable and dull, they may be villains for all that. Keep a gal in the dark, indeed, and give 'er summat to make 'er go to sleep—I've 'eard summat like that afore, Mrs. Blamey, and no good come of it! So if there ain't a key in the 'ouse as will fit that door, I'll 'ave one made, afore I'm a day older. Good-night, and if I discovers any of their willainies, you'll be the first to 'ear of it, you may depend on that!"

Consequently, as soon as the Professor had departed on his round of teaching the following morning, Mrs. Battleby sent Hannah on an errand, and commenced her tour of inspection. As was to be expected, a common house had common locks to the doors, and she soon found that the key of her own bedroom proved an "Open Sesame" to the séance chamber.

On her first view of the interior, Mrs. Battleby screamed aloud, so gloomy and funereal was its aspect. But when she had somewhat recovered her nerve, its appearance inspired her with but one notion——all this want of light and air meant the Devil, and nothing else! They were practising Sorcery in this mysterious little chamber, and had dragged the poor gal, with her dancing tables and chairs, and her "shadders" and "woices" into it, with themselves. And yet, after all, the landlady was not sufficiently sure to feel brave enough to accuse her lodger of mal-practices. So she resolved to wait for the next opportunity, and find out what she could for herself. She had the resolution to hold her tongue about her intentions— not only to the Professor, but to Hannah and her next-door neighbour, and when the Signor's door had been locked upon the succeeding séance, Mrs. Battleby knelt outside in the darkness, with her ear applied to the keyhole.

CHAPTER VII.

AT first she heard nothing but the ordinary salutations that passed between the Professor and the serving-maid, but she was patient and long-suffering in the cause of Curiosity, and after a while, she was rewarded. Silence ensued;—next, furtive whisperings between the two conspirators—then, a few words of awed surprise—and lastly, the Victory!

"Leonora!" she heard the Professor say, "Leonora! come to me!"

"My gracious!" thought the landlady, "if they ain't got another gal in there! 'Oo'd 'ave thought it, and the Sig-nor looking so grave and solemn the while? I was a green'orn to have believed as they would 'ave been satisfied with Hannah between the two. That's the Doctor's doings, I'll be bound! Them medicals are hup to heverythink. 'Ow did 'e smuggle the 'ussy in under my very eyes? In an 'amper, I suppose, which no more comes into my 'ouse. And I, who 'ave tried so 'ard to keep it quiet and respectable! I'll 'Nora' them, when we meets again. And as for that there Hannah, 'ome she goes to-morrer."

Mrs. Battleby, having applied her ear again to the keyhole, and heard Steinberg speak of "Mrs. Carlile," and being convinced that the villainies going on were not confined to unmarried girls, bundled downstairs shaking with indignation, and began to seek industriously for pen, ink and paper, wherewith to inscribe a letter to Mrs. Stubbs of Settlefield.

She was some time before she found what she sought, letter-writing not being an every-day habit with her. At last, however, in a corner of the kitchen dresser, she unearthed the penny bottle of ink, which had remained there, without a cork, a couple of months, and been well thickened by the addition of a dozen flies, and in a drawer of the same article of furniture she discovered a steel pen with only one nib, with which she scratched as with a pin, on a dirty half sheet of paper, the following words,

"DEAR MRS. STUBBS,

"If you will please to come to London tomorrer, and fetch 'ome your daughter Hannah, I shall be obliged, as there is goings on hupstairs wich I don't approve of, and I'm afraid she ain't no good with the gentlemen.

"Your loving friend,
"MARTHA BATTLEBY."

The consternation which this mysterious epistle caused in the cottage home in Settlefield, may be better imagined than described.

Mrs. Stubbs, who was a laundress, and trying hard, with the assistance of her husband, to keep five or six hungry mouths full, was like many ignorant country people, excessively stern upon a lapse from Virtue. These brawny-armed daughters of the soil, who are spoilt for love-making before they are five-and-twenty —who deteriorate in every direction as soon as they become mothers, and remain like sacks of meal for ever afterwards—are invariably unable to understand how any women can be tempted to deviate from the straight and narrow path, from which they have never had the opportunity to swerve by so much as a hair's breadth.

When Mary Stubbs therefore received Martha Battleby's letter and had mastered its contents, she was more than angry with her recreant daughter.

"Look 'ere! John Stubbs," she exclaimed, as she waved the epistle towards her husband, with a hand immersed in soap suds; "just see what your darter 'as been a'doin' of! Gallivanting along with gentlemen, which never did no gal any good yet, and she keeping company with Joe Brushwood all the while. Let me git 'old of the 'ussy and I'll kill 'er—see if I don't. My family 'ave always been brought up honest and respectable, and I won't 'ave any light-a-loves among 'em. I'll go up to Lunnon by the fust train and give Miss Hannah sich a thrashing as she never 'ad in 'er days before."

"Now! now!" replied Stubbs *père*, "be easy, my lass! The gal's done no 'arm as I can see! She's a nice-looking gal, and the gennelmen 'ave paid 'er a compliment or two, p'r'aps. And no wonder! They're all the same when they sees a nice, fresh country lass, a'bringing in their tea, or what-not. Let it alone! The ould woman will write agen and apologise in a day or two."

"*Let it alone!* you fool! What are you talking on? Let it alone, till our Hannah comes back to us with a babby at 'er back, like Emily Marks did last year! Will I let it alone? You wait and see," cried Mrs. Stubbs, as she energetically wiped her steaming arms and hands on a coarse towel. "And there's Joe Brushwood, too," she continued, "I wonders what *he'll* say to Miss Hannah's goings-on!"

"Sure! you'd never go to make mischief atween the young people?" exclaimed the father.

"If anybody makes mischief it'll be Hannah herself. You mind what she left 'er 'ome for, father! She wouldn't give up them devilries of hern, not for Joe, nor me, nor no one, but went on talkin' about woices and shadders till she made me sick. I said I'd 'ave none of it in *my* 'ouse, and so did Mrs. Brushwood, else Hannah might 'ave been a married woman by this time and safe out of 'arm's way. But no! she wouldn't, so I sent 'er to Lunnon to shake the nonsense out of 'er, and this is my reward. She's a'going to the bad! But she is my lawfully begotten child, and I'll murder 'er, but she shall give it all up from this day,—gentlemen and shadders and woices, and the whole bag-o'-tricks!"

"Well! well! I don't say nothing against your going," replied her husband, who like many of his kind was terribly hen-pecked, and afraid to interfere in any matter from fear of making it worse, "but take young Joe along of you. He'll look arter your traps, for you must stay a night in Lunnon, I guess, and he'll be powerfully persuasive with the gal, and help you to bring 'er to 'er right senses, eh?"

"Yes! that be wise on you, father," responded his wife, as she put on her linen bonnet and went in search of her neighbour, Mrs. Brushwood.

It was soon arranged that young Joe, Hannah's sweetheart, should accompany his prospective mother-in-law to Town, and convey the two women safely back again to Settlefield. Joseph Brushwood, the younger, was not a bad fellow for his station in life. His parents were well-to-do farmers, and the young man's prospects were as bright as he had any right to expect. He was good-looking, too, in his countrified fashion, with bold black eyes and a thick bush of curling hair, and a ruddy complexion—a "follower" of whom any girl, like Hannah Stubbs, might have been proud, and for having attracted whom, she was much envied in the neighbourhood of Settlefield. But Joe had been brought up "pious", and stuck to the Bible as his rule in all perplexities of life. He was like many other people in this world. He called himself a Christian, yet possessed not one virtue of the Great Lover of mankind. He did not regard the Almighty as a reality—he only knew Him through the Bible. He never prayed from his heart, nor because he felt the actual necessity of prayer. But he went to church every Sunday afternoon, because he had been reared to consider it his duty. He sat there, with his Sunday clothes on, —his dark hair well-oiled, and a bright blue or crimson tie beneath his turned-down collar, and all the young women thought how nice Joe Brushwood looked and wondered what he could see in that stout, awkward Hannah Stubbs to take his fancy. And Joe slumbered through the greater part of the service, and returned home with the comfortable feeling that he had performed his weekly duty, and was a pattern Christian.

He was the sort of bucolic ignoramus, who would be more "down" upon anything which was Greek to him, than any other man. He had no humility, though he had a good deal of rough good humour. He was flattered by Hannah's undoubted affection for himself, but he did not care enough for her to give up anything for her sake.

He dressed himself in his smartest clothes to go to London with Mrs. Stubbs, though she told him as little as she could of her errand.

They arrived in Soho about five o'clock, and presented themselves at Mrs. Battleby's door. They were received by the landlady herself.

"O! there, I *am* glad to see you!" she exclaimed; "come in, do, and sit down and have your tea. Hannah has just gone on an errand for me, but she'll be back in a jiffey. O! Mrs. Stubbs, ma'am, she 'ave give me sich a scare!"

"Well! I'm sure your letter give *me* a scare, Mrs. Battleby," replied the visitor, as she settled herself in a chair, "and me and this gentleman, which he is my Hannah's young man, started off as quick as we could to 'ear the rights and wrongs of it!"

"Lor! is this 'er sweetheart?" interposed Mrs. Battleby admiringly, "well, she have an inducement to keep straight, if any gal on hearth 'ave!"

Joe settled his collar and tie and looked conscious of the compliment, as Mrs. Stubbs proceeded:

"And keep straight she 'ave, I will take my solemn hoath of it, though I'm her lawful mother."

"Lor! Mrs. Stubbs, you mustn't take my words for more than meant," said Mrs. Battleby, as she placed the tea-tray in front of her guests, "but Hannah, she do give me the squirms, there's no denying of it, what with her ghosties and her woices, and now these gentlemen—till she's a'most too much for me!"

At the word "ghosties" Mrs. Stubbs put down her teacup, and said solemnly,

"You don't mean for to go to tell me, Mrs. Battleby, as she's seen them shadders and things again!"

"*Seen 'em!* why, she's allays on about 'em, till she makes my flesh creep. But I wouldn't have writ to you, Mrs. Stubbs, if it 'adn't been for the gentlemen upstairs—that is my hattic lodger Sig-nor Ricardo, and 'is friend Doctor Steinberg—which they arsks for leave to cure your gal of 'er seeing of things, which they calls highstrikes,—and gets 'er upstairs of evenings to sit with them, under pertence of physicking 'er, so the night before last I makes bold to listen at the door to see what they was a'doing with the gal, and I 'eard—well, Mrs. Stubbs, ma'am, I 'ardly likes to tell you *what* I 'eard!"

"But you must, ma'am, but you must!" exclaimed the other, eagerly, "I've come to Lunnon with this young man, a puppuss to 'ear all as you can tell us!"

"Well! then, Mrs. Stubbs, I must tell you fust, as the Sig-nor kep' one of 'is rooms locked, night and day, but arter 'e got 'old, as I may say, of Hannah, I considered it my dooty to see what they did for myself, and I got another key fitted, and unlocked the door!"

"Which you did right, Mrs. Battleby!" agreed Mrs. Stubbs.

"And what did I find, but the 'ole room was hung with black curtings—walls, floor and winder—

and sich a 'orrid smell, something between musk and cockroaches! Thinks I to myself, this ain't for no good, so I listens to them, as I says before, and it's a mixture, Mrs. Stubbs—a mixture of gals and Sorcery and Magic and the Devil, that's what it is, and I cannot 'ave it in my 'ouse. The Professor 'e must go, and so must Hannah, though I'm sorry to say it of a daughter of yours—but it's right-down wickedness, and I won't countenance it!"

At this Joe Brushwood sprang to his feet.

"I know what it is," he exclaimed, fiercely. "Hannah's been raising them sperrits again, which she promised me to have no more to do with 'em, and if that's the case, it's all over between us, for I won't 'ave a sorceress for a wife, to bewitch me half my time,—not if I dies a bachelor!"

"'Ush!" cried Mrs. Battleby, "'ere's Hannah. Just put it to 'er, Mrs. Stubbs, 'ow she's been employing 'er time with the Sig-nor and 'is friend, and judge for yourself!"

In another moment Hannah entered the kitchen. She had been out for a little walk and it had done her good. Her face was rosy and fresh and beaming with smiles. On her arm she carried a market basket, but as soon as she caught sight of her mother and Joe Brushwood, she threw it on the ground and flew towards them, her eyes sparkling with delight.

"Mother!" she cried rapturously; "'owever did you come 'ere. And Joe too!"—more bashfully—

"O! I *am* glad to see you both again. I cries for 'ome every night afore I goes to sleep, mother!"

She would have embraced her, but the elder woman thrust her away.

"No! Hannah Stubbs, no!" she said, severely, as she glared at her daughter, "not till you gives me a hexplanation of your doings in this 'ere 'ouse— likewise to Joe Brushwood, which we're 'ere for that, and nothink else."

The rosy colour faded from Hannah's face, as she encountered her mother's angry glance.

"What 'ave I been a'doing of?" she faltered, " why, nothink, mother—leastways nothink wrong, as I knows on. I've tried to give satisfaction. Mrs. Battleby knows that, don't you, Mum?"

"Well! I can't say as I do, Hannah," returned that worthy, "if seeing ghosts and sich-like, and playing with the Devil up in the gentlemen's rooms, is giving satisfaction, I can't see it, and that's all!"

"Hannah! what 'ave you been a'doing up in the lodgers' rooms?" demanded Mrs. Stubbs again.

"Only 'aving physic," replied the girl, as she looked down upon the floor.

"Come! that ain't true," interposed Mrs. Battleby, "for you knows you go into a room all 'ung with black, and sees ghosties, which is only the Devil dressed up to deceive mankind."

"Is this the case?" said her mother, sternly.

"I never see none," replied Hannah, "leastways

not in the room, and I 'ates them, mother—I've told you so, scores of times—but they will foller me, I can't 'elp it."

"Does you go to sleep in those gentlemen's rooms?" continued Mrs. Stubbs.

"The physic they gives me, makes me do that!" replied the girl. "'Tain't *my* fault!"

"Then I've done with yer for ever," exclaimed Joe Brushwood, energetically, "a gal as goes to sleep in gentlemen's rooms, ain't the wife for a respectable young man, and it's all over between us, Hannah Stubbs, you mark that! I've told you so, afore two witnesses, so you needn't try for a breach of promise of marriage case!"

"O! no! no! Joe, don't say that!" cried Hannah, tearfully, "I've been a true gal to you all along, Joe, and if—if—I'm so un'appy as to be prosecuted by shadders and things, you did ought to pity me, and not turn against me like that!"

"You leave the young man alone, Hannah," interrupted her mother, "'e's doing the right thing in casting you hoff, and I, for one, won't blame 'im for it! Do you suppose any decent feller will marry you with these devils allays arter you? You're a Witch! that's what you are, and a Sorceress. You've sold yourself to the Devil and ought to be burnt alive, as they did to sich as you in the good old times. Likely a respectable man like Joe Brushwood, would own you now—when your own people won't!

I won't 'ave you a'coming 'ome, contaminating your brothers and sisters with your devilish ways, no more won't your father! You must make your living the best way you can for the future, for you don't see me nor 'ome no more, and that I tells you straight."

"Mother! mother! don't go to say that!" cried Hannah, in despair, as she flung herself down upon the floor and burst into tears.

At that moment, the spare figure of the Professor appeared at the open door of the kitchen.

"Mrs. Battleby!" he commenced, and then perceiving the attitude which Hannah had assumed, he broke off his request with, "Why! what is the matter? Is Hannah ill?"

"No! Sir, she hain't hill," replied Mrs. Stubbs, guessing his identity, "but she's cast off by 'er friends and 'er young man, for hever."

Ricardo looked at the stranger with mild surprise.

"But why?" he inquired, "what has she done?"

"And you can stand there, and arsk me that, you brazen-faced impostor?" cried Mrs. Stubbs, with undisguised fury, "when it's all along of you and your diabolical practices, that the pore gal 'ave lost 'er good name and repitation? What have *you* done—that's more to the puppuss, a'avin 'er up to your rooms a nights—your dark rooms 'ung with black—and playing with 'ell fire as you do? Why 'ave you been a'calling up sperrits and ghosties and sich-like, and frightening us all out of our wits. But since it is so, and Hannah, she 'ave been fool enough to play into your 'ands (wich I'm sure you're old enough to know better than to lead young gals astray), she ain't no more a child of mine, and she don't come 'ome no more, neither, to contaminate 'er brothers and sisters. She belongs to the Devil and let 'im keep 'er! *I* don't!"

"But, my dear Madam," said the Professor, "you mistake altogether! My friend Doctor Steinberg has been trying to cure your daughter of her natural weakness——"

"Bah!" exclaimed the irate mother, more emphatically than politely. "Go along with yer!"

"Mrs. Battleby, *you* can explain this matter," said Ricardo, turning to his landlady.

"No! Sig-nor, I can't," she replied, "I must make bold to tell you that I went into your locked-up room the other day, and I listened at your door last night and I know *all!* And I'll be much obliged if you'll find another lodging, Sig-nor, by this day week. Mysteries as is jined with books I can be easy with, but not Mysteries as is jined with gals!"

"Of what baseness do you suspect me?" said Ricardo, indignantly. "It is true that finding this girl to be a strong medium, my friend and I have used her to assist us in our studies in spiritualism, but if anyone is in fault in the matter, it is I. Hannah is perfectly blameless; indeed, she does not even know what has occurred. Pray, therefore, do not visit the misfortune on her innocent head. If Mrs. Stubbs does not believe in, or does not approve of, Spiritualism, she can at least sympathise with the marvellous power which her daughter possesses, and which is as rare as it is wonderful."

"*Sympathise!*" screamed Mrs. Stubbs. "No! Sir, I don't, nor with any dealings with the Devil, nor witches, nor sorcery, nor——"

"Devils! Witches! Fiddlesticks!" cried Ricardo, impatiently.

"It'll fiddlestick you, Sir, and that misfortunate gal there, if you don't take 'eed to your ways," retorted his irate adversary, "Me and mine 'ave been brought hup Christuns from our birth—in sound Methody principles—and we won't stand no devilry, nor doings of Satan—and no more will this young man 'ere!"

"No! no! certingly not!" exclaimed the chivalrous Joe, "hit's hall hover with me and Hannah from this hour."

"What! are *you*, too, going to turn against her, for a temperament which is no fault of her own?" exclaimed the Professor, addressing the young farmer. "You—who professed to be her lover! Shame on you! You are not a man! Men were different in my day. They stood by the women they had promised to defend, to the very last—I think Hannah is well quit of such as you."

"O! do you, Sir?" interposed Mrs. Stubbs, "and we thinks we're well quit of the Devil and hall his himps! As you've been the means of leading this un'appy gal astray, and 'aving 'er turned out of a good place, and spurned by 'er relations, p'r'aps you'll see arter 'er for the future, and the Devil and you will 'elp 'er to make a living, for no one else will."

The Professor looked like a grand old hero as he replied,

"*I will!* You may depend on that! Whilst I have a crust, she shall share it! I would be ashamed to own so cold and unfeeling a heart as you seem to possess, though you *are* her mother. Do not cry so bitterly, Hannah! I will see that you do not want! As for you, Sir," he continued, turning to Joe Brushwood, "words cannot express the contempt I feel for you! You are a poltroon—a coward—a cur! In my country, they do not let men like you *live!* Mrs. Battleby, I accept your notice, and will leave your rooms as soon as I have found others. Till then, I hope you will allow Hannah to remain under your care, and to-morrow I will tell you with whom I have decided to place her. Good-night!"

He quitted the kitchen with the air of a *preux*

chevalier, and the persons in it felt very small.

"Well! I ain't a'going to stay 'ere any longer," said Mrs. Stubbs, as she bounced up from her seat, "the very hair seems to collaborate me. I'll get a bed at the Pig and Whistle, which the lady knows me well, and to-morrer p'r'aps you'll let me know, Mrs. Battleby, what that old feller means to do for that misfortunate, wicked gal there. If 'e don't provide for 'er, she must just go to the workus, for I washes my 'ands of 'er altogether!"

"Saying as I was no man, indeed," added Joe, indignantly, "I'd like to take the old chap outside for a minute and I'd soon let 'im know which on us was the best man. A dried-up, withered old carcase like that, and an *I*-talian into the bargain, who's been fed on macaroni and snails. I like 'is imperence!"

"Come on, Joe! don't waste no more time 'ere," exclaimed Mrs. Stubbs, "if we make 'aste, we shall be in time for a music 'all yet, and I do love a music 'all. It'll put all this wickedness as we've been talking of, out of my 'ead."

She went into the area as she spoke, followed by Mrs. Battleby, cackling all the while of the Devil and his ways.

Hannah was left for a moment alone with Joe.

"Joe!" she ejaculated, plaintively, as she raised her head, "don't you leave me for a minute. Your words 'ave nigh broke my 'eart. I've allays loved you, Joe, and I've been true and faithful to you, ever since we was little children together. Don't you believe what mother and Mrs. Battleby says—they're talking of what they know nothing. I ain't pretty, I know, Joe, but I've been a good gal to you. Don't go for to forsake me like mother, for I shall kill myself if you do!"

She drew nearer to where the young man stood, sheepishly turning his billy-cock hat round and round in his hands, and laid hers gently upon his.

"Do you mind when we fust kep' company, Joe—when we was nutting in Farmer Burrows' copse, and you ketched my 'and and kissed me afore I knowed what you was after? That was two good years ago!"

CHAPTER VIII.

"WELL! what of that?" demanded Joe, as he twitched his hand away from that of the girl.

"Two years is a goodish time at our age," continued Hannah, "and through it all I've 'oped to be your wife! Be you going to break your word to me now, lad?"

She spoke so wistfully that she made Joe feel very uncomfortable, though if he had had his own way, he would have stuck to her, whatever her proclivities.

"Well! Hannah, you see it's just like this," he replied, after an awkward pause, "Mother, she won't 'ave any sperrits, nor anyone as deals with 'em, in 'er 'ouse, and there won't be no other for me to take you to, till she and father kicks the bucket."

"Not if we worked 'ard for it, Joe?" asked the girl.

"I ain't got no work, nor ever shall, but what's on the farm," returned Joe, stolidly, "besides which, Hannah, I don't approve of sich goings on myself. It'll lead to 'ell some time or other, you mark my word!"

"But, Joe, it ain't *my* fault," cried the girl, earnestly, "by the blessed Cross it ain't. I'se as feared on 'em as you could be! I screams if they come near me! I don't know why they should, or why I sees 'em. It's my misfortune, Joe, and if it loses me you, it'll be my death as well."

And she began to sob afresh.

"Now, Hannah, don't do that, for mercy's sake," urged her lover, "for I must go. Your mother'll be rare fashed at my staying be'ind, as it is. Now, do dry your eyes, like a good lass, for matters is too far gone to be mended by crying."

"You means to leave me then in right earnest?" said the girl. "You sides with mother and the rest, and will turn your back on me just because I'se un'appy?"

"What can I do? my mother, she won't 'ear on't, and yourn is as bad. They'd worry my life out atween 'em, if I went agen 'em, and how should we live then? that's the question. No! no! we'd better be square and part at onst. Besides, the old gennelman says '*e*'s a going to look arter you, and you couldn't do with two on us. So good-bye, Hannah, and I wishes you well, but you mustn't expect to see me any more."

So saying, Joe Brushwood ran after Mrs. Stubbs, and was soon in the full enjoyment of a music hall programme.

Hannah was not a fine lady to faint from her

emotion, but may be she felt it all the same. When Mrs. Battleby returned to the kitchen, she found her standing by the table, with her most sullen look on, as if she dared a stranger to intermeddle with her grief.

"Well!" cried the landlady, coarsely, "I 'opes you're satisfied with the mischief as you've done! There's the mother as bore you, 'alf drownded in grief, and as 'ansome a young feller as ever I clapped eyes on, done with you for ever—and all on account of your goings-on with the gentlemen upstairs. You've made a pretty pickle for yourself, it seems to me."

"Mrs. Battleby," said the girl, suddenly, "can I speak to the Sig-nor afore I goes to my bed?"

"In course, if you wants to! 'E and you leaves this 'ouse as soon as may be, but I've no call to part you, whilst you remains 'ere. The Sig-nor's in 'is room. You can go up if you've a mind to. You're not under my horders any longer. You belongs to 'im now. 'E is to pervide for you, so you needn't arsk me nothink any more."

And Mrs. Battleby turned her back on Hannah and walked into the scullery. The girl went up the stairs and knocked softly at the Professor's door. He was deeply absorbed in a treatise on his favourite study, but he gave his permission to enter, in a pleasant voice.

"Well! my poor girl, and what may you want?"

he inquired, as he caught sight of Hannah's blotched and swollen visage, "I hope you have made it up with your mother and sweetheart. It is better to give in our own wishes a little than to quarrel, Hannah!"

"Yes, Sir," she answered, in a muffled voice. She did not seem like the Hannah of the day before. Something had suddenly gentled her, and cast a soft shadow over her plain face. "But we ain't made it up. Mother, she's firm, and so is Joe, that they won't see me again. I take it rather unkind on their parts, Sir, for I don't know what I've done wrong. But Mrs. Battleby says as 'ow, when the Doctor 'ave put me to sleep up 'ere, ghosties and sperrits walk about the room, dressed in white gownds, and speak with you. Is that true, Sir? 'Ave sperrits come as she say?"

Ricardo looked very uneasy. He would have given a great deal to be able to answer "No!" But he could not!

"Mrs. Battleby has told you the truth, Hannah," he replied, "though, Heaven is my witness, I never imagined I should bring you into such trouble with your family by permitting it. You have different powers from most people, my child! The shadows and figures, that you have seen, you say, all your life, and the voices which you have heard, should have taught you that. Doctor Steinberg and I are much interested in such visions, and we thought by letting your powers have free vent whilst with us, that you would not be so troubled with them when alone. And if Mrs. Battleby had not been so dishonourable as to listen at the keyhole, no one would ever have been the wiser. As it is, it has turned out very unfortunately for all of us. But I will see that you get another situation, Hannah, so don't be anxious about that. You shall not want, whilst I can support you."

"Yes, Sir, thank you kindly! It's very good of you I'm sure, to think to make it up to me like that, but it won't give me back my mother, nor Joe!"

"No! not directly, but surely they will come round after a while?"

"I don't think so," said Hannah, shaking her head, "country folk is very hard to turn. I don't believe as I shall ever see any of 'em again. But I thought I'd just arsk you if it was true, Sir!"

Ricardo hid his face in his hands.

"What have I done?" he murmured. "Fool that I am, I have ruined this poor child's life! Don't you hate me, Hannah, for this?"

"'Ate *you*, Sir?" she echoed, "but for why? You didn't mean to 'arm me, I'm sure of that—nor the Doctor neither! It's Joe as I oughter hate, I s'pose, or mother, but I can't find it in my 'eart to do it! They was so good to me afore these sperrits come round me. Arter all, I oughter 'ate *them* the most, for they's done the mischief for me. Good-night, Sir, and thank ye for what you've said."

She quitted his presence with a kind of rough curtsey, but the Professor could hear her heart-breaking sobs as she descended the staircase. He leant his head thoughtfully upon his hand, and tried to decide what was best to be done. For his own gratification—in order to further his researches into Occultism—he had spoilt this girl's life, parted her from her lover and her home—thrown her, ignorant and without protection, upon a world that did not want her. How could he make amends? He pondered over the question for a long time—then suddenly drew out his watch. It was not yet eight o'clock. He hastily transcribed a telegram to Karl Steinberg, and rang his bell. It was answered by Mrs. Battleby.

"What may you please to want, Sir?" she demanded, "Hannah, she 'ave gone to bed, as well she may. I'm sure if I had been found out in sich practices, I should be glad enough to 'ide my 'ead anywheres, sooner than face honest and God-fearing people!"

"Mrs. Battleby!" replied the Professor, in an unusually stern voice, "I am going to quit your apartments as soon as I can find others to suit me. So long as I remain here, be good enough to spare me the expression of your sentiments regarding Hannah, or anybody else. I wish that telegram to be sent as soon as possible!" and he held out the paper to her as he spoke.

"It's quite unpossible as I can send it, Sig-nor," said the landlady, with asperity, "considering as there's only me in the 'ouse. You've took Hannah away from me, Sig-nor, and so you must please to wait on yourself, and send your own telegrams."

The Professor rose with a sigh, and assumed his coat and hat.

The message was of importance, so he was fain to put up with the woman's insolence. He felt he could not finally decide this momentous question, without the counsel of his friend. The words were transmitted to the Hospital by a little after eight o'clock, and by half-past nine, Steinberg entered the room.

"Why! what's the matter now?" he exclaimed; "not ill, I hope, Ricardo."

"No! but much perplexed," replied his friend, and thereupon he related the circumstances regarding Hannah Stubbs, over which he had been brooding for so long.

Karl Steinberg looked very grave. Here was, apparently, not only the end of Hannah Stubbs, but of their studies in Spiritualism. Where should they ever find such another medium?

"What do you intend to do?" he inquired of the Professor.

"I have been thinking over it for a long time," replied Ricardo, "and I can arrive at but one conclusion. *I shall marry the girl!*"

If he had announced that he intended to murder Hannah Stubbs and all her family, he could not have astonished the Doctor more. He positively leapt from his chair, as he exclaimed,

"Good God! are you mad? Do you know what you are saying? Marry that clod. Bind yourself for life to a mere animal like Hannah Stubbs! O! you are jesting with me!"

"I am doing no such thing," replied Ricardo, "I am in sober earnest! I have unintentionally done this girl a great injury. Through my means she is left without protection, lover, or family affection. I propose to remedy the evil by making her my wife, and providing for her as far as I am able."

"But not as your wife—Ricardo, my dear friend, think! think what you are contemplating! Make Hannah your servant—your housekeeper—your nurse —what you will, but keep her in the station to which she was born. Take other rooms, or a little house, and install her there as mistress of your property, but, for Heaven's sake, do not contemplate such a mad, impossible self-sacrifice as to marry a woman like that!"

But the Professor was firm.

"What did you tell me the other day, that the

world would say if I took Hannah as my servant, and sat, shut up with her alone, night after night? You said it would talk scandal of us, and doubtless you were right! As my wife, no one will dare to say anything against her or what I may choose to do! And do you not guess what is at the bottom of this resolution, Steinberg? I cannot part again with Leonora! She would be lost to me for ever! Where should I find another *rara avis* like this girl, to bring her back from the grave? No! no! I must retain her services, and I see no other way to do it. Leonora has but just been able to manifest herself to us. You saw her beautiful face peeping through the mist last night, but as yet she cannot communicate with me—she cannot set this gnawing doubt at rest. Can I give up my researches just as they are beginning to reward me for my trouble?—just as I am on the brink of ascertaining what I have thirsted to know for so many weary years? No! Steinberg, I feel it to be impossible! I must go on now until I know the truth, and I know of no means of ascertaining it, but through Hannah Stubbs!"

"But make her anything but your wife!" repeated the Doctor, "think of the dishonour—the degradation! *You*—Marchese di Sorrento—the scion of a princely family—to ally yourself with a common serving girl, a clod of the soil! O! it is monstrous. I cannot bear to think of it! It is an infamy—an anomaly—an insult to your birth and your ancestors!"

"I cannot see it in that light," said Ricardo. "In the first place, I am no longer Marchese di Sorrento! I have voluntarily abandoned the title, and Hannah shall never know that it was mine. To her, I shall be no more than Signor Ricardo, Professor of the Italian Language. Taking this away, I do not see that the advantages of such a marriage will be all on her side. I am poor and I am old——"

"Nonsense! a man of fifty! Were you to acknowledge your true rank and status, you might marry a woman with money, to-morrow!"

The Professor smiled faintly.

"And Hannah can give me more than any money can buy—she can give me Leonora! Ah! my friend, you do not yet realise what I suffered in the loss of my wife—in the loss of my faith in her! To regain that, I would sacrifice everything I possess in this world! I am fifty, in years—yes! but in feeling I am seventy—a hundred! Hannah is low born—I admit it—and ignorant, but she brings Youth and Health and Innocence as her portion, and she brings what is better than all—*Leonora!*"

"If you have quite made up your mind on the subject, I suppose it is of no use my talking to you any more," said Steinberg, in a tone of annoyance.

"No! not if you would try to make me give up my wife, who has not yet even spoken to me.

With Hannah always at my commands, what may I not accomplish? I can go on and on, until I hold Leonora in my arms again, fresh, pure and beautiful, as when I first received her as my bride. Do you not see, Steinberg—cannot you understand—that it is not *Hannah* whom I wish to marry, but Leonora whom I wish to call back to my love and my embrace? And how can I accomplish this, except by having the medium under my own control? Were I to engage Hannah as my servant, and give her every comfort, I could never be sure that she would not leave me for a better situation, but as my wife, she—I mean, Leonora—will always be with me to my life's end."

"I understand your feelings perfectly," replied the Doctor, "but I would not have you do this extraordinary thing in too great a hurry. I am not yet satisfied that the pursuit of Spiritualism is entirely without its dangers, or that these spirits are always the persons whom they profess to be! What should you do, if, after you had taken this irremediable step of marriage, you were to discover that the form which looks to you now like that of your lost wife, were that of some stranger?"

"I should try again until I found her," replied the Professor, "I should consider my whole life well spent, if I only caught a glimpse of her at the last!"

"And if this is to be, where do you propose to take Hannah?" continued his friend.

"I have hardly thought of it! I want your advice on several things. First, shall I mention my project of marrying her to her parents?"

"I should not! Since they have cast her off, I should take the girl away with me as my servant, and let the matter alone for a little while. If she is attached to her lover, as you seem to imagine, she will probably refuse to listen to your proposal for some time further."

"True! then as to a residence——"

"I have something to say about that," interposed Steinberg. "Some time ago an acquaintance of mine offered me the lease of a cottage in Hampstead for the rent of twenty-five pounds. I did not care for the idea of setting up house by myself, and I did not think I could afford it, but if you would like me to live with you and share expenses, I believe we might be very comfortable together, and I could still share your midnight studies with Hannah."

"It is the very thing!" cried Ricardo, slapping his knee. "You and I will pursue our several avocations whilst Hannah looks after the cottage, and then in the evenings we will return home, to find all things ready and comfortable for us, and to spend the hours in our favourite pursuit. But supposing you, too, take it into your head to marry, my friend, what then? Will the cottage hold us all?"

"Have no fears on that subject," replied the Doctor, "I am not such a fool! Excuse me, Professor, but you have heard my sentiments regarding Marriage and Women long ago. I am wedded to my profession, and have no wishes outside of Science. If I did not believe Spiritualism to be a very great Science, disbelieved in by many, simply because it is altogether above their heads, I should not pursue the knowledge of it. But as it is——"

"As it is," interrupted the Professor, gaily, "you *do* believe in it, and we will live happily together in the little cottage at Hampstead, with our good Hannah to look after our temporal wants and assist us in our spiritual researches. My dear Steinberg, I know of nothing that has given me so much pleasure as this proposal of yours, for a long time."

"I am looking forward to it also," said Steinberg, "I have long felt the want of a home and a congenial companion in my leisure hours. My quarters at the Hospital are too easy of access. I am never sure of not being disturbed out of canonical hours, and a man does require a few moments in the day that he can call his own. I must leave you now, but I will write to my friend to-night about the cottage, and let you know as soon as possible when we can take possession of it. I have a few articles of furniture—so have you—and the rest I will procure on credit. Have no fears, Professor, the cottage will be ours within the week? But take my advice and think seriously—*very seriously*—before you decide on the step you contemplate."

He ran off, leaving Ricardo with his own thoughts, but when the morning came, he was still of the same mind—he could not part with Leonora, and if a marriage with Hannah Stubbs was the only way by which to secure that end, a marriage there must be. He decided, however, to keep his own counsel on the matter until he had left Mrs. Battleby's house.

When his landlady brought up his breakfast on the following morning, she informed him in a severe tone, that Mrs. Stubbs was down below and would be glad to hear what were his intentions with regard to her misguided daughter, as she had to return to Settlefield by the twelve o'clock train.

"My intentions are, as I told the woman last night, to provide for Hannah," replied the Professor, "Doctor Steinberg and I intend to take a house and live together for the future, and we shall engage Hannah to do our housework, and pay her at the rate of twenty pounds a year. Will that satisfy her mother?"

As Hannah had never received more than ten pounds before, Mrs. Battleby said that she considered the Sig-nor's offer to be very handsome, adding "that she didn't know 'ow it 'appened, but some people was so lucky, they seemed allays to fall on their feet."

But when she rejoined her crony, Mrs. Stubbs, her sentiments appeared to have undergone a change.

"Now! wot wickedness do you think them two is up to?" she commenced. "The Professor's been just a'telling me that 'e and 'is accomplish the Doctor, is going to set up 'ouse and keep Hannah atween 'em, and won't they be up to all sorts of mischief, the three on 'em together! I'll tell you what it is, Mrs. Stubbs, that gal of yourn is right-down 'ardened, she is, and don't want no 'ome, nor mother, nor nothink! She'd rayther be off with them two old scamps, so let 'er go, says I, till she comes back to 'er senses."

"Well, if she's got another sitivation, it's all as I looks for, for the gal must earn her living and learn to look arter 'erself into the bargain. Joe Brushwood, he seems quite set against 'er like, and wouldn't come over this morning, though I arsked 'im ever so! 'Owever, if Hannah's pervided for, that's all I arsks and I shall tell 'er father as it's all right, and she don't want to marry Joe, for men are so inquisitive and troublesome, there's no a'bearing 'em. Well! good-bye, Mrs. Battleby, and please to tell my gal as she's seen the larst of me and the rest, for we repugniates 'er!"

And gathering her Scotch plaid shawl about her, Mrs. Stubbs laboured up the area steps and was lost to view. Hannah did not come down to her breakfast that morning, but appeared an hour later, with red eyes, a swollen nose, and blubber lips that looked as if she must keep them open in order to breathe.

She did not speak for some time after she entered the kitchen, and when she did, it was to ask when Mrs. Battleby expected her mother to call.

"Your mother!" exclaimed the landlady, in her shrill voice, "why, she's been and gone this hour!"

"*Gone!*" cried Hannah, "and won't she come back? Shan't I see 'er again?"

"Not you, I guess, and she was glad enough to go, pore creetur, and 'ide 'er shame in the country. Your young man too—though in course 'e ain't your young man no longer—'e wouldn't step in, not for a minute, 'e was so afeared of seeing you again. You've disgraced 'em all, Hannah Stubbs, that's the long and the short of it, and they don't want to look upon you no more, so the best thing you can do is to go arter your old gentleman and see what *'e* can do for you."

"What old gentleman?" inquired the girl, "the Professor? O! 'e is good, I know, and kind. 'E said that 'e would see as I never wanted nothing, but 'e ain't mother and 'e ain't Joe!"

And she commenced to weep afresh.

"Now, look 'ere," said Mrs. Battleby, "it's no good your doing that. It won't bring 'em back to you, nor wipe out the 'arm you've done 'em. You'd much better go upstairs and clear the Signor's breakfast things, for that's what you've got to do for the future, 'e tells me. It's your business now, plain enough, so just dry your eyes and do your dooty, for I've got no time to waste over it to-day."

Hannah did as she was told, and the Professor took the opportunity to tell her about the new cottage and what he intended her to do for him there, and she went downstairs again, satisfied, that if she had lost the good-will of her friends, she had not, at least, the prospect of starvation before her eyes.

CHAPTER IX.

KARL STEINBERG'S negociations for the cottage at Hampstead, proved eminently successful. The rooms were too small for most tenants, so it was still unlet, and before the end of the week, he had signed the agreement for it, and had such articles of furniture as were absolutely necessary, put in. Ricardo and Hannah moved to their new abode on the appointed day—their departure being loudly lamented by Mrs. Battleby, who, finding her quiet, well-behaved lodger had taken her at her word, was very doubtful where she should find such another occupant for her attics.

The Professor was delighted at the prospect of the change. He had seen the black draperies carefully taken down from the séance chamber—had packed his precious books himself—and put together his few articles of furniture, and now had the pleasure of looking forward to arranging them in their place again, without any prospect of being turned out at a moment's notice.

Hannah also, though still in great grief for the loss of her young man and the anger of her mother, was much cheered by the idea of having twenty pounds a year, and reigning sole mistress over the little domicile at Hampstead.

It was a tiny house, consisting of a sitting-room and kitchen on the ground floor, with two bedrooms and two dressing-rooms above—the larger of which were to belong to Ricardo and his friend, whilst Hannah slept in one of the smaller, and the other was to be hung with the black draperies and devoted to their séances.

There was so much to do on first taking possession of the cottage, that they determined to postpone the pursuit of their studies until they felt more at home. The Professor had his teaching to attend to, as usual, and the Doctor his hospital, and when they met in the evenings they were too much engaged in carpentering and painting to be able to attend to anything else. Meanwhile, however, the resolution he had arrived at respecting Hannah Stubbs, had not deserted the Professor's mind, and it was not long before he mooted the question to her.

He saw more of the girl than the Doctor did. Steinberg had his hospital duties to attend to, and occasionally they kept him from home all the evening, but Ricardo's work was more irregular. Sometimes he had but two or three lessons to give during the day—sometimes eight or nine. One day he would be employed all the morning and have his afternoon free—on another, he would lounge in his arm-chair, robed in a dressing-gown, and reading his favourite authors, until noon, and rush away directly after his luncheon, not to appear again until it was time for supper.

Hannah had but little hard work to do, as neither of the gentlemen took dinner at home, and their morning and evening meals were very light.

She had the whole day to scrub and polish the rooms, and being a clean girl by nature, she took a pride in making them as bright as it was in the power of soap and water to do.

It was one of the Professor's afternoons at home, and she was in the midst of cleaning her little kitchen when he called her into the front room.

"Hannah, I feel lonely," he said, "I want you to leave off work and come and sit with me!"

"Lor! Sig-nor, it's impossible! I'se all of a muck, and the kitchen's flooded with water!"

"Then wipe it up as soon as you can, and come to me. I want you to sew some buttons on my clean shirt!"

The girl did as she was desired, for amongst the anomalies that beset this strange creature, was her capacity for needlework, the most delicate of which did not seem to come amiss to her clumsy fingers. As soon as she had mopped up her kitchen floor, she put on a clean apron and brought her work basket into the Professor's room. There she found various articles awaiting her, to mend, and taking a chair at the furthest end of the little apartment, she applied herself to her work.

"Hannah!" said the Professor, presently, between the puffs of his meerschaum pipe, "have you ever thought about getting married?"

The girl reddened; looked up quickly; and then dashed her hand across her eyes to brush away a tear.

"Lor! Sir, in course I 'ave! You're a'forgetting of Joe!"

"To be sure! You must forgive me, Hannah! But you will never see any more of Joe, you tell me!"

"I don't think so, Sig-nor! 'E's a young man of 'is word, Joe is, and what 'e says 'e sticks to," replied Hannah, with a heavy sigh.

"But you don't mean to remain unmarried for ever, for his sake, do you, Hannah? He is not worth it!"

"I don't suppose as any one else will want to marry me," replied the girl, humbly, "I knows as I ain't much to look at, nor clever, nor nothink of that sort, but I loved 'im, Sir, true, only 'e didn't seem to vally it!"

"No! He was a fool," said the Professor, "but all men are not the same, Hannah! There are plenty that may want to marry you yet—and I am one!"

Hannah looked up quickly, as if she did not believe she could have heard aright.

"I begs your pardin, Sir, what did you say?"

"I said that *I* would marry you, if you are willing, Hannah, and then you will at least be provided for, for life!"

"But you're quite an old man," replied the girl, naïvely.

Ricardo winced under the truth.

"You are right," he answered, presently, "I am old, at least compared with that young cub who has kicked you off. But men older than myself marry young wives every day, and I should make you a kind husband. I am a gentleman also—you know that without my telling you—and a gentleman raises the woman he marries, to his own position, and though I am not a rich man, I am better off than you would ever be if you married a man of your own standing. I am a very lonely man now, Hannah, and you are a kind, amiable girl, and I am sure you would make me a good wife. What do you say to my proposal? Shall we be married?"

"You're joking with me, Sig-nor," said Hannah, "it can't never be!"

"Why not?" inquired Ricardo.

"O! 'cos I'm so different from you every ways, and you'd be ashamed to say I was your wife. And what would the Doctor say, too?"

"Never mind the Doctor! This is a matter that

concerns you and me only. I don't mean that we should go on differently from what we are doing now. I am not rich enough to keep a servant to wait upon you! You would have to look after the house and get the breakfast, just as you do now. Only—you would be my wife and bear my name, and if I am ever better off than I am at present, you will share my good fortune with me."

"O! I'd be glad and proud to do all I can for you and the Doctor, Sig-nor,—now and allays—" replied the girl. "Only—for 'tother—why I can't speak like a lady—you'd laugh at me for my hignorance and I'd be shamed to open my mouth afore you, if so be I was, what you say."

"I know you have not had any advantages in the way of education, Hannah, but I should be willing to teach you many things, and being always with me, and hearing me talk, you would soon improve yourself. Is it a bargain, or not?"

"O! lor! Sir, I don't know what to say, sure," cried Hannah, in a frightened voice. "It's a honner, I know, but it don't seem nateral-like. And I'm not sure as it would be right, neither, for I can't 'elp thinking of Joe, and his falseness to me, and I can't promise to give it up, neither!"

"I like you all the better for saying so, Hannah, and don't imagine that I shall expect you to love me! If you continue kind and attentive, that is all that I shall ask. And if I did not believe that you would be so, I should not wish you to be my wife, even if you were a Princess of the Blood Royal. Cannot you make up your mind on the subject?"

"Well! I don't suppose as I could do better," replied the girl, with another deep sigh, "so p'r'aps I'd better say 'Yes', Sir!"

It was not a very ardent way of accepting his proposal, but Ricardo wanted no more than her acquiescence. He did not even put down his pipe to kiss the girl, nor press her hand. He only smiled and said,

"Well! I'm glad you've come to that conclusion, and you and I will go out together some day and get it quietly over."

He said nothing to Karl Steinberg on the subject until a week afterwards, when he came in one morning, with the girl, from the Registrar's office, and told him that they were man and wife.

Hannah grinned as the news was made public, but disappeared immediately afterwards into the kitchen, to prepare the family breakfast.

Ricardo waited for Steinberg to speak, but he sat silent and apart, with knitted brows, and a perplexed countenance.

"And so, my dear friend, you have no congratulations to offer me?" said the Professor at length.

"Frankly, my dear Ricardo, no! You know what my sentiments are regarding the step you have taken, which appears an act of madness to me. However, it is done and cannot be undone, so the less said the better."

"And you know the motives which induced me to propose it," replied the Professor. "They are not altered, Karl, they never will be! I feel as if the ceremony of this morning had united me to Leonora over again. I am as rapturously happy as if the grave had restored her to me. There is no such thought as love, or any other nonsense, for this girl. I will be good to her, but to me she is Leonora's medium—nothing more! Come! at least congratulate me on having reached the climax of my desires regarding Occultism."

"I wish you all happiness and success in every possible way, my dear Ricardo," exclaimed Steinberg, as he stretched his hand across the table and grasped that of his friend. "But here is Mrs. Ricardo with our breakfast. I hope your morning stroll has given you a good appetite, Professor!"

"The best in the world," cried the older man, gaily, as he drew his chair to the table.

Hannah had placed the coffee and rolls and eggs before them and was about to return to the kitchen.

"But surely your wife will breakfast with us, now?" remarked Steinberg.

"Of course! to be sure," said the Professor. "Hannah, my dear, sit down and take your breakfast with the Doctor and me!"

"O! no, Sir, indeed I'd rayther not!" exclaimed the girl, as she beat a retreat to her own quarters. Her husband smiled and shrugged his shoulders.

"Let her do as she likes," he observed; "she will be happier in the pursuits of her old life. And it would be most awkward to have her always listening to our conservation, particularly at this juncture. Steinberg, I must have a séance to-night. Will you try and come home early? I have married to-day, not Hannah Stubbs, but my Leonora, and I shall not close my eyes until I have seen and spoken to her again. The last séance! I shall never forgive Mrs. Battleby for having interrupted us! In another moment I should have held my wife in my arms. But I will sit and sit for her, until that happy moment arrives. Is the room quite ready?"

"I finished it yesterday, and it is one of my leisure evenings, so that I shall be back as soon as yourself. Tell Hannah—I beg your pardon, I must call her Mrs. Ricardo now——"

"No such thing!" cried the Professor, "continue to call her Hannah as usual. I wish all things to go on exactly as before!"

"Tell Hannah, then, to be sure and get us a good supper, for I feel so much exhaustion after these séances, as if my brain and body were alike scooped out and empty."

"Yes! yes! I will see to all that!" replied Ricardo, as they parted to pursue their avocations.

The Professor ordered his wife to procure a couple of fowls for supper, which Hannah quite imagined was in honour of the morning ceremony, and gave her five pounds as a wedding present, which delighted the simple creature as much as if he had settled an income upon her.

But when he and Steinberg returned home and intimated their intention to hold a séance in the dark chamber, Mrs. Ricardo showed signs of insubordination, and vehemently opposed their desire.

"O! no!" she exclaimed; "nothink won't ever make *me* henter that dark 'ole again! Wasn't it that as brought the whole of my misfortins on my 'ead? It lost me Joe and mother and the rest, and I won't never try it again. You didn't ought to arsk me, Sig-nor! You deceived me onst, and I said it should be for the larst time. If I'd a known as when I went to sleep, ghosties and sperrits and shadders walked about the room, I'd 'ave chucked all the physic out of the winder. But never again—no! not if you paid me a 'undred pounds!"

And turning her back, Mrs. Ricardo walked away into her kitchen.

The Professor and the Doctor looked at each other with comical dismay.

"Is she in earnest, do you think?" whispered Ricardo to his friend.

Steinberg made a grimace.

"I don't know I'm sure. I don't know enough of women, but one thing is certain—performing the office of a medium does not come within the legalities of Marriage, and if she will not do it of her own free will you have no means by which you can compel her!"

The men were silent for a few minutes, and then the Professor exclaimed,

"Karl! don't look at me in that way, as if you thought I'd bought 'a pig in a poke!'"

"I don't say that, but I think you have a difficult task before you—to convince Ignorance that it is a duty which it owes to Mankind, to sacrifice itself for the good of the Human Race. However, Hannah has a kind heart and an amiable nature, and if you will have patience, I daresay you may be able to induce her to do, for love of you, what she would refuse on compulsion. Cheer up, Ricardo. Don't look so down-hearted, man, but tell your wife to get the supper ready and let us all try to be jolly together!"

"But I shall not see Leonora!" said the Professor, in a tone of disappointment.

"Not to-night, that's certain, unless she comes to you in your dreams. But it is only a pleasure deferred! Hannah will come round after a while. Take my advice, and don't mention the subject again to-night."

Ricardo did as his friend suggested, and when the supper was ready, he insisted upon Hannah coming into the room and sitting down to table with them. She was very shy and awkward, and looked all the time as if she longed to bolt back to her own domains, but the two gentlemen reassured her, by taking no notice of her ignorance of their ways, and talking to each other, rather than to her. When the supper table was cleared, Ricardo asked her to bring in her needle-work and sit with them, but though she acquiesced in his desire, she did not reappear, and the friends finished the evening alone.

She felt that she had wounded her husband, and disappointed him in some way, by refusing to go into the séance chamber, and she was fearful of the request being renewed.

The next day passed much the same. The Professor spoke kindly to her, when he had occasion to speak, but he addressed her as seldom as possible, and sat for the greater part of the time that he spent at home, with his head buried in his hands.

On the third day, whilst the Doctor was out, Hannah brought her husband an apple-green merino dress, and a bright blue bonnet, and some underlinen which she had purchased with part of the money he had given her.

"I never 'ad sich beautiful things in my life afore," she said, with a broad grin, as she displayed them for his approval, " ain't they 'ansome?"

"Very pretty, indeed, Hannah—very pretty!" replied the Professor, as he returned to his book.

"I never 'ad so much money in my 'and at a time afore either," continued Hannah, "and I thought these would be nice for me to walk out with you, Sig-nor, in the Parks or elsewheres!"

"Yes! my girl, yes!" he said, as he raised his head for an instant and smiled at her.

Ricardo's smile was very sweet. It broke Hannah down completely, and she began to sob.

"Why! what's the matter now?" he inquired. "Is there anything more that you want, my dear? If there is, and I can afford it, it shall be yours."

"O! no! no! 'tain't that," cried the girl, "but you've been that good to me, Sig-nor, and I can see as you're not 'appy, and I'm afeared you're sorry now that you was so foolish as to marry a pore, ignorant creetur like me. I'd been fitter for Joe, Sir, but even 'e didn't think me good enough, and I'm so feared you've repented of your goodness to me."

And Hannah wept unaffectedly. The Professor drew her towards him and kissed her wet cheek. "You are quite mistaken, my dear. I do not regret, nor repent, anything. But if you really think that I have been kind to you, wouldn't you like to do something for me in return?"

"I'd cut off my right 'and for you this moment," replied Hannah, with fervour.

"Well, sit down by my side, and let me tell you a little story. When I was a young man, Hannah, five-and-twenty years ago, I married a young lady, whom I loved very much indeed!"

"Lor!" cried the girl, "you was married to a real lady, and yet you can bear with me!"

"Well! she died! I need not tell you how she died, but her death made me a very miserable man, because we had had a little misunderstanding beforehand, and it happened so suddenly, that there was no time for a reconciliation. The wish to see her, or hear from her again, haunted me for years, but I thought there was no hope of it, until I fell upon some old scientific books and learned that it is possible for those whom we call dead, to re-visit this earth!"

"Lor!" exclaimed Hannah, with wide open eyes, "but that's all rubbidge, sure-ly!"

"Why! how can you ask me such a question? What do you suppose the apparitions—the ladies and gentlemen—whom you see sometimes, are?"

"I dunno, I'm sure! Shadders, I s'pose, but they gives me the creeps! O! Sig-nor I can't abear 'em! I'd rayther run a hundred miles the other way."

"But why do you fear them, Hannah? They cannot harm you!"

"I dunno that! They looks very queer sometimes, and the woices as I 'ears—gruff 'uns and squeaky 'uns!

—they makes me trimble all over, as if I'd got cold!"

"But they cannot hurt you, Hannah," persisted the Professor, "and when I met you at Mrs. Battleby's, and heard that you possessed that wonderful capacity for seeing spirits, I was delighted. I felt that my dead wife would come back to me through you, and she has! On three occasions I have communicated with her, but not long enough to hear her say that she has forgiven me, and loves me still—and now, just when I hoped I should see her as often as I chose, you tell me you will not sit with me any more! That is what has made me sad, Hannah."

Notwithstanding her rough training and ignorance, Hannah had much natural intelligence, and she realised the situation at once.

"That's what you married me for, then," she remarked.

The Professor felt ashamed. He did not know what to say. He began by answering, "No! no!" but broke off short.

"I will not tell you a lie," he said. "When I married you, my dear, I certainly did hope that, having you always with me, I should also have the constant pleasure of communicating with my dead wife. For I am getting an old man now, Hannah, and I should like to make sure that there is another life, before I quit this one. But all that

I said to you, when I asked you to become my wife, was true. I will make your future my care to the utmost of my ability, and when I die, you will find that you are not left quite penniless. My savings have been scanty, but, such as they are, they will all be yours. It was your mediumship (by which I mean your power of seeing and attracting spirits from the other world), that first drew me to you, Hannah, but if you really dislike sitting with me, I will not ask you to do so again. And in all other things, you will find me the same, I hope, and your friend, my dear, till Death parts us."

"I see," said the girl, thoughtfully, "I'm to take all, as you may say, and give nothink in return. I see it plain now, Professor, and I'm not that sort, as you'll find. I know you're good and true, and that you'll take care as the sperrits and things don't 'urt me, while I'm asleep. So, if you please, I'll sit as often as you wishes, and we'll go into the dark room to-night, as soon as the Doctor returns 'ome. I couldn't 'ave ever wore this beautiful gownd," added Hannah with a sob in her throat, " and remembered the while as you give it me, and I 'ad done nothink for you in return. So that's settled, ain't it?—and you won't never 'ear me say again as I won't do anythink as you arsk me!"

And from that day the séances commenced anew.

CHAPTER X.

NOTWITHSTANDING her acquiescence, Hannah displayed such genuine terror at the idea of entering the dark séance room, that Ricardo had pity on her, and held a sitting downstairs first, at which he consulted "James" as to what was best to be done. By his advice, the black hangings were taken down, and a cabinet formed by a curtain hung across one corner of the apartment, behind which was placed a chair. A lamp was lit and the two men were directed to sit at the table, holding Hannah's hands in either of theirs. Feeling herself in the presence of her husband and his friend, the girl's fears were allayed, and in a few minutes, she went under control, and wresting her hands from their grasp, rose and entered the cabinet of her own accord. Then "James" told Ricardo and Steinberg to lower the light until it was a mere glimmer—to close the door—and to seat themselves at the further end of the little chamber.

Steinberg was earnest in his pursuit of Science—

Ricardo, in his pursuit of Leonora—so they did as they were directed, and waited patiently for the result. In an incredibly short space of time, the curtain was shaken—then pulled asunder—and the laughing, mischievous face of Leonora peeped out. The Professor was in ecstasy. He knelt down upon the bare floor, as though he were worshipping a divine creature. But his adoration was not given, because the appearance of a spirit from the dead endowed him with the blessed certainty of Everlasting Life, but because the materialised spirit was the creature of his imagination. Steinberg, on the other hand, regarded the appearance of Leonora with unstinted wonder and satisfaction, simply because her coming was another step gained in the difficult task which he had set himself to learn. As a Spirit, he hailed her advent with the keenest interest—as a Woman, he did not admire either her person or herself. She evinced none of the sorrow which a wife, whose thoughtlessness at the least, had led her husband into a serious crime, might have been supposed to feel—neither did she exhibit much pleasure at meeting him again. Her behaviour was more that of a coquette, who wished to regain the admiration she had forfeited, than of a loving woman. She smiled and beckoned to Ricardo, but as soon as he approached the cabinet, she would dart inside and be lost to view. Apparently she was, or had been, a very handsome woman, but there was nothing attractive in her appearance. Her large black eyes were void of tenderness—her smiles were affected—each motion of her supple body seemed made in order to raise Ricardo's ardour, without gratifying it. Had she not been his friend's wife, the Doctor would have called her by some opprobrious epithets—as it was, he regarded her simply as a curiosity, and hailed her coming only because she came.

The advent of Mrs. Carlile had a different effect upon him. She had been only his friend—scarcely that. Had she lived, he would have spoken of her as his patient. But her unfortunate and early death, occurring, as it did, under his own hands, had invested her memory with a certain tender compassion, which gave him the right, as it were, to hail her as a friend from the other Land. She came, not only to convince him of the Great Truth, but to console and comfort him under his disappointment. She came with pity and forgiveness beaming from her eyes, and trembling on her lips, and made him feel, each time he saw her, that Earth was valueless and the next World the Haven to which we must look for consolation.

The sittings, once more begun, were continued steadily every evening. Neither Ricardo, nor Steinberg, were aware of the danger that might accrue to the medium from these frequent séances. Hannah did not seem to suffer from sitting, and once she had overcome her childish fear of the Invisibles, declared herself ready to gratify their curiosity, whenever they asked her to do so.

Doctor Steinberg was only at home three evenings in the week, but the Professor sat with his wife, whether his friend joined them or not, and frequently in the daytime he would take Hannah up into the séance chamber, and hold converse with Leonora all by himself.

She did not always come to him. These things are not ordered by our earthly wishes, and we have no control over them. Often, when Steinberg was anxiously awaiting the arrival of Mrs. Carlile—sometimes, when she had even promised to come to him—a figure would emerge from the cabinet, and on inspection prove to be that of an old man, utterly unknown to either of them—or a child would run across the room, as if in play, and, startled by their addressing it, run behind the curtain again and be seen no more. To the doctor, who looked upon these manifestations as fresh proofs of Immortality, one spirit was as good as another, but to the Professor, whose whole thoughts were fixed upon Leonora, such disappointments fell keenly, and he would not be satisfied until he had sat again to give Leonora an opportunity of manifesting her presence to him.

Accordingly, he took to having séances by himself, and Hannah, who had never objected to doing as he asked since that first day, became his willing victim. Indeed, the girl even seemed to grow to like being a medium—her low spirits disappeared—she often went singing about the house—and no more was heard of her false young man, nor of her mother.

One afternoon as the Professor sat alone in the séance chamber, with Hannah entranced behind the curtain, the now familiar form of Leonora stepped out of the cabinet. She was clothed in some soft, clinging white material which showed plainly the lissom figure beneath it—her dark hair was unbound and fell below her waist—her small white hand beckoned him to approach her. Ricardo crept on tiptoe to the dark curtain that divided them. He was quite alone—Steinberg was miles away and Hannah lay unconscious in her chair—there was none but Heaven to listen to what he might say to his lost wife.

"Leonora!" he exclaimed, "my one, only Darling! Come to me and lay your cheek on mine! Whatever you were, whatever you did, you are still the same to me—the peerless, beautiful bride, whom I held to my heart during so many blissful years! Do you remember the villa down in Parma, to which I took you for our honeymoon, Leonora? Do you recall the happy evening that we were first man and wife—how we wandered into the gardens, and sat down on a bank, covered with delicious violets whose breath intoxicated us with pleasure. You cast yourself across my knees, and laid your lovely head upon my breast—then I seemed to realise, for the first time, that you were all my own. Our lips met—I drank in your sweet breath, sweeter than the violets upon which we sat—and we mutually trembled with the ecstasy of the contact. Ah! Leonora, my dearest, that was twenty-five long weary years ago! I am an old man now, but I have never forgotten—I never shall forget! Come once more and press your sweet lips to mine as you did in that unforgotten moment, and I shall be rewarded for all the efforts I have made—the sacrifice I have gone through—in order to draw you once more to my heart again!"

The tantalising face peeped out from the curtain—the lips pouted—but as Ricardo drew near to kiss her, Leonora darted like an arrow into the cabinet and evaded him. It was like the cup of Tantalus, ever presented, brimming with sparkling liquid, only to be withdrawn as soon as approached.

The Professor breathed a heart-felt sigh as he leaned against the curtain, to see if he could hear any movement going on behind it. But all was still as the grave!

"My wife—my wife——" moaned the unhappy man, "speak to me, if you cannot touch me. I feel the reason. My contact is too earthly for you, pure as you have become!—the hands that slew you are too foul to clasp with yours. But tell me—Leonora!

I am hanging on your words—tell me the whole truth. You know I could not be angry with you now! *Were you guilty with Centi?*"

The mobile face again appeared round a corner of the curtain, and the rosy lips murmured, "No!"

"*No?* O! my God! then I am a murderer of the deepest dye! I have slain my other half—she, whom I had sworn to love and cherish! What Hell will be deep enough for me? What devil urged me on to strike that fatal blow? Heavens! I can see it now, your pallid, startled face—the crimson blood that stained your white breast—that issued from your livid lips—can hear the sigh with which your pure spirit took wing, to bear witness against me before the Throne! O! Leonora, my wife! my angel! say that you forgive my rash act—my unfounded jealousy!"

The Spirit again appeared, and nodded its head solemnly.

"I knew you would forgive, dear Angel, who were so much too good for such a wretch as I am, but will Heaven forgive? that is the question? Shall I join you wherever you may be? Shall we be lovers and friends again in the Eternal World?"

But to this question there was no reply. Ricardo knelt where he had stood, and wept like a child. His life had been one long suffering for the awful deed he had committed, and now, to hear that it had been done in vain—that he had murdered an innocent woman—she, who, but for his insensate jealousy and fury, might have lived to be the mother of his children and the pride and comfort of his old age—was too much. It smote him to the ground, and struck a blow at his heart, from which he never recovered.

He felt that he could bear no more and left the séance room, without further comment. Even to Steinberg, he never revealed what had taken place between himself and Leonora that day, but he seized every opportunity of communicating with her, until he came to spend half his leisure moments in the séance chamber.

Doctor Steinberg perceived the alteration in his friend's spirits, but attributed it to his health, which was not satisfactory. The Professor still went about his daily work, but he taught in a spiritless, listless fashion, and his pupils were not so quick to follow his instructions as they were wont to be. When he returned home, instead of interesting himself in a book, as he had been used to do, he would sit for hours with folded arms, silent and meditative. The only times when he evinced any enthusiasm, were those spent in the séance chamber, though Leonora came no oftener than the other influences who controlled Hannah, and when she did come, gave scarcely any information on subjects connected with her present life.

But if the Professor's health and spirits appeared to fail, those of Mrs. Ricardo rose in proportion. She seemed to have entirely overcome her dread of the "sperrits" and "shadders" and "woices", and often said it was unfair that the Doctor or the Professor did not sit in their turn, and let her share their privilege of interviewing the friends from the other World. From having been heavy and somewhat sullen, she developed quite a lively disposition, and Steinberg was astonished sometimes on reaching home, to hear her singing over her work, an accomplishment for which she had never exhibited any taste before.

She became less shy also of remaining in the society of her husband and his friend, and made a point of taking her meals with them, by which means she soon got in the way of joining in the conversation, and dropped many of her coarse sayings and mispronounced words.

She improved so quickly indeed, as to surprise Steinberg, who had imagined her hitherto to be one of the dullest mortals in creation. It was not long before he mentioned the subject to the Professor.

"How wonderfully Hannah has improved in her pronunciation, lately," he remarked. "I couldn't have believed it possible that any one could have made such rapid strides. Have you been giving her private lessons during my absence, Ricardo?"

"No! indeed," answered the Professor, in the

weary tone he had assumed of late, "I seldom see her, except in the séance room. Has she improved, Steinberg? I had not noticed it. But there was room for it, Heaven knows! I suppose it is listening to our conversation."

"I suppose so too, but Hannah must be very clever naturally, to have caught our accent so soon. And she is so much more lively into the bargain. I heard her singing, or rather humming, the air of '*Au clair de la lune*,' yesterday. Now, where can she have caught that up? It is essentially French. She must have heard you, or me, whistling it. And did you observe this evening that she has plaited that mass of hair of hers, and twisted it round her head at the back? We shall see her wearing kid boots with heels next. Bravo! Hannah!"

"You look at her more than I do," replied Ricardo. "She is a good enough girl, and I have no fault to find with her. But I hope she will not get any extravagant ideas, because I cannot afford to humour them. I wonder who can have been putting such absurd notions into her head."

"No one, unless it be yourself. You should feel flattered, Ricardo, that your wife shows any wish to please you. She is certainly vastly improved. You cannot find fault with her for that! What have you been doing with yourself to-day? Talking with Leonora, eh?"

"I entered the séance room, but she did not

come," replied Ricardo, in a discontented tone, "she has not been so regularly lately. I cannot understand the reason. Can it be any falling-off in the medium? Would her want of interest in Spiritualism account for it?"

"No! no! certainly not!" Steinberg quickly exclaimed. "How can you expect the poor girl to take any interest in it, when she is under control all the time, and knows nothing of what occurs. Hannah has more than once expressed her disappointment to me, that she should be so completely shut out from what seems to give us so much pleasure. I think it is most unselfish of her to sit so often and so cheerfully. Besides, she is as strong in health as ever! How can she be responsible for Leonora not coming so often?"

"I don't know," said Ricardo, peevishly, "but the fact remains. An old woman whom I cannot recognise, seems to have taken her place the last few days. I dare not show my impatience at the change, but I am longing all the time for her to go away and let my wife come instead."

"Ah! my friend, you are not a Scientist! You do not pursue this interesting study in order to find out the secret of Everlasting Life, but only to gratify your personal longing to see your dead wife again. And now that she has come, you are less satisfied than before. What is the reason? Has she not spoken to you? Has she not solved the mystery that oppressed you? Are you not yet aware whether that blow was struck with justice, or not?"

"If I were, I should not feel inclined to discuss the question with one who was a stranger to her," said Ricardo, in a tone very unlike himself. "The confidences which pass between husband and wife should be sacred."

"I agree with you there, so let us say no more about it. You mooted the subject to me, or I should not have presumed to mention it again. But I think you sit too often. These researches, if carried to extremes, are apt to prove harmful to both mind and body. Come to the theatre with me this evening! It will divert you. I have a box for the Adelphi. Let us take Hannah with us. She is so much more lively lately, that I think it will interest her. She seems to be enjoying life, poor child, for the first time."

The Professor being agreeable, Steinberg's plan was carried out, and Hannah thoroughly enjoyed her evening. The Doctor was not mistaken. The change in her was quite as palpable as that in her husband. Live as long as she might, she would never have a lissom figure, nor a beautiful face, but a kind of brightness had settled over her features, which much redeemed their homeliness, and her attempts at tidiness did not at all events deteriorate from them.

She laughed and cried at all the right places throughout the melodrama and returned home in high good humour with both her friends.

But what still more surprised Steinberg, as time went on, was to see the gross humility that had overpowered the girl, entirely disappear, to give place to a species of pride in her attainments as a medium—as if she had suddenly waked up to a consciousness of the value she was to Ricardo, and the difficulty he would find in replacing her, if she were gone.

"I can't sit to-day," he overheard her say to the Professor, "so it's no good your asking me! Can't you see that I'm dead tired from sitting so long yesterday? Do you suppose that I don't waste my strength, as well as yours, over these séances? And what is it all for?—so that you may see the woman you cared for, and talk love nonsense to her! I tell you, Professor, there ain't many wives in this world who would do as much for their husbands. You treats me as if I had no feelings. I'm making a dress for Sundays, and haven't been able to put a stitch in it all the week, so you must wait for your séance till I choose to give it you."

"Very well," Steinberg heard Ricardo answer meekly, "never mind, my dear! I'll go for a little walk instead."

As soon as he had left the house, Steinberg took Hannah to task for her treatment of him.

"I am surprised to hear you speak like that to your husband, Hannah! Do you know what I should have done if you had been my wife?"

"But I ain't your wife," replied Hannah, with a certain arch look that startled him—so little had he considered the girl capable of giving it with her usually dull, lack-lustre eyes.

"I am quite aware of that! You'd have to obey me if you were! But you have no right to speak so rudely to the Professor, especially when you consider that you owe everything to him."

"Do I?" retorted the girl, "I think the boot's on the other foot! I consider that he owes everything to me! Haven't I brought his wife back to him, that he was hankering after for years. Who else could 'ave done that, eh? Why! I've heard you say yourself, that I'm the most wonderful medium in the world! I think it's six of one and half a dozen of the other, when you come to look at it."

"Maybe, Hannah, and I know you make him a good kind wife on the whole. But you mustn't forget that he's an old man now, and has broken down considerably during the last few months. So you must be more considerate of him than ever. He works too hard for his strength. Sometimes I am afraid it will not hold out much longer!"

"O! he's all right," said Hannah, with a lack of feeling that struck the Doctor as not only very unlike her usual disposition, but very contemptible into the bargain. "Them old men never die! Though I don't s'pose there'd be much left for me, if he did!"

"You are unfeeling—unnatural—I am ashamed of you, Hannah," exclaimed Steinberg, as he rose to leave her, "and you forget that you are speaking of *my friend.* I have a great affection for the Professor, and if anything happened to him, I should be deeply grieved."

"Well, I didn't say any 'arm," replied the girl sullenly, as she returned to her work.

This conversation did not seem to make any coolness on Hannah's part towards the Doctor—on the contrary, she appeared to like him all the better for speaking in defence of his friend. She commenced to hang about him more than usual, on the occasions of his being at home, and once or twice Steinberg detected a tone in her voice, or a glance in her eye, which struck him unpleasantly at the moment, and still more so, when he came to reflect upon the cause. What could she mean by them? Surely, she could never imagine that he would play his nearest friend false, for the sake of a face and figure like hers?

He put the idea away from him, again and again, as derogatory to himself and the honour of Ricardo's wife—but it haunted him all the same. Has the reader ever encountered pictured eyes of villainy or lust which have seemed to follow him wherever he went? So did the eyes of Hannah Ricardo follow Steinberg, until he was fain to remember them, whether he would or no. She never betrayed herself, nor said a word that might be construed to her own undoing—but she gave Steinberg the impression, that the feeling was there, all the same.

He began to avoid her, as much as possible, leaving the cottage as early as he could, and returning late. He was rather an attractive young man, as has been said before—being only thirty years old, and having a fair German face, which struck most people as pleasant to look upon.

He was just pondering upon the best excuse for dissolving partnership with the Ricardos altogether, when the Wheel of Fortune did for him what he was contemplating doing for himself. He had come to London poor and without expectations, when by one of those strokes of good fortune that do occasionally happen in this world, a rich uncle of his died suddenly in Berlin, and left him his entire fortune. He rushed to the Professor with the news, almost unable to believe it to be true.

"My dearest friend, I am a wealthy man! My good uncle the Baron von Steinberg, who was the richest publisher in Berlin, has died and left me everything—everything! Congratulate me! Give me your hand! Let me feel that my best friend is glad with me! *Ach! Himmel!* we will be happy now, and have a good time together."

"A thousand congratulations, my dear Steinberg," cried the Professor, warmly wringing his hand.

"But I must leave you! I must go to Berlin without delay. The lawyers have written for me. As yet I know nothing but the fact, but when I get there, I will write to you, dear Ricardo, and tell you all."

"And won't you come back to the cottage?" inquired Hannah.

"I do not know, Hannah. All is vague at present, except that this good luck has befallen me! My uncle's fortune amounted, so I am told, to many thousand pounds a year, so perhaps I may have to live in Berlin. I cannot tell, but be sure of one thing—that I will never forget you, my dear Ricardo, nor all the interest you have shown in me. Farewell!"

The men grasped hands again, whilst Hannah looked on and murmured,

"Thousands of pounds a year! Some people are lucky! Why didn't *he* take a fancy for me, instead of the other?"

CHAPTER XI.

THE Professor felt very dull for the first few days after Karl Steinberg had left them for Berlin. He rejoiced at the good fortune that had befallen his friend, but he feared it might prove a separation between them. With only Hannah to talk to, he felt more lonely than he had ever done in Mrs. Battleby's apartments.

He watched for the post eagerly, to bring him news of his absent companion, and in about ten days his patience was rewarded by receiving a letter from Steinberg.

The Doctor wrote gaily and enthusiastically. He seemed not to have a care left in the world.

"Congratulate me, my very kind friend," he commenced; "I am a wealthier man than I imagined. We laid my good uncle to rest in the family vault of the Von Steinbergs, three days after my arrival in Berlin. He was a childless man, and when the will was read I found that (with the exception of a liberal life-allowance to his widow) he had left everything, without reserve, to your humble servant. His house in Berlin—his château at Wiesbaden—his fortune, amounting to between three and four thousand a year—and all his personal property, which includes one of the finest private picture galleries in the country.

"Am I not lucky? I feared at first lest this generous bequest should involve my living in Germany, perhaps looking after landed estate or farming country property (which is not at all in my line, my dear Ricardo, as you are aware). But no! Even here, I am fortunate, as the greater part of the legacy is in hard cash, and the houses can readily be disposed of. I am free, therefore, to do as I like and live where I choose, and all my wishes tend towards London, the grandest city in the world. You may expect, therefore, before very long, to see me again.

"I shall take a house in Town, and collect around me all those whom I love, or take an interest in. And for the future, I shall resume my right of writing 'von' before my name, which I dropped when I entered on my duties at the Hospital. Ah! those dreary days and sleepless nights! Thank Heaven! they are over for ever! I can, at least, live the remainder of my life as best pleases myself. But I can never, never, under any circumstances, forget my very best friend, and you know what his name is, without my telling you.

"The first place I visit on my return, will be the little cottage at Hampstead, when, tell Mrs. Ricardo, I shall expect her to brew the very best cup of tea of which she is capable, in honour of my uncle's fortune and title.

"Ever yours, with warm affection,
"KARL VON STEINBERG."

The Professor read this letter to himself—then aloud to Hannah—finally laying it down upon the table with a deep sigh.

"Ain't you glad?" demanded his wife, shrewdly regarding the old man, "the Doctor'll 'ave a fine 'ouse now, and everythink of the best, and that's as good as saying as you'll 'ave it,—and me, too, eh?"

"I don't know, Hannah," he replied; "when men grow rich, they are too often apt to forget their poorer friends. Besides, Von Steinberg's fortune will attract people of equal position round his table, and we are not fit to associate with such."

"Why not?" asked Hannah, broadly.

She had a household broom in her hands at the time, and she leant her chin upon the handle, and stared the Professor well in the face.

"Why ain't we as good as any other of 'is friends—let them be who they may?" she asked, fixing her large eyes upon him.

"Well! my dear, it is rather unnecessary to put such a question," replied Ricardo, "money makes money, you know, and we have none. Karl will have a grand house, doubtless, and give big parties, and rich and titled people will attend them—people with whom you and I have nothing to do! He is not only rich, you see! He is no longer a doctor, but a Baron, and can hold his own with any one in the land."

"Ain't a Markiss higher than a Baron?" demanded Hannah, and her husband, not dreaming in what direction the conversation was tending, answered gravely, "Why! of course!"

"Then, you're higher than him," retorted his wife, "so why shouldn't you mix with any nobs as he gets round him?"

Ricardo looked up in amazement.

"*I* am higher than Von Steinberg? What do you mean?" he said.

"Why! ain't you a Markiss?" reiterated Hannah, still sturdily regarding him from over the broom; "the Markiss of Sorrento? If you're bigger than the Doctor, why should you mind going among 'is friends? Money don't count beside name. I've often 'eard you say that to me."

"But who—*who*—" said the Professor, stammering, "ever told you anything about my having a title? Has Steinberg betrayed my trust? You have never known me, except as Professor Ricardo! What do you mean by all this talk about a Marquis?"

Hannah looked as if she had been suddenly struck

foolish. The light faded out of her flat, unmeaning face—she seemed as if she were scared at what she had been led into saying.

"I don't know, I'm sure," she replied, with a quivering lip, as if she were about to cry, "unless I dreamt it! Some one must 'ave told it me. Markiss dee Sorrento! Yes! that's it! Markiss dee Sorrento! There's a woice repeating it in my ears now! And—and—*the proof of it* is in that drawer," she continued rapidly, as she slapped her hand down upon a small writing-table where the Professor kept his private papers.

Now the title deeds of the marquisate and lands of Sorrento were still in the Professor's possession, lest a change of dynasty might restore his family rights to him. But he always kept them in a small iron safe under his bed. He had destroyed every other trace of the rank and position he had once held amongst men, and felt certain that nothing could be found in his desk to betray them. So he answered, somewhat pettishly,

"These voices in your ears, Hannah, are not telling you the truth! You had much better go and attend to your household duties, and leave off talking rubbish!"

But at these words Hannah turned a face upon him, which he could hardly recognise as her own. Her usually dull eyes were blazing with passion—and her tones were loud and authoritative, as she exclaimed,

"It is *you* who are not telling the truth! The proofs of what I say are in that drawer, and I will not leave the room until you open it!"

The Professor was really frightened. He felt confident that nothing was in the drawer that could identify his name and title, so, more to pacify her and restore peace between them than to prove his word, he drew forth his bunch of keys, and inserting one in the keyhole, pulled the drawer open. It apparently contained nothing but odd sheets of writing paper, and a few old letters.

"Now! are you satisfied that you are wrong?" he said, turning to his wife.

But Hannah seemed possessed by the fury of a demon. She flew at the papers and scattered them all over the floor by a twist of her hand. Still she was not content, but scratched about the bottom of the receptacle as if she were blind or acting under some spell, when she suddenly ceased, and drew from the inmost recesses of the drawer, a small card, yellow with age, which had become wedged at the back. She held it to the light with a discordant chuckle of triumph. On it was printed in flourishing Italian characters, "Marchese di Sorrento."

"What is that?" she cried, holding it out to the Professor, "is that your name, or is it not?"

Ricardo was fain to confess the truth.

"Sit down, Hannah, my dear," he said, "compose yourself, I beg of you! There is no need for you to be angry with me! Be patient and I will tell you the whole story."

"Is that your name, or is it not?" repeated the girl, as she flourished the card in his face.

"Yes! yes! it is, will that content you? But I shall never use it again, Hannah! I have very good reasons for not doing so, and you must regard this discovery on your part as if it had never been. Do you understand me?"

"I don't know as I do," said Hannah; "this is your true name, you say?"

"Yes! I am the Marchese di Sorrento," replied Ricardo, with some degree of pride, "but, as I said before, I have discarded the title and consider that it is no longer mine! I am sorry you ever found it out, my dear. I should never have told you myself, but as it is, you must forget it as soon as you can."

"If it's your name, it's mine too," said Hannah, with an obstinate look about the mouth.

"It *would* have been so, had I retained it," interposed the Professor, quietly, "but since I choose to be known only as Signor Ricardo, my wife is Madame, or Mrs. Ricardo—nothing more!"

"If it's mine, it's mine," returned Hannah, doggedly, "and I don't see why I'm to be called out of my name! Why should Mrs. Barnett, the grocer's wife, call me 'Missus', when she ought to say 'my lady?' I 'eard 'er telling another customer larst night, as I was a foreigner! Like 'er impidence! I'll shew 'er if I'm a foreigner! I'll make 'er say 'my lady' next time she speaks to me, or I'll get all our things from Addison's."

"Hannah! Hannah! for Heaven's sake, don't make us the laughing stock of Hampstead," exclaimed the Professor, in genuine distress, "however true the story may be, no one will believe it from your lips. They will ask you, if you are a lady, *why* you do all the house-work by yourself. Such people as you speak of, only value their acquaintances by the amount of money they may happen to possess."

"And I don't see why I shouldn't 'ave a servant to help me!" replied Hannah, boldly. "If I'm a Markiness, it isn't fit as I should cook and scrub and what not, making my 'ands filthy, and spoiling my complexion. I've been going to speak to you about that afore, Professor—I mean Markiss——"

"O! Hannah! for God's sake, don't call me by that name!" cried poor Ricardo, with both his fingers in his ears.

"Well! I'm sure!" exclaimed his wife. "I s'pose *she* called you by it, or summat very similar, but I ain't good enough, eh? Well! since I've a right to it, I'm going to use it, and so I tells you straight, and the sooner you gets accustomed to it, the better. 'Tain't much as I got by marrying of you, Markiss, so you might as well leave me the name. 'Twon't bring in bread and butter anyway!"

"I know it, and what is the use of using a title which you cannot keep up in appearance? We have only enough money to live on, and I see no chance of our ever having more."

"I don't know about that!" replied the girl, with a cunning look, "I know of a way by which money could be made, and pretty sharp, too."

"What do you mean? If you are correct, you will find me willing enough to take advantage of it!"

"Well! you just give out as I can make the sperrits and things walk about the room, and make folks pay to come and see them, and you'd make a fortune. I've 'eard Steinberg say so, times out of mind!"

"O! no! no!" exclaimed the Professor, in disgust. "What! make the vision of my Leonora common property? Let every Jack and Jill, who has the money to enable them, come and gape at her, sharers with me in this heavenly pleasure! Never! Hannah, never! I cannot prevent your adopting my title if you refuse to comply with my request that you should not do so, but I utterly forbid your turning your divine gift into a merchandise. I am afraid you have never estimated it at its real value!"

"No! I can't say I see much fun in it myself," replied Hannah, grinning, "but it got me out of a precious muddle, didn't it? I don't know what I should have done at that time, Professor, if you 'adn't taken a fancy to sperrits and things!"

"You appear to have conquered all your fear of them, Hannah," remarked the Professor, musingly. "You have altered in many ways lately! I never hear you object to the cabinet now, nor express terror of the spirits, in any way."

"I've no call left to be feared of them," replied his wife, still grinning, as if her mediumship were an excellent joke. "They're allays after me, day and night! I've got so used to them, that I don't take no more notice of them than I do of you. Let them go on with their larks, and leave me to go on with mine!"

"And your father and mother, and Joe, Hannah?" continued the Professor, a little wistfully; "do you never think of them now, either?"

It seemed as if he would have liked to hear her say that she still hankered after her people and her home. But her grin remained unabated.

"Not often," she replied; "they ain't no good to me now! As for Joe, he may go to the devil for aught I care!"

"O! hush! hush! hush!" cried the Professor.

"It's of no use your saying, ''ush! 'ush! 'ush!' to me, Sig-nor! You don't want me to be 'ankering after a young man now that I'm the Markiness dee Sorrento, do you? Which I don't, I'm sure! I often wonders 'ow I could ever 'ave fancied Joe, with his coarse 'air, and his pig's eyes! I'm sure if I 'ad my rights and a 'ouse fit for a Markiness,

I would never arsk 'im into it! I'd 'ave no one under a Barrow-knight, or a squire, within the walls. I should know 'ow to play my part, you bet, Professor—I means, Markiss!"

Ricardo sighed.

"Well! my poor girl, I fear you will never have the opportunity of trying it," he said. "But will you give me a séance this evening! I feel rather low-spirited, and it will cheer me and do me good."

"O! you can 'ave it and welcome," replied Hannah, "but, I say Markiss, it do seem a pity now, to 'ave all this fuss, and two good hours wasted, only for you, don't it? And if we 'ad a dozen or so of strangers with their 'alf guinea each, why, I'd make more in a night than you can do in a week."

She hung coaxingly over him, as she spoke, but Ricardo put her away, as though the suggestion had come from the Evil One.

"I have said 'No!' already, and I would repeat it a thousand times!" he ejaculated. "You don't know what you are talking of! Your insinuation is a desecration of the angel, for whom alone I value your services."

"Didn't *she* like being a Markiness?" asked Hannah, as she left the room to make some little preparations before the séance.

Her remark set Ricardo thinking how much all women are alike.

"How they love a title!" he pondered inwardly.

"Although Leonora was of noble birth, I can well remember her pleasure, less roughly expressed than that of this poor untutored girl, but still the same, when she first assumed my name, and heard herself called Marchesa di Sorrento.

"And how proud I was of her, with her lovely face and swan-like figure, all life and grace! She looked a Marchioness, from the crown of her noble head to her dainty feet. But this poor, uncouth child of nature! I never thought of the disgrace to my title, when I married her! Steinberg reminded me of it, but I considered it dead, and myself only as a drudging teacher! How did she find out about it, I wonder! It is inconceivable—still more, that she should take such a keen pleasure in assuming it! Well! it is a misfortune, but I cannot prevent her! It *is* her name beyond all dispute, and if she will use it, she must!

"But how changed she has become during the last few weeks. Sometimes I regard her with amazement and cannot believe she is the same Hannah I married! Where is her timidity—her stolidity—her implacable good humour—her fear of me and Von Steinberg, flown? She has become brisk and pert, almost dominant in her manner— and at times I catch a look in her eye, as though her soul had but just waked up and was astonished at its own power. Yet with it all, I like her better—yes! there is decidedly something that I like better in Hannah now, than when I first married her!

"But this folly about assuming her title! How I wish Von Steinberg would hasten home, that he might reason her out of it!"

Here, his wife's voice summoned him to the séance chamber, and he was soon absorbed in watching for the wonders which his sittings with her revealed to him.

One point had rather worried him lately, and that was the defection of his beloved Leonora, or rather, the little advance which she made towards development. Ricardo had imagined on commencing his studies in Occultism, that the apparitions would grow with the growth of his knowledge of them, and from being visible but silent, would progress in language, as in familiarity, until they would converse with him as easily as if they stood face to face on earth, or in Heaven.

He had a thousand things to ask of Leonora. He yearned to ascertain where she now lived—how she employed herself—what associates she had—and how her spirit life was sustained in her; above all, by what mystical wonder, she managed to leave her Heavenly dwelling-place and visit him in the little dark chamber, which he called his séance room, and through the instrumentality of so rough and untutored a medium as Hannah Stubbs.

But though he addressed such queries to the apparition of Leonora night after night, he never received any satisfactory reply. A shrug of the shoulders—a shake or nod of the head—a whispered "Yes!" or "No!" seemed to be the extent of information he could receive from her.

Naturally, having been her husband, he longed to touch her again, to put his lips to hers, or to grasp the little white hand which was invariably thrust through the curtain to greet him.

But such favours were sparingly accorded him. If he were permitted to touch her hand, it was only to pat the outside of it—if her face were advanced to meet his, it merely brushed his cheek, like the fluttering of a butterfly's wing. And, as he had complained to Von Steinberg, her visits had become far less frequent than they had been at first. Strangers, in whom he felt but sparse interest, had taken her place and usurped the time and power, which he considered Leonora's.

But this evening, after an interval of several days, she appeared. Her dark eyes peeped at him through a veil of gossamer, which fell to her feet, and her lissom form swayed itself to and fro, as though loath to leave the sheltering curtain.

Ricardo was in the lowest spirits. He could think of nothing but the subject that immediately disquieted him.

"My beautiful Marchesa!" he said, as Leonora's form appeared at the entrance of the cabinet, "can you guess how distasteful it is to me to hear the title which you adorned, usurped by another? *She* a Marchesa! O! it is impossible!—degrading—poor uncouth, ignorant creature! she little knows the height to which she aspires. She could as soon sit as Queen, upon the throne of England! Forgive me, sweetest Love, that I should have given this ungainly servant the semblance of your position. But she is not *my wife*, Leonora! You know it! Her name is but an empty sound! I have been widowed since the fatal night that saw your pure spirit wing its flight to Heaven, and I shall remain widowed till we meet again. But tell me, dearest, what shall I do? What do you advise me to do? Is Hannah to have her own way in this, or not?"

The form of Leonora nodded its head.

"Is it part of my punishment for having sent you to your account, whilst still in the bloom of your youth and beauty, to have brought this trouble on my head? Must I endure it, as a penance, that shall bring me, all the sooner, to your dear feet?"

The figure nodded its head a second time.

"Then I *will* bear it—even to hear her called by the title which I was so proud to bestow upon you—if it will only reunite us one moment sooner than I hoped for."

The Professor, in his anxiety to gain the approval of his former wife for all he did and said, did not consider that he put the words he wished to hear her say into her mouth, or, rather, that he accepted her acquiescence as a sign that she understood the case, and his reasons for it. If Leonora approved of Hannah being styled Marchesa di Sorrento, it should be exactly as she wished and vice versa. The next question was put with some amount of trepidity.

"And do you consider that she ought to have a servant?—that the work is too hard for her, and unbefitting her position as my wife? Ought I to allow her to make her powers public, or shall I keep them entirely for myself, as now?"

Leonora shook her head vehemently.

"It will not militate against our meeting, Leonora, nor interfere in any way with your appearance? Ah! my beloved, think what I have sacrificed, in order to obtain this great privilege! It would break my heart if you were to desert Hannah, because others kept you away."

The figure bent forward until its lips touched the Professor's face, and whispered,

"Better! much better!"

"Then it shall be so!" exclaimed Ricardo, though he sighed whilst he said the words; "I will put no further obstacle in the way of her wishes. Anything—anything—that shall make your path more easy to you, and bind us more nearly together. But O! my Leonora! how I long sometimes for the happy day when Death, like a kindly friend, shall lead me out of this world of perplexity, into the Land of Light, where I shall meet you again, in all the radiance of your spiritual youth and beauty!"

The Spirit patted him gently on the head, but Ricardo did not raise his face from his hands for the remainder of the séance. When Hannah came to herself, she found him sitting so, almost as lost to all external things as she had been.

CHAPTER XII.

A FEW weeks after the events related in the last chapter, as Mrs. Battleby was helping her wretched drudge to wash up the miscellaneous assortment of plates, dishes, cups, saucers and tumblers, sent down by her various lodgers, and harrying the girl's soul out, by constant adjurations to make more haste, she was startled by the sound of a loud double knock on the front door.

"Now! 'oo on hearth can that be calling at this time o' night?" she exclaimed testily, as she wiped her hands on her canvas apron. "'Ere, 'Liza, 'and me over that clean apron *do*, and don't stand gaping at me there! I declare, you put me ever so much in mind of that great, hulking fool, Hannah Stubbs, which I've never forgiven 'er mother to this day for putting her upon me! It might be some one arter the hattics, for I've known 'em to come, when pressed, as late as ten o'clock at night, Now! go on with your washing-up, and don't be a'follerin' me to hear what they may say, for it's no concern of yourn any way."

Saying which, Mrs. Battleby left the lower regions and ascended to answer the hall door.

It was a dark night, and all she could distinguish at first was, that a female figure stood on the door steps.

"Who do you please to want, Ma'am?" she inquired.

"Is Mrs. Battleby at home?" asked the stranger, in her turn.

"Yes! Ma'am, I be Mrs. Battleby, but if it's rooms as you want, I've none to let but the hattics, which was occupied last by a gentleman of very high degree!"

"Lor! Mrs. Battleby! I don't believe you know me!" exclaimed the visitor, as she pushed her way into the passage, and leant up against the wall, laughing.

"Why, it's never!—No! it can't never be—*Hannah Stubbs!*" cried Mrs. Battleby, too much astounded to be angry at being taken in.

"Yes! it is," replied Hannah, still laughing, "but I ain't Hannah Stubbs no longer, Mrs. Battleby! I'm a married lady now, and able to hold my own with anybody. But ain't you a'going to arsk me to take a chair? Ain't the parlours vacant? Can't we go in there?"

"The parlours!" repeated the landlady, with a sneer. "Well! I wonder what we're coming to, next! I should 'ave thought as the kitchen was good enough for you, Hannah Stubbs, though you *be* married!"

"Well! then, let me tell you, Mrs. Battleby as it ain't! And I'll thank you not to call me out of my name. I'm married to a nobleman, and I'll stick up for my rights. 'My lady' is the proper way for you to address me, Mrs. Battleby! I'm a Markiness!"

"A *what!*" exclaimed Mrs. Battleby, as she pushed her visitor into the back parlour, which lacked an inmate. "Are you mocking me, Hannah, or 'ave you gone clean off your chump? A markiness! You must be daft! They belongs to the highest of the haristocracy. What 'ave you been a'doing of, since you left this 'ouse?"

As she lighted the gas, and was enabled to have a good look at her late slavey, the landlady perceived there was a great difference in her appearance. Hannah wore the famous apple-green merino, with a silk mantle over it—a small black bonnet, crowned with scarlet poppies, and a pair of brown silk gloves. Altogether, though she did not look like a marchioness, she had the appearance of a very respectable servant.

"And now do tell me the rights of all this, for you've took my breath away," said Mrs. Battleby. "What's become of the poor Professor, and his friend the Doctor, and 'ave you left them for good, and where are you living now?"

She pushed Hannah into a chair and took one opposite herself, so eager was she to learn how this wonderful transformation scene had come about.

The Marchesa di Sorrento was wonderfully self-possessed. She drew off her silk gloves and folded them neatly on her lap—placed her umbrella in a safe position—and settled herself down for a good talk.

"I have not left the Sig-nor at all, Mrs. Battleby," she commenced; "we've been married for a long time now, and our 'ouse is at 'Ampstead."

"The Sig-nor has *married* you!" exclaimed the landlady, gasping in her surprise. "Why! I allays thought as 'e was a real gentleman! Actually *married* you! Well! wonders never cease!"

"A real gentleman," cried Hannah, sharply, "I should think he was—a better gentleman than you'll ever 'ave in your attics agen, Mrs. Battleby. He's more than a gentleman, a good deal! He's a real Markiss! What do you think of that! The Markiss dee Sorrento! And I'm a Markiness! The Markiness dee Sorrento! And that's why you'll 'ave to call me 'my lady' if ever you speaks to me agen, Mrs. Battleby."

"I don't believe as I could ever find it on my tongue to do it, Hannah—not if you was to give me a 'undred pounds," said the landlady, as she sank back in her chair with surprise.

"Are you satisfied I speak the truth," asked

Hannah, presently, "or must I bring the Markiss here to tell you so, himself? He was always a Markiss, of course, but he didn't choose to let on to you about it. But as soon as we was married, he told me the truth! It was a fine surprise for me, as you may be sure, but I'm quite accustomed to it now."

"And he actually married you—that quiet old gentleman! Well! if you'd told me marriage was in his line, I'd 'ave said you was quite mistook. And the Doctor—what did 'e say to it, eh, Hannah?—I mean—my lady!"

"You don't go to suppose as we asked the Doctor's leave, or anybody else's?" replied the Markiness, with a fine scorn; "the Markiss was old enough to know his own mind, I s'pose! And the Doctor ain't a doctor any longer either! He's a Baron—the Baron von Steinberg, and 'as come into a big fortune of thousands and thousands of pounds a year."

"O! you don't go to tell me as the Doctor's a haristocrat, too?" cried Mrs. Battleby, who felt as if all her old acquaintances had suddenly drifted from her into realms above. "'E who was such a nice-speaking young gentleman! A Baron! Well! I never! And money into the bargain! No wonder as they both left the hattics!"

"The Baron 'as a lovely 'ouse in Portland Place," continued Hannah, "the most beautiful 'ouse as you ever see—all statues and pictures and flowering plants. You can't 'ear your feet in 'is carpets, and 'e keeps ten or twelve servants. He's rolling in riches, is the Baron."

"My!" gasped Mrs. Battleby, too exhausted by astonishment to be able to say any more.

"And you, my dear," she resumed, after a pause, "'ow do you git on with the cooking and that? The Sig-nor, 'e wasn't very particular, but if I remembers rightly, you didn't know nothink of cooking, or of much else when you fust come to me—did you?"

"No! nor now either," responded Hannah, with her grandest air, "I 'ave no call to do anything of the sort. My servant does all that for me!"

"*Your servant!* Lor! and you keep a servant!" echoed the landlady. "I never! But in coorse the Sig-nor, being a Markiss, would now, wouldn't 'e? And 'ave you told all this to your pore mother and father, who 'ave been sadly about you, ever since you runned away from me!"

"No! Mrs. Battleby, and don't mean to, neither! You don't suppose as the Markiss would let such people as my mother and father come about the 'ouse! It would bemean his rank! They carst me off and they must keep to theirselves—as well as that ill-mannered young man Joseph Brushwood! I wouldn't stop to speak to 'em, not if I met 'em in the road."

"Well! Hannah, you 'ave grown 'igh," replied the other, " but I 'opes as you've given up all them sperrits and devils and things as beset you 'ere. The Markiss won't allow them about 'im, I expect!"

"You only says that because you're so ignorant, Mrs. Battleby," said the Markiness, tossing her head; "those who know about the matter says they're Science, and all the aristocracy are running after them like mad! They call them 'angels' not 'devils', and they *do* say," continued the girl, lowering her voice, and bending towards the landlady, "that Royalty's crazy about it, too, and that if I chose to go to the Palace and show 'em what I can do, that I should be made a duchess in my own right!"

"O! Hannah—my lady—don't you go for to do it!" cried Mrs. Battleby, "for what's the good of being a duchess, if the Devil 'as got hold of you! Better remain as you are—a plain markiness! O! I 'ad 'oped as you'd given it all up and lived quiet and sober, like a married woman should!"

"O! that would never do!" replied Hannah, "Why! do you know, Mrs. Battleby, as it's the best thing I've got! The Baron says I'm the grandest medium in the land, and there ain't another as can make the sperrits walk out so soon, and so nateral like! His friends is all mad to meet me, and I'm to go to 'is 'ouse next week, and sit for the Russian Ambassador, and the Duke of Standingstone, and two foreign Princes! Sometimes I wish I hadn't been so quick to take the Markiss, for I should 'ave 'ad no end of chances, if I 'adn't been a married lady!"

"Ah! well! I 'opes it will all end satisfactory," sighed Mrs. Battleby, "but it don't seem right to me! Sperrits is sperrits all the world over, which we're told not to meddle with in holy Scriptur, and I should never be surprised to 'ear as they'd taken you away with 'orns and a tail and a smell of brimstone!"

"I ain't afeared of that!" said Hannah, "the sperrits are more afraid of me than I am of them!"

"Of *you*—who used to shriek if you saw 'em!" replied her companion, incredulously.

"I know! but they says as use is second natur. Anyways, I don't mind 'em one pin now! The Doctor says they 'ave seen the most wonderfullest things through me—his dead patients and others—and that if anythink 'appened to the Markiss, my mediumship would be worth its weight in gold. So I'm not going to throw it away—you bet!"

"O! well! and I'm not the one to blame yer. We must all look arter ourselves in this world. But 'ow improved you are in your speaking, my dear! 'Ave you been to school since the Sig-nor married you?"

"Am I improved?" demanded Hannah, with a look of surprise; "I don't see any difference myself!

P'r'aps it's talking so much with my 'usband—not that the Markiss is a great talker, but still I don't hear anyone else."

"You are altered in many ways," continued the landlady, thoughtfully, "you've lost the scared look you used to 'ave on your face, and the dull look too, I may say, for we never considered you over-bright, you know, Hannah! But now—I ain't good at describing—but you seem to me to have wakened up, as if you'd seen a lot of the world and its ways. And it's improved you, Hannah—wonderful!"

"I'm glad of that," replied the markiness, "for now that I am a lady, I has to speak like one. Well! I'll say good-night to you now, Mrs. Battleby, for I must be going 'ome! But I thought, as you'd known the Markiss for so long, you'd like to hear the news, and that we're all so 'appy together!"

Hannah had risen to go, but Mrs. Battleby detained her for a moment.

"You 'aven't told me nothing of the Sig-nor's 'ealth," she said; "'as 'e got rid of them dreadful fainty attacks as used to take 'im sometimes, when 'e lived with me?"

"No! not quite! He had one yesterday. The Baron says it's 'is 'eart, and that 'e's 'ad it a long time. But all we 'ave to do is to be careful, and 'e'll last as long as any."

"And may I come up and see you some day,

Hannah—my lady?" inquired the landlady. "I should like to 'ave a look at the Sig-nor, I must say."

The Markiness dee Sorrento hesitated.

"I s'pose I must say 'yes', Mrs. Battleby, because of old times, but you must please not to call me 'Hannah' before my servant, or she may think it disrespectful. I 'ope you understand the motive!"

"O! yes, my lady—certainly, my lady!" replied Mrs. Battleby, as she curtsied the newly-made peeress out at the hall door, and retreated to the kitchen again, to try and solve the marvellous riddle which had been presented to her.

Meanwhile the marchioness took an omnibus back to Hampstead, where she found Karl von Steinberg, who had been home about a week, in close conversation with her husband.

"I am trying to combat Ricardo's objection to your giving my friends a séance next week, Hannah!" he said, as she appeared, "but he is very obstinate! He seems to imagine that if your powers are made public, they will deteriorate in some way. I—on the contrary—think they will improve with practice, always provided that we see you are not overtaxed. And *I* shall be present to prevent that! I have not given up being a doctor, at all events for the benefit of my friends, though I have become a Baron!"

"Of course not!" replied Hannah, "and I've told

the Markiss so a hundred times! Haven't the sperrits said the same thing? They're more likely to desert me, if I disobey their orders. Don't waste no more time over the Markiss, Baron! I'm going to give your friends that séance next week, and as many more as you choose—so there's an end of the matter!"

"But we must follow your husband's wishes in this respect, Hannah," said Von Steinberg. "I should not enjoy the séance, for one, if he disapproved of your giving it! He will never shut me out from your home sittings, I am sure, and if he is determined, my friends must go without it, or get another medium to sit for them!"

"And where will they find another like me?" replied Hannah, with that strange look in her eyes—half sensual and half cunning—which he had noticed before his departure for Germany. "You know yourself there is not such another in the country! No! I shall sit at your house next week, whatever any one says. Besides, if I do not, Leonora will not come again, and how will you like that, Markiss?"

"Did she tell you so?" cried Ricardo, in alarm.

"Indeed, she did! She says my gift was given me for the good of humanity and not merely to gratify your selfish wish to see her again."

"O! I will not—I will not—be selfish then," exclaimed the poor Professor. "Von Steinberg, she is right! This wonderful gift was never intended to be hidden under a bushel! I give my consent to her using it for the benefit of mankind. But—if you will forgive me—I will remain at home! I could not bear to see my Leonora disporting her lovely form for strangers to gaze at. No! let Hannah wait upon your friends, and I will stay here until my Angel deigns to come to me again."

"But why should Leonora appear at all in my house, Ricardo?" remonstrated his friend, "if you do not care to attend the séance, you can at least bring your wife to my house and take her home."

"No! no! I would rather that she went alone!" persisted the Professor.

"O! let him be!" cried Hannah, impatiently, "if the markiss has got a crotchet in his head, it'll take more than you and me to dig it out again. It'll be his own loss—not ours!"

At this Ricardo rose, and, without another word, walked up stairs to his own room.

"You are wrong, Hannah," remarked Von Steinberg, "you have no right to speak before your husband like that! You should be doubly forbearing towards him just now, for I don't think he is well."

"What's the matter with him?" asked the girl.

"His heart is weaker than usual, and he has other disorders which complicate it. I think your determination to assume his title has worried him more than you imagine. It rouses unpleasant memories in him, and keeps the Past always before his eyes. Besides, it is not yours to use! It was confiscated years ago by the Italian Government, and does not belong to Ricardo himself any longer!"

"O! that's rubbish!" cried Hannah, "it wasn't lawful of them to take it away, and so it's his still! Besides, what 'arm does it do to anybody, my calling myself a markiness? It's little enough I got by marrying 'im, I'm sure! He needn't grudge me that!"

"You got an honest, brave, honourable gentleman, Hannah, which is a thing to be proud of!"

"But it won't do me 'alf the good that being called 'my lady' will, all the same," replied Hannah, with one of her cunning looks. "I mean to make my way in the world, Baron, for he won't leave me much butter for my bread, and it's the only crutch I've got to walk with! It'll go down better than money with 'alf the fools I meet."

"I think you're a very clever woman," said Von Steinberg, regarding her with admiration. "I had no idea when I first saw you, that you had such a quick wit and brain. And you are improving fast in your manner of talking! If it were not for dropping an *h* now and then, when you get excited, you might really hold your own with many a lady in the land!"

"I mean to, too, you bet!" said Hannah. "I ain't—I mean, I haven't—married an old man for nothing! I've got something to set against his age, eh, Doctor? And if you'll stand my friend, and introduce me to some of the big people at your séances, you see if my 'wonderful gift' (as you call it) won't land me some day in unexpected places."

"By Jove! I believe you're sharp enough for anything," exclaimed Von Steinberg, "and if I can help you, I will! But it must be with Ricardo's consent."

"Didn't you hear him give it? He'd sell me to the Devil, if it would bring his Leonora to him! He doesn't care a hang about me! He only cares for her!"

"You mustn't say that!" replied Von Steinberg, though he believed it to be true.

"And I'll tell you a secret, Doctor! I don't believe that Leonora will come to him much longer, either! She's pretty well sick of being prayed and slobbered over, and called an angel! She wasn't an angel—not by no manner of means—and it wearies her! She liked life, did Leonora—domestic happiness wasn't in her line at all."

"I believe you are correct there," replied the Doctor.

"And can't you see how sitting by himself, night after night, is drawing all the strength out of the Markiss. It doesn't signify about *my* strength—he has never thought about that—so long as he can see Leonora—but it'll chaw him up before long, if he don't look out. It'll be for his good to take me away a bit—mark my words!"

"By Jove! you're right again," replied her companion, "and it is wonderful I did not perceive the danger to him before! You've done Ricardo a great benefit by your astuteness, my dear, and I shall not fail to tell him so! But you are sure you have not hurt yourself! You do not feel at all weak, or ill—not as if a tonic, or stimulant of any kind, would do you good?"

"O! no! Doctor, I'm all right, thank you," said Hannah, smiling at the anxiety depicted in his face; "only you get me to your fine house and it'll do me all the good in the world!"

"I am delighted to think that you are coming," said Von Steinberg, "and, Hannah, at this or any time, remember that anything I may have, or can procure, is at your service! I can never sufficiently thank you for the grand insight you have given me, through your mediumship, to the truth of Immortality, and anything I could do for you in return I should esteem a great favour!

"And now one word of advice, my dear girl, which I know you are too sensible to resent. Try to correct the few errors of grammar which you still retain, and the sooner will you gain admittance into the houses you aspire to be invited to, on an equal footing with their owners."

Hannah stood, for a moment, as if dumbfoundered.

"I don't get on as fast as I should, do I?" she said at length. "It seems queer, but there's something in my tongue as won't sound some words. I s'pose it's all habit, and I haven't much opportunity for improving myself now!"

"How's that?"

"Why, the markiss has gone dumb! 'E never opens 'is mouth 'ardly from morning till night! 'Ow is a girl to learn anything from him? I can read a little, you know, Doctor, but not enough to improve myself, and I carn't go back to school, now I'm a markiness!"

"No! you're too old for that! Well! we must see what we can do together, Hannah, you and I! Your husband is out almost all day, so I could come over here sometimes, and give you a lesson in conversation, that is, if you really wish to learn."

"I'd like to learn Italian with you," said Hannah, softly.

Von Steinberg stared.

"Italian, my dear! What are you talking of? I think we had better get on with a little English first! When shall it be? Shall I come up to-morrow morning and begin our studies?"

Hannah approached him, and laid her hand gently on his arm.

"I shall like to learn with you!" she said, softly, in the same voice she had used a moment before.

"You are good. I feel it! I shall love you for your kindness to me."

Karl von Steinberg started away from her, as if he had been stung.

What was the expression in her face, which had so improved its expression? Rough Hannah Stubbs seemed to have gone away, and a gentle-featured, alluring woman to have stepped into her place. Her eyes, always beautiful, glowed with gratitude and sensibility—her touch was tender—her smile had become plaintive and appealing.

The doctor shook off her grasp rather rudely than otherwise, and, rising, declared it was time he returned home, and left the cottage without another word.

CHAPTER XIII.

KARL VON STEINBERG was naturally a great lover of Art and Beauty, but hard work and want of means, had prevented him hitherto from indulging his taste for either. Now, however, that he had money at his command, he took the keenest pleasure in surrounding himself with everything that struck his fancy, or pleased his eye.

His house in Portland Place was furnished with æsthetic taste and delicacy. The wide hall and staircase were laid with the softest carpets, and decorated with towering palms and hothouse flowers. The salons were hung with rich tapestries, and ornamented with *objets d'art*, whilst the pictures, transported from the Berlin gallery, formed an uncommon attraction in a private house.

The Baron did not indulge in these expensive luxuries for his own gratification only. He had a liberal and expansive heart, and loved to gather round him as many of his countrymen as he knew in London, as well as all those who had been kind to him in his poorer days.

His sudden accession to Fortune soon drew a crowd of acquaintances to share in his good things, whilst his rank attracted men of good birth and position amongst them.

Over his dinner-table, he had discoursed to scientists and others, of the marvellous powers of Ricardo's wife, and many had eagerly desired to witness them. This was the reason that he had obtained his old friend's permission to ask Hannah to his house, to meet some people who were interested in the matter with himself.

On the evening in question, he entertained at dinner the Persian Ambassador, one of the Gentlemen at Arms from the Royal Household, a celebrated brain doctor, who had long made abnormal cases his study, and three or four medical men with their wives, who had all promised to submit to such conditions as he should impose upon them.

In an ante-chamber to the drawing-room, he had had a cabinet prepared for Hannah's use. A dark velvet curtain drawn across one corner of the apartment, and covered in at the top, proved all that could be desired for the occasion, whilst a moderator lamp, shaded by red silk, cast a subdued light upon the proceedings.

He had not invited Hannah to be present at the dinner; firstly, because he did not like to ask her to leave her husband for too long a time, and secondly, because he thought the presence of his company might intimidate her and make her feel uncomfortable, and perhaps have a bad effect upon the subsequent sitting. He had prepared his guests for her advent, speaking of her as a very quiet body, unaccustomed to society—the wife of an old friend of his, who did not care about her sitting for anybody but himself, but had kindly given permission for her to come there that evening.

He did not exactly ask their indulgence for the roughness of the medium, but he led them to expect a person much their inferior in position—one to whom they might be kind and condescending, but with whom they need not think to associate. She was "the medium"—nothing more.

The men were prepared to stare at her with curiosity, and the women to patronise her, as they might a housemaid who had been endowed with a miraculous voice, or anything else which they did not possess themselves.

No one seemed disposed to sit long at dinner that evening, and they had all assembled in the drawing-room, before Hannah was announced. At last there sounded a cabman's knock and ring at the hall door.

"There is my medium!" exclaimed Von Steinberg, with alacrity, as he rose and advanced to meet her. The guests all looked up curiously, expecting to see a dowdy, scared-looking person enter the room, with an air of fright at finding herself in the presence of so august a company.

What was their surprise, as their host reached the door, to see it thrown open by the footman, and admit a woman, stout, fleshy, and dressed in rather an incongruous manner for the occasion, but to all intents and purposes as self-possessed as any one amongst them.

Karl von Steinberg was so astonished, that it was with difficulty he could restrain himself from giving open vent to his surprise.

On the threshold stood Hannah—arrayed as he had never seen her before—as he had not believed it possible she would ever think of arraying herself! Her abundant hair, which she had gone to a coiffeur to have dressed, was piled upon the top of her head, thus adding height to her stature—her coarse complexion had received a touch of powder, which softened its natural bloom. On her back she wore a white dress, hanging in straight folds from her shoulders to her feet, and thus leaving her waist and general contour undefined, whilst above it rose her well-covered, pinky neck and arms—looking very youthful and healthy, if somewhat countrified.

Had Hannah added jewellry to this new attire, she would have spoilt it and herself. But luckily for her appearance, she had none to wear—the white, straight, unadorned dress and her abundant hair were positively her only ornaments, and strange to say, notwithstanding her birth and antecedents, she looked exceedingly well in them.

Her manners, also, seemed improved to match her dress. Instead of grinning from ear to ear, as was her wont when pleased, she stood like a young Juno on the threshold, as if she knew she was there to confer a favour, not to receive one. She almost took Von Steinberg's breath away, but he managed to collect himself and murmur,

"My dear Hannah!——"

"The Marchesa di Sorrento, if you please!" she replied, and taking her cue, he turned, and presenting her to his guests, repeated,

"Allow me to introduce to you, the Marchesa di Sorrento, who has been charming enough to come here for our amusement this evening. Marchesa!" he added, turning to Hannah, "can I offer you nothing in the shape of refreshment, before you undertake your arduous duties on our behalf?"

"Nothing—nothing!" replied Hannah, as she sank into the seat he offered her.

"And how is the Marchese?" demanded Von Steinberg, willing to humour her, whilst his eyes were roving all the while over her pink neck and rounded arms. "Is he feeling pretty well? I was so sorry he would not join us to-night!"

"It is better so! He is not very well," replied the Marchesa, in a low, modulated voice.

The doctors' wives, who had come to the gathering in high dresses, and lace caps, were beginning to wonder by this time, if they had done wrong and whether the Marchesa would consider they had committed a breach of etiquette.

They sidled up to the Baron and whispered him to present them more particularly to his friend, and then they tried to "pump" Hannah as to her spiritualistic powers and how she developed them, but the Marchesa was unusually silent. Von Steinberg, who had rather dreaded her becoming communicative, could not sufficiently admire her reticence; she was a deucedly sight cleverer than he had ever given her credit for, he said to himself—and in order that the favourable impression she had evidently made, might be kept up, he was not long in leading the way to the séance room.

Here, the guests having been arranged on seats at one end of the apartment, and cautioned not to stir on penalty of being sent away, Hannah was escorted to the cabinet by Karl, who could not help whispering as he affected to be arranging her comfortably in her chair,

"You are marvellous—you have astonished me—I never knew what a handsome woman you were, before!"

To which compliments she answered by half closing her eyes, as she ejaculated,

"You may be very clever, my friend, but you do not know everything that there is in this world yet," and immediately shutting her lids, she fell into a profound sleep.

"How unlike Hannah!" thought the Baron, as he mingled once more with his company— "not even like her voice. The accent too—I could have sworn that it was foreign—it is too marvellous—it is past finding out!"

His friends were full of curiosity.

"What a fine woman!"

"We never expected anything of this sort!"

"Has she gone to sleep already?"

"How soon will they appear?"

"What a remarkable power to possess!"

These were among the remarks that poured in upon Von Steinberg, almost in a breath, from his various friends.

"Ladies! Ladies! I can tell you nothing more than I hope you will see for yourselves before long! Have patience, and I think you will be rewarded! Yes! the Marchesa is a very fine young woman, Derrick, as you say. Her age?—between eighteen and nineteen! Where was she educated? I really cannot say. Somewhere in the country, I believe! She is quite new to London, and has been kept in such close attendance on her husband, since her marriage, that she has had no time, nor opportunity, to go into Society.

"But stay—hush!—I think I saw the curtain move. Yes! I am right! There is her principal control, who calls herself, 'Leonora!' Mrs. Atkinson, cannot you see the form from where you sit?

Draw your chair nearer mine! That is better! You can see the whole figure now!"

"But," argued the lady, with her glass raised to her eye, "isn't that the Marchesa? Surely, she is very like! Should you have known them apart, Mrs. Derrick?"

"Why! where are your eyes?" demanded her husband; "the Marchesa struck me as a stoutly built young lady, with light brown hair! This figure is extremely slim—I should say, thin—and her hair is jet black! I cannot discern any resemblance between the two!"

"O! she is certainly thinner," acquiesced the lady, "and the hair is darker—I admit that—yet the expression, and something about the features, strikes me as resembling the medium. I wonder what sort of feet she has!"

At this hint, Leonora thrust her little bare foot beyond the curtain, for the satisfaction of the sitters. It was a lovely foot—white as marble, slim and smooth, and excited the universal admiration of all the gentlemen present.

"There can be no mistake about *that*, I think!" exclaimed the Baron eagerly.

"But we did not see the Marchesa's feet!" grumbled the incredulous lady.

"But surely you could judge by her build, that her feet would not be as small as those!" argued Von Steinberg, who began to wish, as so many have done before him, that he had never invited his friends to a séance.

"My dear! you are making a fool of yourself!" whispered Mr. Atkinson to his wife, "and if you can't say anything more sensible, I'll be obliged by your holding your tongue altogether!"

After this, the lady's remarks were made in the strictest confidence in her neighbour's ear, and Leonora showed her feet and her hands, and smiled her saucy smiles for the edification of the male portion of the assembly, who were all ready to swear to her beauty and distinct personality from that of the medium. Several other forms made their appearance—one being that of an old man, between whom and the Marchesa, even Mrs. Atkinson could not trace any resemblance, and the séance closed with the apparition of a little child—a boy of four years old, who ran across the room towards Dr. Derrick, and was fully recognised by his wife and himself, as their little Lawrence, a child whom they had lost some twenty years before.

After this apparition, which fully proved the claims of the Marchesa di Sorrento to be one of the most marvellous mediums in the world, the meeting broke up and the sitters dispersed into the adjoining room, Karl van Steinberg alone remaining behind for a few minutes, to see the medium recover from her trance.

As soon as he found himself alone with her, he

gently raised one end of the curtain. There lay Hannah in her easy chair—one pinky arm thrown across the velvet elbow, the other beneath her head. She was breathing heavily still and her mouth was slightly open, showing the large, firm, white teeth within.

It had never struck Von Steinberg that she was even good-looking before, but now she looked positively handsome—an embodiment of youth, health, and vigour—more admirable in a doctor's eyes, than all the anæmic, bloodless, white flesh in the world.

He regarded her quietly for a moment—then yielding to an unaccountable impulse, he stooped and kissed her rounded arm. Hannah woke and caught him—she did not speak, but lay there, with her eyes open, gazing at him—with a languid smile upon her lips.

"Come! come! you are yourself again now!" cried Von Steinberg, quickly, "let us go into the next room! We have had a wonderful séance, and my friends are waiting to congratulate and thank you!"

He dragged her to her feet as he spoke, and led her into the drawing-room.

Here, the scientific men present crowded round her, eager to ascertain if her condition were normal, or if they could trace any lingering remains of the super-human faculty she possessed.

The women looked at her furtively and from a little distance. They could not understand what they had seen—they could not believe it possible, and were more ready to ascribe uncommon cleverness and cunning to the Marchesa, than uncommon powers.

They gazed at her, and whispered to each other, and were generally disposed to consider that the gentlemen were making too much fuss over the matter, and that there was an excellent solution of it, if it could only be found.

Meanwhile their husbands were pressing Hannah to fix an evening to give a sitting at their own homes, and promising her all kinds of preparations in honour of her compliance with their entreaties.

The Baron stood by listening, and a strange feeling of jealousy came over him, that his guests should attempt to monopolise the powers which he had had so much difficulty in securing for himself.

He was determined that Hannah should go to none of their houses.

"Excuse me, gentlemen!" he said, laying his hand on her arm; "but you must allow me to have a voice in this matter! I hold the Marchesa in trust for her husband. It was after much persuasion that he permitted her to attend here this evening for the purpose of pleasing my guests, but I am sure he would never hear of her visiting strangers on the same terms. You must forgive me for saying that she can accept no invitations without the Marchese's leave!"

Hannah did not resent his interference, nor withdraw her arm from his grasp—but only murmured, "That is so!"

"I had hoped," said Dr. Derrick, with some degree of offence, "that the Marchesa would have regarded us as friends, after the delightful evening we have spent in her company."

"But not to the extent of giving you sittings for the investigation of your family," replied Von Steinberg; "the Marchesa is not strong, although she appears so, and as her medical adviser, I am obliged to limit the amount of her séances. Goodnight, Doctor! some other time perhaps I may be able to ask you to repeat the experiments of tonight."

The visitors departed, and the butler had announced that the Marchesa's cab was at the door, when Von Steinberg told him to let it wait.

"You must come in here, Hannah, and have a glass of wine or some refreshment after your labours," he said, leading the way into his diningroom. "I hope you were not vexed at my interference just now, but these people would drain you dry, if you allowed them—not caring one whit, if you sank from fatigue and exhaustion, so long as they gratified their own curiosity concerning you. We must take better care of you than that."

He poured out a glass of wine, and whilst she was drinking it, he put his finger gently on the folds of her white dress and asked,

"What made you put on this pretty frock to-night, Hannah? I did not know that you possessed such a one! I hardly recognised you at first—you looked so nice! What a difference dress makes. Forgive me for saying, that I really did not know before this evening, that you were a handsome woman!"

"Am I?" said Hannah, with the old, broad grin. "No one ever told me so afore! I thought as I was coming amongst grand folks, I ought to 'ave a nice frock, so I went to Madame Cusada and she made me this. I did feel so queer coming out to see you, as if I'd got next to nothing on."

"Never mind! It's quite the fashion, you know, and you will soon get accustomed to it! You have a lovely neck and shoulders, Hannah! Who would think to see your hands, that they were so pink and soft! You must try and get your hands to look like them. They will soon, now that you do no rough work. I should like you to look nice always."

"Should you?" said Hannah. "I don't think the Markiss cares 'ow I look! I 'ad to take the money out of 'is trouser pocket to buy this. I arsked 'im for some, but 'e's so close, 'e wouldn't give me any, so I just helped myself!"

"O! Hannah! you mustn't do that again. It's

stealing! And how vexed Ricardo would be, if he discovered the theft! Promise me, that you will never take his money again, without his leave."

"O! that's all very well, but 'ow am I to get things else?" grumbled Hannah. "What's the good of being a Markiness, if I'm to go about in the same old clothes day after day?"

"Well! come to me when you want money! Treat me like a brother, and tell me all your troubles! I have more than I want—a great deal more—and will gladly supply anything that your husband is unable to afford you. For, you must remember, Hannah, he is very poor."

"Beastly poor!" echoed Hannah. "What a different life *your* wife will lead! She'll 'ave everything as 'er 'eart can wish for! Well! some people is borned lucky!"

"But are not much the happier, all the same," replied Von Steinberg, "if ever I should have a wife, as you suggest, she may envy you your robust health, and your youth, and your mystical powers, Hannah."

"Lor! they ain't much good to me," said the girl, but if you likes 'em, you're welcome to 'em, that's all!"

The Baron took out his purse.

"That is very good of you to say, and if you will not feel offended, I should like to make you a little present in return for your kindness to me. You needn't tell Ricardo, you know! Let it be a secret between you and me, and when you buy a pretty new frock or a hat with it, think it is a present from your old friend Karl von Steinberg."

He laid a note for twenty pounds upon her lap as he spoke, and as Hannah's eyes fell upon it, the expression of her face changed. She took the note in her hands—smoothed it out lovingly—and turned eyes up to his, that were full of something more than gratitude—something, that made the young man stoop down and kiss her; then draw back, as if he had been shot.

"That was wrong of me, Hannah," he said, "I should not have done it! Will you forgive me? Ricardo would be awfully angry if he heard of it! He would say I was a traitor!"

"He won't hear of it," replied Hannah quietly, as she gazed at the bank note.

"Well! put that away safely, and my man shall summon the cab for you, and to-morrow I am to come and give you a lesson in reading and conversation, is that not so? I very much want to cure you of some of your funny little ways, Hannah, and it is so strange to me, that sometimes you appear to have quite cured them for yourself, and then you break out again, as bad as ever. Here is the cab! and here is your wrap. Well! Good-bye till tomorrow, and mind you remember me to Ricardo."

He watched her drive away in the direction of her home, and walked back into his own, dissatisfied with himself, and all the world.

What on earth, he thought, had made him give way to that impulse to kiss his friend's wife twice in one evening? He did not admire her! How could he admire a coarse, under-bred woman, with huge hands and feet, and an accent that set his teeth on edge?

And yet there had been something about her that evening, that had attracted him more powerfully than he had considered her capable of attracting anybody—than he had considered himself capable of being attracted. It was not entirely her appearance, though she had looked better than he had ever seen her look before—it was a kind of animalism and magnetism, combined, which had made his senses reel, and caused him to forget her position and his faith to his old friend, Ricardo.

Karl von Steinberg hated himself for what had occurred, and yet he felt that, should the time come over again, he should behave in exactly the same manner. She was a wonderful combination, he thought, of sorcery and coquetry, and gross, inanimate earth! He knew that the Professor did not love Hannah as a man should love his wife—he had told him so direct, yet should he find out that she was tampered with by his friend, he might be provoked into jealousy and view the matter in a very disagreeable light. So that—Von Steinberg decided—for the future, Hannah should be sacred to him!

At the same time, he could not endure the idea

that she should do for his acquaintances what she had done for him—go to their houses and make herself as common as a professional medium! He was resolved that, at all costs, he would put a stop to that, even if he were compelled to side with Ricardo, and resolve she should never sit, except at home.

He tried to disgust himself with her, but he could not! He recalled all the deficiencies of her womanhood—told himself that she was coarse, ignorant, and cunning—that she was a woman to be ashamed, not proud, of—and yet he felt drawn back and back to thoughts of her, as though she had been the Goddess of Love herself!

He had said at first, that he would not visit the cottage on the following day, but with the morning's light, his resolution had faded, and as soon as he had bathed and breakfasted, he called a cab and drove out to Hampstead.

CHAPTER XIV.

As he alighted, he perceived Ricardo at a little distance, coming towards him. The man's aspect was most lugubrious. His head was sunk upon his breast. His eyes were cast upon the ground—his hands hung listlessly by his side. He came close to Von Steinberg without seeing him, and when he did see him, he started, as if he were the last person he had dreamt of encountering.

"Good Heavens! Von Steinberg!" he exclaimed; "where have you sprung from? Hannah told me but just now that you were leaving Town for the day."

Karl von Steinberg stopped one moment to consider why Hannah should have taken the trouble to tell a falsehood, but recovering himself replied,

"Ah! I was thinking of doing so, but changed my mind! She has forgotten that I also said, that if circumstances permitted of my remaining in London, I should run over to give her a little lesson in polite conversation. Your wife is eminently teachable, Ricardo! It is a real pleasure to me to help her a little on her way."

"For my part, I think you had better let her alone," returned the Professor, gruffly, "I don't see that polite education improves her."

"My dear Ricardo, what is the matter? Have I offended you in any way? Pray tell me at once, if it is so!"

"Since you demand it, I will. I must beg that you will not ask Hannah to your house again, for whatever purpose. It does her no good, but only inflates her foolish head with an idea of importance, which she does not possess, and introduces her to society in which she can never hope to mix.

"Besides, Von Steinberg, my means will not admit of buying her dresses, and paying for her cabs—and when I mention the subject, however gently, she insults me to my face. No! no! it was with much reluctance that I gave my permission for her to attend your party last night, but it must be for the last time—the very last time!"

"I am sorry to hear you say that," replied Von Steinberg, gravely, "and still more that Hannah should appear ungrateful for your indulgence."

"But it is ridiculous—absurd—" exclaimed Ricardo, passionately, "that she should pass the evening with such people as you gather round you. Remember what she was—a common scullery maid! She can only bring disgrace on you and me and herself!"

"But you are really mistaken," said the Baron. "I acknowledge that Hannah is uneducated, but she has much shrewdness, and knows when to hold her tongue. She behaved admirably last evening, and my friends were delighted with her—so much so, that had I not interfered, she would have been overwhelmed with invitations to their houses."

"Only to save themselves money," sneered Ricardo, "to procure her services for nothing! She is a curiosity—a new toy—nothing more!"

"I don't think you quite do justice to Hannah," observed Von Steinberg, "she is more than a mere machine! She is naturally clever, and can be very amusing and original. And she really looked superb! I was quite astonished at her appearance!"

"She doesn't go out again. She has done it for the last time!" persisted the Professor, doggedly.

"My dear friend, there is something more the matter than you have told me," said the Baron, looking anxiously into Ricardo's face; "you are not yourself this morning! Is there anything else, beside your wife's very natural desire to see a little of the great world, that troubles you?"

"A great deal more," exclaimed the Professor, "my life with her is becoming a hell upon earth! I can stand it no longer! You know why I married her, Karl! A coarse, uneducated, ignorant clod (as you yourself called her)—I gave her my name and the sanctity of my home, because she brought my Leonora to me. The great object of my life seemed about to be realised—my yearnings set at rest! I made this clod my wife—no! no! not my wife; I will never give her that sacred title—but I made her mine by law, so that I might keep Leonora ever by my side. And now—can you believe it?—she refuses any more to sit for Leonora!"

"O! you must be mistaken," cried Von Steinberg, "Hannah may be tired of sitting for a while—you forget the strain it is upon her constitution—but she can never have intended you to understand that she would never sit for you again."

"She said it, and she meant it. I could read it in her evil eyes," replied Ricardo, steadfastly. "She told me only this morning, when I asked if we could have a séance together this evening, that she had made up her mind to sit with me no more. She said worse than that," continued the Professor, in a breaking voice, "she declared that Leonora—my Leonora—was sick and tired of me—that she said she had come often enough—and expressed her determination not to appear again, unless it were for the amusement of a crowd, such as you gathered round you last night—a crowd who cares nothing for her personally, —only to see the wonder of her materialisation. And I—*I*—loved her so!" he gasped out, as he hid his face from observation, and gave vent to a weak flood of tears.

Karl von Steinberg was much shocked. He was

really attached to the Professor, and his conscience pricked him sorely, lest he should, by indirect means, have had some share in bringing this trouble on his head. He turned with him down a narrow lane, where they would be more sheltered from observation, and waited silently until Ricardo's emotion had subsided.

"How weak—how unmanly—you must think me!" he said at last, as he lifted his worn face and smiled faintly at the Baron, "but I have been much shaken lately! Hannah's insolence to me—her over-bearing manner—the way in which she uses Leonora's sacred name in my presence—has sapped my courage!

"O! what an egregious fool I was, not to listen to your kindly advice, when you warned me that to marry her would ruin me, soul and body! It has been just that! Were it not for cowardice, I would put an end to my life to-morrow! There is nothing left me worth living for!"

"My dear friend! I cannot hear you talk like that! I must prescribe a tonic to strengthen your nerves! You are run down, that is all. I am afraid that you work too much and worry too much. Do you know, Ricardo, that these constant séances are very debilitating for you, and though she might have conveyed the intelligence in milder language, Hannah is quite right in saying, that you must not indulge your fancy so frequently.

"I was speaking to her of the danger of it, the other day, and I daresay she was only repeating my sentiments on the subject to you. If she failed to express them rightly, you must remember that she has not been reared in a polite school, and make allowances for her!"

"It is not that!" replied the Professor, shaking his head; "Hannah is not the same woman she used to be—she is altered in every way! Do you remember the first time we saw her at Mrs. Battleby's?—how shy and awkward she was—how terrified at the effect of her own power—what an unmeaning, but amiable smile, irradiated her dull vacuous countenance?

"Where has all that gone? She is still somewhat clumsy and coarse, but her temper is hasty and uncertain—she has developed the cunning of the Devil—and she will have her own way in everything! It is of no use my trying to guide, or advise her. She considers she is quite capable of doing all that for herself."

"Well! you could hardly expect her to remain for ever, the dull clod you rightly say she was, when you first fell in with her! She had had no advantages then, nor opportunities of improving herself! Now—she has lived for more than twelve months in your daily presence, and must have been dull indeed, if she had not picked up something of your ways and manners!"

"But she need not *insult* me!" cried Ricardo, vehemently, "I tell you, Karl, there is hardly a day goes by, but she stings my pride with some covert allusion to the Past! What does she know of it? Have you ever spoken to her of Leonora?"

"*Never!* beyond her name!" replied the Baron, decidedly, "what you related to me of her life and death, I have kept sacredly to myself!"

"Yes! yes! I am sure of it! I should not have put the question to you," said Ricardo, feebly, as he wiped the sweat off his forehead; "but, O! Von Steinberg, I am utterly miserable! I cannot bear my life much longer! The sooner it is ended, the better!"

Whatever thoughts had run riot through the Baron's brain as he set out for the Cottage, were all merged now in the desire to redress the wrongs of his old friend, and bring Hannah to her senses. He parted with Ricardo affectionately—told him that he should speak to his wife on the subject—and extracted a promise from him, that he would come the following day and dine quietly with him in Portland Place. And then he hurried on to the Cottage, determined to give Hannah such a roasting as she had never received from him in her life before.

He found her dressed in a sort of loose tea-gown, seated in the Professor's arm-chair, and apparently engaged in reading one of her husband's scientific works.

"Isn't it strange," she said, as soon as the usual morning salutations had passed between them, "that I can't make out half these words? I seem to have forgotten how to read!"

"I don't suppose that you ever knew!" returned Von Steinberg, who was disposed to be rather curt with her on the occasion.

"Then you are mistaken," she said, without offence, "for I could read very well—but English is so hard," she added, pathetically,

The Baron stared at her. Hannah was in one of those queer moods which were so unaccountable to him.

"Never mind that now!" he said, "I want to talk to you upon another matter. I met your husband as I was coming up just now, and had some conversation with him. I think he is looking very ill, and he seems very unhappy! Why are you treating him so badly, Hannah? What has he done, that you should make his life a misery to him?"

"Who says that I have?" she answered.

"He did! He told me that you have refused to sit any more with him. Is that true?"

"Yes! He is wearing me and himself into the grave! He is never contented, but must sit every night. I shall be ill, if it goes on. *You* must prevent it, Karl!"

It was the first time she had ever presumed to

call him by his Christian name and it pleased, whilst it startled him. He drew his chair nearer to hers.

"I will if I can! I have just been telling Ricardo how bad it is for you both! But you are not kind to him, Hannah! He says you insult him, how is that?"

"Bah!" said the girl; "I am sick of his reproaches! They are all on account of Leonora! If I tell him what is the truth, that Leonora is a very violent spirit, and that I am more tired after one of her visits than after twenty others, I have insulted him!

"He is angry now, because you asked me to your house last night, and I was happy to go. He wants to keep me shut up here all day, whilst he gives his lessons. It is intolerable! Does he think I am not made of flesh and blood? But what I told you once before, is true—he married me, not to get a wife, but a medium! Well! he has got a medium, and perhaps he will find after all, that a wife might have been a better thing!"

"Hannah! I am so sorry for all this," said Von Steinberg, thoughtfully, "Ricardo is a dear, good fellow in reality, but his nature has been soured by adversity. He has lost everything,—wife, fortune, and title—and it has weighed upon his mind. You must bear with him—he is an old man now——"

"I hate old men!" interposed Hannah.

"No! don't say that, for I was going to add,

that he is much older than his years, and that I don't think that he will live for many more! He is in such a despondent condition too, that I feel very anxious about him, and I want you to watch him carefully. Have you any poison about the premises—beetle poison, or oxalic acid, or any of those mixtures, that servants use for cleaning?"

"What do you mean?" inquired Hannah, with open eyes.

"I mean, that if his distresses weigh too heavily upon his mind, he may get up some night and take anything that comes to hand, to end his life. If you have any such dangerous mixtures in the Cottage, Hannah, you must throw them away, or lock them up. And you will be very kind to Ricardo—for my sake, won't you?

"Get him a nice little hot supper, and meet him with a kind smile, when he comes in, for he is very low-spirited to-day, and if he asks for a séance, give him one. He has promised to dine with me alone to-morrow, and then I will have a serious talk with him, about all this, and show him the folly of endangering your health and his own for the sake of his occult studies. Will you do this—for *my* sake?" he concluded, looking in her face.

"Yes, for *your* sake, Karl," she answered, in a low voice.

"Ah! why didn't *I* see the beauties in your undeveloped character, when we first met, and marry you, instead of Ricardo?" exclaimed the Baron, "there should have been none of this forcing of your inclinations then! I would have carried you abroad, and let your natural talents have full sway, until they had blossomed into fruition. You have a big heart and soul and brain, Hannah! They only require opportunity, to keep pace with those of anybody."

"And would you have taken me there?" demanded Hannah, with sudden interest.

"There—or anywhere!" cried Von Steinberg, rashly.

Hannah made no answer, except what was conveyed by putting her huge hand into his. He glanced at it, as it lay in his slenderer palm. It was less rough, and of a better colour, than it had been, but it was still very, *very* far from what a lady's hand should be! As he regarded it, the same feeling of wonder that had assailed him before, rose in his breast, as to *what* it was, that fascinated him in this woman.

At times he felt an intolerable repugnance to her—at others, he was drawn towards her, with an irresistible attraction!

Was she a witch? Had she exercised any unholy spell over him? He looked up in her face with its large, heifer-like eyes—so simple, so bovine, it appeared—but as he gazed, an archness stole into the eyes—a wicked smile hovered over the lips—

and the Baron felt he was victimised once more.

"And when are we to begin this wonderful lesson?" asked Hannah, presently.

"You don't seem to require any lesson to-day," replied Von Steinberg, "you are the most unaccountable creature I ever met in my life! If you would only always remain the same!"

"Then—you would tire of me. It is the way with men."

"Never!" replied the Baron, after the fashion of lovers; "you are the one only woman who could never tire me! You are unlike all the rest."

"So you *say!*" returned Hannah. "But with regard to my husband—he is very despondent, you tell me?"

"Terribly so! He frightens me! Do all you can to cheer him, Hannah."

"And he is likely to attempt his own life?"

"O! no! no! I hope not, most sincerely! But it will be as well to keep all dangerous articles, such as razors, etc., out of his reach, until his fit has passed away."

"*Che sarà, sarà!*" murmured Hannah, languidly.

Von Steinberg started again. Had her lips really uttered Italian words, and with a foreign accent.

"You frighten me sometimes," he said, with a gasp. "Where on earth did you pick up that Italian proverb? We shall have you talking Greek next."

"Is not the Professor Italian?" replied the girl. "Am I always to listen and never to learn? What a fool you must take me for?"

"I take you for the sharpest woman I ever met in my life," exclaimed the Baron, as he kissed the large hand which he still retained in his. "And now I must go, as I have an appointment at one. Good-bye! Think a great deal of what I have said to you, Hannah—and *think a little of me!*"

His eyes said more than his words, as he walked hastily out of the Cottage, as if afraid to trust himself any longer in her presence.

Hannah looked after him lazily.

"He will be mine, when I choose it," she said to herself, "and it may not be long first! Ah! to have that house and all its contents placed at my feet, as a free-will offering! I should feel as if I were in Heaven!"

She rose slowly from her chair, for Hannah had become very lazy in those days, and putting on her walking things, left the Cottage also. When she returned, she found the Professor had reached home before her.

It was one of the days on which he had his afternoon to himself.

Hannah was well pleased with the turn her fortunes seemed to be taking. She was disposed to be amiable, but Ricardo had already been too deeply wounded, and received her advances with repugnance.

"Leave me alone!" he said, testily, "I require none of your attentions! I suppose my friend Von Steinberg has been talking to you, and you feel ashamed that he should have heard of your bad conduct. But I told him all! There is no need for me to conceal anything.

"He saw you with me first—an ungainly, ignorant, uncouth clod of the earth—they were the very words he used with regard to you—and he knows what I did, in raising you to the position of my wife! He prayed and implored me to pause and consider what I was doing before I brought disgrace on my name and my birth and my family connections, by linking myself to a maid-of-all-work. But I was mad—I wouldn't listen to him. Had I done so, I should have been spared the awful shame you have put me to, since! I married you, because I believed you to be a simple, amiable, kind-hearted girl——"

"You didn't!" interposed his wife, "you married me, because you saw that I was a wonderful medium, and because you were always crying after your beloved Leonora, and hoped, through me, to have daily intercourse with her! Why don't you tell the truth, whilst you're about it?"

"Well! then, that was the truth, since you will have it," replied the Professor, "but I wish now that I had died before I ever met you. You refuse to give me séances—you even say that Leonora is tired of coming to see me—you are not commonly grateful for the benefits I have bestowed upon you."

"Where are they?" cried Hannah, insolently. "I should like to see them. Do you call it a *benefit*, for a young, hearty girl to be married to an old dotard, who makes about enough money to keep himself in victuals and drink, and no more?

"Do you think it is any pleasure to me to be shut up in this little hole, whilst you're at work, without money, or amusements, or friends, and when some one is good enough to take pity on me and ask me to a pleasant party, you declare that it shall be the last time, and you will never let me go out again."

"And I repeat it," said Ricardo, "you are not fit for such gatherings. They only make you insolent and over-bearing at home. I told you when we were married, that you would have to perform the household duties, as I could not afford to keep a servant. You persuaded me to go against my own word, but it is over. I shall dismiss the girl this evening, and for the future you shall do your own work.

"No more parties, nor dresses for you, Madame Ricardo! You are not fitted for them. One might as well bring a cow into a drawing-room! I have burned the dress you wore last night, and no money will you ever get out of me to buy another!"

"That will be no obstacle!" exclaimed Hannah, triumphantly. "I have money of my own—more than you are ever likely to have to give me."

"Where did you get it?" said Ricardo, curiously. "Who gave it to you?"

"That's my business, and not yours," cried the woman, "if you are such a beggar, that you cannot afford to give your wife a new dress, she must get it how she can!"

"My God!" he cried, "what do you insinuate? What do you mean me to understand?"

"What you like! You can prevent my leaving the house, p'r'aps, but you can't make me open my mouth, if I choose to keep it closed."

"You are a devil! You are not fit to live!" exclaimed the Professor, as he rose from his chair, as if to advance towards her. But Hannah was already round the other side of the table.

"You'd like to kill me, wouldn't you?" she cried; "as you killed Leonora, but you would find that I wouldn't take it quite as quietly as she did!"

At that name, and the announcement that Hannah knew how his first wife had left the world, Ricardo sank down into the chair, from which he had risen, trembling like an aspen leaf.

"Leonora! *Killed* Leonora!" he gasped, with a face of ashes; "who told you such a—a—lie? What do you mean by speaking to me like that—of accusing me—of—of——"

Hannah stood where she was, and laughed at him.

"Ah! who?—*who?*" she said. "Find out! It isn't all jam to have a medium in the house, Professor!

If sperrits come for one, they will for another, and you don't s'pose they'd keep any secrets from me! Poor Leonora! I wouldn't 'ave been 'er, by long chalks! And *you*—who pretended to be so fond of 'er! Ugh! go along with yer! If you'd had your rights, you'd been hung on a gallows tree long afore this!"

The wretched Professor could not answer her! He could only hide his face in his hands, and groan. His dread secret dragged from him, as it were, and spread out for the coarse criticism of Mrs. Battleby's maid-of-all-work!

He did indeed feel at that moment, as though his punishment was greater than he could bear.

CHAPTER XV.

"It's of no good crying over it now," taunted Hannah, as the unhappy man stirred in his seat; "you didn't mind how much *she* cried—did you? You found her on a sofa with young Centi, singing a song for him, maybe, or playing at cat's-cradle, like a couple of babies together—and you took out your knife, and ran her through the 'eart, without a thought, or a pang——"

"No! no! not without a pang, God knows!" moaned the unfortunate Professor.

"You drove your murdering weapon through 'er 'eart," continued the girl, without noticing his interpolation, "with no more mercy, than if she had been a dangerous animal.

"She 'ad youth and beauty, and all 'er life before 'er, but you cut it short, without waiting for an explanation of what you saw! Do you know what she was thinking of, just as she was dying, and you watched the film steal over her eyes and the blood spirting in little jets from her blue lips. If she could 'ave spoke to you in that moment, 'er last words would 'ave been, '*I 'ate you!*'"

"Let me go! Let me go! I can stand no more!" cried Ricardo, as he rushed past her, and mounted the stairs to his own room.

Even there, Hannah would have followed him, and continued her mental torture, but he was too quick for her, and had locked the door before she reached it. So she was compelled to go downstairs again, and think of some way of passing the afternoon.

The Baron had begged her to provide a tasty supper for Ricardo, and she would not have liked him to hear that she had neglected his advice, so she arrayed herself in her walking attire and sallied forth to purchase it.

The Markiness had made quite a little circle of acquaintances in Hampstead, where her manners and her title, so incongruous with each other, had excited a great amount of curiosity and interest. Mrs. Barnett, the grocer's wife, declared that she had quite turned her ideas regarding the aristocracy, she was so affable and friendly-like, and Mrs. Thomson, the butcher's lady, said that if she had not known that she was a marchioness, she should have taken her for one of themselves.

So Hannah, after having enjoyed an hour or two of converse with these amiable creatures, returned to the Cottage with her little basket on her arm, well primed for supper.

First, there was a fowl, ready roasted, which she had bought at the ham and beef shop, with a pound of cut ham to eat with it—a crisp lettuce and some ruddy tomatoes, which were Ricardo's greatest luxuries—and half a dozen cheese-cakes—which were hers.

When, with the aid of her little maid, Charlotte, who numbered fifteen years, she had set these dainties forth upon the table, Hannah sent a message up to her husband to say that his supper was ready, but in a few minutes Charlotte returned, gaping, with the intelligence that the Markiss wouldn't answer her, and she thought he must be asleep. Then Hannah piled a plate with something of everything on the table, and carrying it upstairs herself, thundered such a tattoo upon the Professor's door, that he was obliged to answer it.

"Who is there?" he inquired.

"It's me—Hannah!—I've brought you up your supper!"

"I don't want it! I don't want anything! Go away!" was the reply.

"Come on! Don't be foolish! You'd better eat it!" said his wife.

"No! no! All I want is to be left alone!"

"All right!" exclaimed Hannah, as she placed the plate with a loud clatter on the floor, "there it is, anyway, so don't go and say you haven't had it!"

She bounced downstairs again, with the tread of

an elephant, which Ricardo, hearing, turned on his bed and sighed.

Hannah, however, did not sigh, but applying herself to the remains of the supper, soon left nothing but the chicken bones for Charlotte to dispose of. Then she took out some of her needle-work, and toiled industriously for the best part of an hour.

But her mind was not entirely easy the while. She was fidgety and anxious. More than once she rose from her chair and, casting the embroidery aside, paced up and down the little room.

"What a fool I am!" she thought, "why should I have any scruples on the matter? Had *he*? Ha! ha! ha! had he?"

When nine o'clock struck, she took a spirit flask from the cellaret and called to her little maid to bring hot water.

"I am going to mix the Markiss a glass of whiskey and water, he is sure to drink it during the night, if not now, and he will want something to make him sleep. Go and fetch a tray—now, make haste, and bring it to me!"

"Yes! Mum—my lady!——" replied Charlotte, who had never been able to acquire the proper method of addressing a Marchioness.

When she had left the room, Hannah put sugar and lemon and whiskey and hot water into the tumbler—but then she seemed to hesitate for a moment.

"Folly!" she said to herself, "*che sarà, sarà!* I *must* be free!"

She dashed a small quantity of white powder into the glass, as she thought thus, and a moment later Charlotte appeared with the tray.

"Take that up to the Markiss," she said; "and if he don't answer you, say you've a message for him from the Baron, and when he opens the door tell him the Baron ordered me to send him up that the last thing. Do you understand?"

"Yes! Mum—my lady!"

"Now, don't forget. Say first—'Please, Markiss, the Baron has sent you a message'—and when he opens the door, hand him the tray and say, 'The Baron begged as you would drink this,' and leave it there."

"Yes! Mum—my lady!" repeated the child.

The ruse succeeded. Ricardo at first refused to unlock his door, declaring he wanted nothing more that night, but when he heard that Von Steinberg had a message for him, he left his bed to hear what it was.

When Charlotte, faithful to her orders, thrust the tray and tumbler into his hands, and repeated the message, Hannah heard him grumble,

"What did you disturb me for such nonsense for? Here! put the tray down, and don't you dare to come near me again to-night, or I'll send you home to your mother. Do you understand?"

"Yes! Markiss—yes! my lord!" stammered the

child, as she scuttled down the stairs again, and ran into the kitchen.

All was silent in the Professor's room, and Hannah went back to her needlework. It was the time that she usually went to bed, but she did not feel as if she could sleep that night. At ten o'clock her little maid crept into the parlour, white and trembling.

"Please, Mum—my lady——" she commenced, half crying, "there's sich a rum noise going on upstairs—like a dog moaning. Please, do you think it can be the Markiss!"

"The Markiss, child!" said Hannah, who had also suddenly gone unaccountably white, "why! what do you mean? Why should the Markiss make a noise? It's most likely the wind you hear through the trees!"

"O! no! Mum—my lady—please! there's no wind to-night, and I'm afraid to go up to bed," continued Charlotte, weeping.

"What nonsense!" exclaimed her mistress, "I'll go with you, then, but what you have to look so scared for, I can't imagine!"

In consequence, she mounted to the upper storey, with the shrinking little maid in front of her. Since Von Steinberg's departure, Hannah had occupied the room which had been his, whilst her servant slept in that which had been hers. As they gained the head of the stairs, a deep, low groan issued distinctly from Ricardo's apartment, and made Charlotte burst out afresh.

"O! please, Mum, please, Mum—there it is again! O! I'm sure the pore Markiss must be very bad in his insides! Won't you knock at the door and see?"

"Yes! yes! as soon as you have gone to bed," replied Hannah, who was looking almost as frightened as her handmaid. She pushed the girl into her chamber and turned the key on the outside. Whatever was happening in her husband's room, she would see by herself. She tapped lightly on the door, but no answer proceeded from the bed, only another low half-stifled moan, as though an animal lay dying there.

Hannah flew downstairs again and passed out of the front door into the fresh evening air. She was not afraid of Charlotte turning witness against her; the child would accept any explanation she chose to give—she was only afraid of encountering those hollow groans again.

After half an hour's suspense, she re-entered the cottage. A violent tapping was proceeding from Charlotte's door. Hannah went first to inquire why she made such a noise.

"O! please, Mum—my lady—'is groans is dreadful! Won't you give 'im a drop of ile, or a pen-north of peppermint?"

"He has locked his door, Charlotte, you know, and I can't get in. But if he is not quiet soon, I must send for the Doctor!"

She conjured her little maid to be easy, and went downstairs in search of a box of carpentering tools. Here she found a crowbar, with which she knew she could force the Professor's door. She crept up again with it in her hand, and listened attentively. There was not a sound in the room of any kind.

"Either it is over," she thought, "or he is asleep! Ought I to send for assistance, or force the door myself? Should I not be justified in any circumstances in entering the room, considering the groans that have proceeded from it? Charlotte will be my witness to them! And if a stranger went in, and *he*—should—should be still alive—alive enough to give evidence against me—O no! at all risks, *I* must be the one to see him first, and then I can judge what is best to be done."

She applied the crowbar to the door with her vigorous hand as she thought thus, and the lock gave way before it. For an instant, she hesitated on the threshold—then summoning her courage, dashed in and approached the bed.

The Professor was just dying—his eyes were glazed—his hands fallen lifeless by his side. The sight, instead of inspiring pity in Hannah's breast, roused a demoniacal fury there. Her husband looked at her as though to say "*You have done this*", and she bent over him and hissed one word into his ear — "*Leonora!*"

At the mention of that name, which had been his

pride and his shame throughout his life, the Professor gave a final moan and slightly turning over—*died!* His wife gazed at him for a moment, as if she could not believe the truth—then, with a shudder, she flung the blanket over his staring eyes, and rushed from the room.

Her next move was to unlock Charlotte, and order her to dress herself as soon as possible and go to Portland Place to summon the Baron.

"To Portland Place, Mum—my lady!" exclaimed the little maid, who had hardly ever walked out by daylight, alone.

"Yes! the Markiss is very ill! You must take a cab and go there as quickly as you can, and beg the Baron to come to me at once! Say that your master is in terrible pain—tell him of the moans you heard—and that I am very unhappy about it, and must have a doctor at once. Mind you say how dreadfully anxious I am, Charlotte, and that I have done everything I can, but it is of no good!"

"'Ave you been into 'is room, Mum?" demanded Charlotte, with surprise.

"Yes! yes! but don't stand chattering there! Go as quick as ever you can, and don't forget one word of what I have told you."

When the child was gone, Hannah sat down in the parlour to await the issue of events. She could not return to the bedroom nor draw the blanket off those staring eyes. There Von Steinberg found her, an hour later, when he returned with the little maid.

"Why! what is this?" he exclaimed, as he took her hand; "is my poor friend ill? Where is he? Let me see him at once!"

"There!" replied Hannah, pointing upwards with her finger; "He looks dreadful! I can't stand it! Whatever has happened, that he should be like this?"

"And you have left him alone, when he is so ill?" said the Baron, reproachfully, "O! Hannah! I did not think you would do that!"

"He has locked himself into his room all day—Charlotte will tell you so—and wouldn't come down to supper, or take anything—and just now I forced open the door, and he swore at me—so I was frightened, and sent for you!"

"You did right!" said Von Steinberg, as he ran up the stairs to Ricardo's room.

But the first glance told him that his services would be of no avail. The Professor was dead as a doornail. His head was thrown back—his eyes were wide open and starting from their sockets—his body had half fallen from the bed.

Karl von Steinberg felt his heart—pressed his eyeballs—laid his hand on his pulse—and uttered a deep sigh.

"Gone! my poor Ricardo!" he exclaimed, "and

I fear, by your own hand!" He caught sight of the tumbler, which had contained the whiskey and water, and raising it to his nose, shook his head mournfully.

"As I thought!" he mused. "O! I should not have left him alone, after what he said to me this morning! It is half my fault that this has happened. I shall never forgive myself!"

He lifted the poor wasted carcase on to the bed, closed the eyelids, laid the arms by his side, and softly closing the door, went downstairs again.

"My poor girl!" he exclaimed, as he rejoined Hannah, "you must prepare yourself for a great shock. Our good friend has left us, Hannah! He is dead!"

"Quite dead," repeated, Hannah; "are you sure?"

"Quite sure! and, what is worse, I am certain he took his own life! O! I blame myself so much for leaving him, after the conversation we held this morning. I should have watched over him better. But I did not think he was really in earnest. My poor Ricardo! I think his work and these séances have been too much for him, and over-taxed his brain. He was the last man that I thought would have contemplated suicide! But it is too evident! The glass on his table contains the remains of arsenic—I could tell it at a glance!"

"Arsenic!" echoed Hannah, "but where can he have got arsenic?"

"Anywhere! It is used for so many things. Doubtless he bought it to-day whilst he was out. How did he appear on his return home?"

"Very queer!" replied Hannah, "he wouldn't speak to Charlotte or me, but went straight up to his room and locked the door. I went out and got him a nice little supper, as you told me——"

"Good girl!" interpolated the Baron——

"But he wouldn't touch it, though I took it up to him myself, but I thought he would like some whiskey and water. So Charlotte and me, we mixed it for him—didn't we, Charlotte?—and she carried it up, but even then he wouldn't open his door, until she told him that *you* had ordered him to take it! And then I suppose he—he——"

"Yes! there is no question about it. He mixed the poison he had purchased, with the whiskey, and drank it off. My poor friend! Little did I think he would come to so sad an end! Well! I suppose the hankering to rejoin his Leonora was too strong for him. I only hope he is happy with her now!"

"I fancy she has had enough of him," remarked Hannah.

"Anyway we shall hear the truth from him when he comes back to us! I should think he was sure to come back through you, Hannah!"

Hannah gave a visible shudder.

"O! don't speak of such a thing pray! I shouldn't like him to come back. I don't think he behaved well to me at the last! I don't never want to see him again."

"Don't say that! You will think differently after a time. You mustn't blame him, Hannah! The very fact that he has taken his own life should convince you that he was not completely in his right mind. Poor Ricardo! He suffered much in his lifetime, and endured many losses. We must think as kindly of him now, as we can."

She seemed so visibly affected, and displayed such a horror of going upstairs, that the Baron took all the arrangements that were necessary in his own hands. Before nightfall, everything was settled regarding the inquest, which was to take place on the following day—the remains of the poor Professor were placed in a coffin—and the ground was purchased wherein he was to be laid.

Von Steinberg had sufficient influence to prevent a verdict of *felo de se,* being brought in, and his friend was allowed to be buried with the rites of the Church.

As soon as it was possible, he erected a handsome monument above his grave, which detailed his real name and rank, and then the Baron turned his attention to Hannah. She still remained in the Cottage and appeared to have no intention of leaving it.

Von Steinberg knew that in order to accomplish this, she must have some assistance. All the Professor's modest savings did not amount to a couple of hundred pounds, and these the widow was very anxious should be deposited in a bank for her against a time of need.

"But how are you to live meanwhile, Hannah?" questioned Von Steinberg who was most anxious for her welfare; "you have never kept house for yourself yet, you know, and money goes a very little way in London. You must let me help you! I will take no denial! Look on me as a brother, and let me have the pleasure of doing for you, what dear old Ricardo would have done for a friend of mine, left in similar circumstances."

"But I do not need it. I shall have enough!" persisted Hannah.

"How do you intend to get it? What do you mean to do?" he asked.

"Heaps of things," she replied; "I am a good needlewoman and a good cook!"

"Needlewoman! Cook!" exclaimed the Baron, indignantly, "do you suppose for an instant, that I will allow the widow of my dear friend Ricardo to engage in such menial pursuits? You are much mistaken if you do. Besides, you have adopted his title. How do you suppose that will accord with the occupations you speak of?"

"Never mind!" said Hannah, decidedly, "I know what I'm about, and I don't want any money from you."

She was obstinate, and he ceased to worry her on the subject. All the same, he often wondered how it was, that she continued, without aid, to occupy the cottage and retain the services of her little maid.

Once or twice he questioned Charlotte, but could get no satisfactory information from her. "The Markiness goes out to see her friends in the evenings mostly," she said, "and all day she works at her dresses, and shows me how to cook the dinner."

This reticence on the part of the Marchesa di Sorrento, made Von Steinberg all the more eager to pursue her and win her to be his. Perhaps she knew this, as well as he did himself, at any rate it had the effect of binding him more closely to her.

Shortly after the Professor's death, his friend felt anxious to communicate with him. It would be the best test he had ever had in his life, he thought, if dear old Ricardo would come back in a recognisable form and assure him of his identity.

He never doubted but that Hannah, when the first shock of her husband's death was over, would gladly fall in with his wishes and hold a séance, so that the Professor might have an opportunity of communicating with them both again.

But, to his surprise, she steadfastly opposed the idea.

She didn't want to sit at all, she said. She had had more than enough of that sort of thing during her married life, and never even wished to hear the subject mentioned. She no longer believed in it—the spirits were not the people they professed to be—she had come to the conclusion that her father and mother were right, and that they were devils sent by the Evil One himself to lure her soul to hell.

Von Steinberg reasoned and argued with her to no effect. She remained unmoved by all his persuasions, and since he had only pursued the subject, as a science and not a sentimentality, he gave in to her wishes and said no more about it.

He was convinced that Spiritualism was a fact, and resolved to remain satisfied with that knowledge. So—although he longed to see his old friend again, and learn the true reason of his rash act—he decided that it was not worth while annoying Hannah to obtain it.

The circumstance, however, made him turn his attention in the direction of other mediums, and in talking with his acquaintances he said, more than once, how anxious he was to fall in with a reliable one.

In consequence of this, a man named Colonel Roster said to him one day,

"By the way, Von Steinberg, my wife has got hold of a most wonderful medium, and she is to sit at our house this evening. Would you care to join the party?"

"Thanks! I should like it exceedingly! There is

nothing interests me more. Does this medium produce materialisations?"

"O dear yes! Nothing else, I believe! The last time she sat with us, my sister appeared, exactly as she was in life. I could have sworn to her anywhere, and several of our friends have seen their relations. Do come! Mrs. Roster will be delighted to see you!"

"I will, with pleasure!" replied the Baron.

At the appointed time, he presented himself at the Rosters' house, and found a large party assembled there, all of whom were talking of nothing but the marvellous powers of Mrs. Brown, the medium who was expected that evening.

"Where did you pick her up?" asked the Baron, of the lady of the house.

"Through an advertisement in one of the spiritualistic papers," she replied, "she is rather uncouth at times, but essentially reliable. Indeed, I never met anyone like her before. But here she comes!"

Von Steinberg looked up with curiosity, and encountered the form and face of Hannah.

CHAPTER XVI.

As is usual in such cases, the woman was the first to regain her presence of mind. The encounter was as unexpected to Hannah, as to the Baron, but she evinced no visible sign of surprise. She only stood quite still, as if she had never seen him before.

Von Steinberg, on the contrary, was nearly betraying her and himself. He stammered and stuttered and coloured rosy red, but at last managed to utter,

"Ah! Mrs. Brown! Of course! I think we have had the pleasure of meeting before," and advanced towards her, holding out his hand.

Hannah accepted the hand, without comment.

"Met before!" exclaimed Mrs. Roster. "O! where? I flattered myself that I was the discoverer of Mrs. Brown's remarkable talents,—at least in our own circle. I suppose then, Baron, that you have already been present at her marvellous séances."

"Mrs. Brown is the widow of an old and dear friend of mine," he answered, evasively.

"A widow!" echoed the lady of the house; "and does your husband ever return to you, Mrs. Brown? How intensely interesting! This will make the third time we have sat with her, Baron," she continued to Von Steinberg, "and each time we have seen the form of a man whom no one in the party recognised. I wonder if it could have been Mr. Brown."

"Hush!" said the Baron, cautiously, and indeed the pallor which had suddenly stolen over Hannah's usually rubicund countenance, quite justified him in saying so.

"O! I am sorry!" returned Mrs. Roster, as she busied herself in pressing the medium to take some refreshment before she entered the séance room.

Hannah faintly asked for a glass of water, and sat down apparently exhausted in her chair. When the water was brought to her, she drank a little, and finally declaring she felt too ill to sit, and must postpone the séance to another day, she rose and quitted the room and house.

The disappointed sitters gazed at each other in consternation. Colonel Roster attributed all the blame to his wife.

"What on earth made you allude to her dead husband in so indiscreet a manner?" he demanded, sharply. "You have just spoilt our evening! What widow ever wanted the return of Number One, to spy out her doings with Number Two? We have no one but you to thank for this disappointment!"

"O! I am sorry," cried his wife; "I thought as everybody's relations came back through her, Mr. Brown would be sure to have done so. And it was only a surmise on my part after all. You say you know her, Baron! Is she always as sensitive as this?"

"By no means," replied Von Steinberg, "and I think she must really be feeling ill. Besides, she has no reason to fear the return of her husband, who was very good to her! I cannot believe that your allusion had anything to do with her defalcation. She felt unequal to the sitting—that is all!"

"You take a load off my mind by saying so," said Mrs. Roster, "and I can only hope that when she comes here again, you will be with us, as on this occasion."

"You are very kind," returned Von Steinberg, "but may I ask you one question? Mrs. Brown was going to sit with you professionally, of course! What is her fee? I should like to ascertain, for the information of my friends!"

"Two guineas!" replied the lady, without hesitation. "She did not ask more! I heard of her through my dressmaker, Mrs. Folkstone, but I understood that she gave her services somewhat secretly, and it was not to be talked about. I am so sorry you have missed seeing her—but perhaps you have sat with her already."

"Once or twice," said Von Steinberg, carelessly, and then the subject dropped.

His friends detained him so late that he could not get out to the cottage at Hampstead that night, or he certainly would have followed Hannah to her home, and asked the reason of what he had seen and heard. He could hardly understand why, but he disliked the idea of her selling her services to the public, exceedingly.

It was no matter to him that she was dowdily dressed, and known as "Mrs. Brown";—he could not bear to think that she placed herself under such an obligation to strangers—that she should belong, as it were, to the public, when he wanted to have her entirely as his own.

His meditations that night revealed the truth to him. He was so fascinated by Hannah Ricardo, that he wished to marry her, and shield her for ever from the slights and obligations of the world. No one could have been more amazed than himself, when he had arrived at this conclusion. He had been a student of men and manners, but he had never lit on anything more incomprehensible than this before.

He wanted to marry Hannah Stubbs—he, who had so opposed the same idea in his friend. Ricardo had formed the wish, in order to keep Leonora by his side, whilst he, Von Steinberg, desired the same thing solely for Hannah.

He longed to possess this woman, with her overwhelming personality—her clumsy movements—her broad smile—her arch looks and witching eyes—for herself alone, and himself entirely.

He tried to recall her, as she used to be, but failed to do so. She seemed to have cast aside her chrysalis shell and emerged (in mind at least) a butterfly! And yet outwardly, there was no difference!

Where did the fascination lie? He could not determine, but felt that it was there, and that in her was contained the happiness of his future life.

He rose early, and was at the Hampstead cottage by eleven o'clock.

His first words to her were those of reproach.

"Hannah! how could you do this thing without letting me know? It nearly paralysed me to meet you at the Rosters last night in the capacity of a public medium. What would dear old Ricardo say, if he could know it?"

"Then he should have left me enough to exist upon," replied Hannah, "Charlotte and I can't live on dry bread—even if we got enough of that!"

"But I have asked you again and again, in case of need, to apply to me. What is the use of being your friend, if I may not have the pleasure of helping you out of your difficulties? You deprive me of one of the great privileges of friendship! And to sit when you are ill too! It is so unlike you to turn faint! You must have been sadly overworking yourself! Are you quite recovered this morning?"

"Quite, thank you," replied Hannah, reservedly—reservedly on purpose to make him speak out.

"I am glad of that," said Von Steinberg, "but to return to our subject;—I trust you do not intend to follow up Spiritualism as a means of livelihood for the future!"

Hannah lay back in her chair, lazily, and fixed her large, full eyes upon him.

"Why not?" she demanded.

"For a dozen reasons! Principally, because your husband so decidedly set his face against it, and then because I—I, who am your greatest and truest friend, Hannah, think it is beneath you, and degrades you."

"But I must live!" persisted the woman.

"Are there not other ways? If your money will not suffice to keep you comfortably for a year or two——"

"And what after that?" she exclaimed.

The Baron hesitated. Should he make the fatal plunge?

"My purse is always open to you, Hannah," he faltered.

"I have already told you, Baron, that I cannot consent to be a pensioner upon your charity," she replied. "You speak of what the world will say!

The world would talk a great deal more of your paying my bills, than it would of my giving séances to keep myself! It can never be! That is decided!"

"Then give me the right to empty the contents of my purse at your feet, Hannah," cried Von Steinberg, losing control of himself. "Come to me as my wife, and the mistress of all I possess! Marry me—be the Baronne von Steinberg, and let us pass the rest of our lives together."

"I could not give up my title of Marchesa for that of Baronne," remarked Hannah, coolly.

"You may call yourself what you choose, so long as you will be my wife!" repeated the Baron. "Hannah! I have longed to ask you this ever since you were free. Crown my happiness by giving me your promise now!"

"It is too soon to think of such a thing," argued Hannah—"only three months after my husband's death!"

But her reluctance only urged him on to fresh entreaties. Perhaps she was clever enough to know it would!

"What does that signify?" he said, "what is Time to dear Ricardo now, and whose opinion do we care for, but his? He is happy, I am sure, and would wish to see you happy, and well provided for, too. Come! Hannah, do not let any absurd scruples stand in the way of my proposal. No one need even know when the ceremony takes place. We are both almost strangers in London!

"Who is to be the wiser what we do, or leave undone! Let me marry you quietly some morning, as poor Ricardo did, and carry off at once to the Continent. There, we can stay a month, or a year, as pleases us best, and when we return, I will instal you as mistress of my house in Portland Place, and all I have. Come! is it a bargain?"

As Von Steinberg mentioned his property, Hannah's eyes glistened with pleasurable anticipation. *This* was what she had been working for—what she had known she would gain at the last. She turned her voluptuous orbs upon him, and languidly held out her large hand.

The Baron seized it and kissed it with rapture. It would have signified nothing to him at that moment, had it been twice as large. The woman had magnetised his every sense, and he was a tool in her hands.

"And when shall it be, Hannah?" he asked, as soon as he had recovered his powers of speech. "To-day?—to-morrow?—it cannot be too soon."

"Not for you, perhaps," she replied, with all the airs of a grand lady, "but you forget, Baron, that I cannot start on a wedding-tour, in a black dress and a widow's bonnet! You must be good enough to draw my small principal from the bank for me, and allow me a few weeks in which to spend it, so that I may be able to appear as your wife should do!"

"A few weeks!" exclaimed Von Steinberg, with really comical dismay, "I will send you the money this afternoon, and surely a few days should see you fully equipped. You need not wait to have things made in London. Get just what may be necessary for the moment, and buy your wardrobe in Paris!"

"In Paris!" exclaimed Hannah, "will you really take me to Paris?"

"Certainly! and to stay there if you desire it! There is no place on earth to which I would not take you, Hannah, if you told me to do so, but I think a residence in Paris will suit us both entirely."

He lavished kisses on her flat, good-humoured face, and Hannah returned them in kind, for a passionate temperament was not the least of her virtues.

Before they parted that morning, it was decided that the marriage should take place privately in a fortnight's time, and that they were to leave England the same day for the Continent. Hannah promised she would give no more public séances, and really looked quite handsome under the prospect of renewed happiness—not to say the acquisition of the house in Portland Place, and all its treasures, to which her eyes had so longingly turned.

Once more by himself at home, Karl von Steinberg had leisure to wonder if his action of the morning had been wise. Hannah had not proved, in all things, quite amenable to the discipline of his old friend, but then Ricardo *was* old—he told himself—and May and December never did hit it off well together yet. He was far more suitable in age to Hannah, and would prove a livelier companion.

It was astonishing to remember how young she was—only nineteen—and yet so worldly-wise in some things, and in others so quick and cunning! She had wonderfully developed since her marriage —no one would know her for the same girl—she doubtless possessed vast capabilities, which travel and his society would tend to unfold. The Baron quite anticipated bringing back an accomplished lady from the Continent.

And he was not far wrong! Hannah *had* developed powers of observation and attainment, which bid fair to let her stop at nothing short of excellence. Each time the Baron met her, face to face, the half-formed doubts which he held, as to the wisdom of the marriage, faded away, and left him with but one certainty—that he could not live without her. The plans they had formed, then, were faithfully carried out, and within a fortnight, the same Registrar who had married her to Signor Ricardo, transformed Hannah Stubbs into the Baronne von Steinberg—though (as she had previously informed her husband) she always intended to retain her old title of Marchesa di Sorrento.

Are the raptures which we anticipate in marriage, or any other exploit, ever realised to their full extent? As a rule, surely not, and Von Steinberg was no exception. Hannah remained the same after marriage as she had been before, but the novelty of possession soon wore off, and when that occurred, Von Steinberg of all men, with his cool, calculating German temperament, was the most likely to see the spots upon the sun.

However, they established themselves in Paris, and a few months of the gay city did wonders for his wife in the way of polish and manners. Naturally quick and cunning, and with a remarkable facility for the acquisition of languages, the Marchesa soon lost most of her vulgarisms and became quite *au fait* with great people and their ways.

The English who met her abroad, put all her eccentricities down to the fact that she was an Italian Marchesa, and the Parisians ascribed them to the misfortune of her having been born a Briton. But Hannah made the most of her opportunities. She went out whenever she was invited, mixing freely with foreigners, as well as her own countrymen, and in consequence, gathering knowledge and information wherever they were to be found.

By this means, when, after a year's residence abroad, Baron von Steinberg brought his wife back to England, if not still in love with her, he had ceased to be ashamed of her. But the same perplexity which had puzzled him in Ricardo's time, still stirred in his brain. *What* was it in Hannah that attracted him, spite of himself? Sometimes he felt ready to lay down his life for her—at others, he regarded her with disfavour, almost with repugnance!

But as the mistress of his house—the dispenser of his hospitality—she was perfect. She had a courteous and gracious manner, which she extended equally to peer and peasant, and which made strangers, who had never seen another side to her character, consider her the most charming hostess under the sun. Whilst when at other moments she spoke her mind freely—far too freely—concerning people and their actions, her visitors still ascribed it to her genuineness and total disregard of what the world might say, or think.

What astonished Von Steinberg more than anything else, was the complacency with which she accepted the fact of his wealth, and the nonchalance with which she treated his pictures, and statues, and hothouse flowers. She took everything that he gave her, as if she had been used to it all her life—she accepted it from him graciously, but she was not overwhelmed with gratitude for his generosity. He would not have had her betray her lowly birth and breeding, by expressing ignorance of such luxuries, but it amazed him, all the same.

He thought his wife had everything she could

have expected, and a great deal more than she had any right to demand, but yet Hannah was not satisfied. As soon as they were settled in town, they commenced to give a series of magnificent parties, and their rooms were crowded with sycophantic guests, mostly of the middle class—the sort of people who will go anywhere—to whom a party means a dance, or a supper, and who care nothing who gives it, so long as it is given.

His visitors satisfied the Baron, but the Marchesa had higher views—she aspired to see the aristocracy sitting round her dinner-table, and quoting her hospitality as the freest in London—her cook as the best to be got anywhere. It was all very well, she thought, to be entertaining Colonel and Mrs. Langley, or Mr. and Mrs. Belleville, but what use were they to her in return?

She wanted Dukes and Duchesses and Earls and Countesses at her receptions, and to make them not only come, but *ask* to come. She racked her clever brain over this many a time and oft, without letting her husband into the secret, and one day the opportunity came to her.

She was receiving a number of ladies at afternoon tea, when the conversation suddenly turned on Spiritualism.

The Marchesa, who was leaning back on a settee, arrayed in a tea-gown of maize coloured satin, trimmed with costly lace, affected to know nothing of the matter.

"What is it?" she inquired, languidly, "nothing wicked, I hope, Mrs. Mostyn."

"O! dear me, no! Marchesa, how could you imagine such a thing?" replied her guest. "It is only a game, you know! Sitting round a table and making it spin and answer questions, and all such nonsense!"

"It is a great deal more than that," interposed an unmarried lady, named Selwyn, "it is a very serious thing! Spiritualism is raising the spirits of the Dead, and our clergyman, Mr. Tennant, says it is sorcery, and condemned by Scripture. My mamma will not hear of my having anything to do with it, which has been a great disappointment to me, for the Countess of Loreley——"

"Well! if you are interested in the pursuit, I am sure there can be no need to wait for your mamma's permission," interrupted Mrs. Mostyn, rudely, "you are surely old enough to judge for yourself. I do think it is so ridiculous of mothers, trying to keep their grown-up daughters in leading strings. Why! I had a couple of children before I was your age!"

"You were speaking of the Countess of Loreley," said the Marchesa, with the apparent view of changing the conversation, "does her Ladyship take an interest in the subject?"

"O! yes, she is quite wild about it," replied Miss Selwyn, who was looking red and confused from Mrs. Mostyn's attack; "and mamma has prevented my going there as often as usual, in consequence. Lady Loreley is my godmother, you know, and I used to be always at her house, but now——"

"Has Mrs. Selwyn compelled you to give up the Countess's acquaintance?" asked Hannah, indifferently.

"O! no, but I do not see her so often, and never when there is to be a séance! Very unfair, isn't it? not that I care so much about the séance, but I would not lose Lady Loreley's goodwill for all the world."

"The Countess believes in Spiritualism then?"

"O! yes! entirely! She is always sitting with some medium or other, but she says they are very unsatisfactory. She told me yesterday, that she would give hundreds of pounds to find a medium, who could bring her little Rosie back to speak with her again."

"Much better leave the poor child in peace—wherever she may be!" remarked Mrs. Mostyn with a sneer.

"Perhaps you have never lost a child, Mrs. Mostyn," said the single lady.

"No! nor you either, I conclude, my dear," replied the other, "but all this talk about Spiritualism is only got up, for want of a better excitement. For my own part I don't believe a word of it, and I am sure the Marchesa agrees with me!"

"One should be careful to reserve one's opinion,

when one has not inquired into a thing!" replied Hannah, as she reclined on her couch and gently fanned herself.

But when her visitors rose to depart, and Miss Selwyn was about to leave the room with the rest of the party, she detained her by a gentle pull at her sleeve.

"Wait a moment longer," she whispered, "I want to speak to you," and Miss Selwyn, who was only too pleased to be singled out for favour by the Marchesa, dallied with a book of engravings, which lay upon a side table, until the rest were gone.

"Tell me more about this poor Countess," said Hannah, drawing nearer to her; "I feel so interested in any one who has lost a dear child—a girl, I think you said."

"O! yes, Marchesa," replied Miss Selwyn, "Lady Rose Charleville—such a dear little creature. She died of scarlet fever at seven years old, and though Lady Loreley has married daughters, she has never forgotten her. She always cries when Lady Rose is mentioned."

"Poor dear!" said Hannah, sympathetically, "how I wish I could help her! And I think I could, if she would come and see me!"

"Could you *really?*" cried Miss Selwyn, clasping her hands, "O! Marchesa, how she would bless you for it! She would worship you! But how is it to be accomplished?"

"That is *my* secret, my dear! I know more of this matter than I chose to say in public, and if you like to bring your Countess here, I will introduce her to some one who may put her in the way of seeing her child again! But you mustn't chatter on the subject, for if the Baron heard that I encouraged anything of the sort, he would be very angry. It is not only your mamma, Miss Selwyn, who disapproves of Spiritualism."

"O! I know that, and I would not mention what you have told me for all the world. But when may I bring the Countess here!"

"On second thoughts, I think you had better tell her what I have said, and leave her to make her own appointment with me. I could not permit you to assist at our conference, you know, for fear of offending your mamma."

"Perhaps it will be better not," replied the girl, in a disappointed tone, "for I have promised mamma never to attend a sitting again. May I tell Lady Loreley that you will have the medium here to meet her, Marchesa? I shall see her this evening!"

"You had better say nothing, but what I have told you—that if she wishes it, I think I can help her to see her child again. Then she can make an appointment with me, or not, as she chooses!"

"Fancy! her *not* choosing!" exclaimed Miss Selwyn, "why, she will rush to you as soon as ever she can!"

And in effect, the very next day Hannah received a coronetted note from the Countess of Loreley, to say that, with her kind permission, she would call in Portland Place that afternoon.

CHAPTER XVII.

No one who had seen the Marchesa, as she sat in her drawing-room, awaiting the arrival of the Countess of Loreley, would have recognised her as the maid-of-all-work, Hannah Stubbs, who had married Signor Ricardo, from Mrs. Battleby's lodging-house, less than three years before. She wore a robe fashioned by a dressmaker, chosen for her by the Baron; her abundant hair had been arranged by her lady's maid in the height of the prevailing style; she displayed one or two articles of costly jewelry; she was neither under, nor overdressed.

Her personal appearance, also, was wonderfully improved, Hannah was not yet twenty-one, but she looked thirty. Her figure was still unshapely and abundantly covered with flesh, but her skin was smoother, and her complexion and hands properly attended to.

She was still a coarse specimen of her sex—there have been such anomalies in this world as coarse and vulgar duchesses, and when bred to the position into the bargain—and she would never be really handsome, but there was a bonhomie in her expression, and a frank good-humour in her smile, which was, perhaps, all that remained of Hannah Stubbs in her composition.

Lady Loreley, who had been led by Miss Selwyn, to expect something altogether out of the common in the Marchesa di Sorrento, (—" Awfully good-natured, dear Lady Loreley, you know, but O! such a moving mass of flesh—like a female elephant—and says such queer things at times, but she thinks she can help you and so," etc, etc,—) was quite taken by surprise, when Hannah, perfectly at her ease, but with unquestionable welcome beaming from her eyes, rose from the sofa to say how pleased she was to make her acquaintance.

The two women sat down to afternoon tea together, and were soon on friendly terms. Naturally, the topic which engrossed Lady Loreley's thoughts was not long in coming to the front.

"Miss Selwyn delivered your most kind message to me, Marchesa," commenced the bereaved mother, "and you must not be surprised at my availing myself of your kindness at so early a period. My dear child was my idol, the youngest of my large family, and I lost her in so cruelly sudden a manner Only four days ill of scarlet fever, and she had gone from us. She could not stand up against it! She was always delicate, my poor little Rose! And is it possible that you can help me to see her? O! Marchesa!" cried the Countess, seizing her hands, "if you can, I shall be your debtor to the last day of my life. Only one glimpse, that is all I ask, one glimpse to assure me that she lives and that I shall meet her again, and I shall die content!"

The Marchesa did not release the Countess's hands—on the contrary, she retained and pressed them firmly.

"Is your Ladyship aware of the method pursued in such cases? Do you know that the services of a materialising medium are necessary, and that often even they are not successful?"

"Yes! yes! but I should not mind how often I had to sit, if I only succeed at last! And expense is no object whatever! I have tried all sorts of mediums, dear Marchesa, but have never heard a word, nor seen a sign of her! O! it has been heart-rending—discouraging—but I shall never cease trying till I succeed!"

"I think I know a way by which you can see her!" replied Hannah, whose eyes had been dreamily fixed upon space for the last minute.

"Pray, pray, tell it to me!" exclaimed the Countess, with agitation.

"One moment! I must ask you first to bind yourself to the strictest secrecy! My husband, the Baron, is like many in the present day, most averse to my mixing myself up in Spiritualism with any but himself, and if he heard that you and I had been sitting together, he would certainly forbid me to help you any more!"

"I will be secret as the grave!" said Lady Loreley, fervently; "no one shall ever hear a word of it from me!"

"Not even the Earl, or Miss Selwyn?" asked Hannah.

"No one! Not even my nearest and dearest, unless you give me leave!" was the reply.

"Then you must come with me to my private boudoir," said the Marchesa.

"What! is the medium there?"

"Yes! she will be there!" replied Hannah, as she rang the bell and desired the servant to deny her to any other callers.

Then, she led the way up to her little boudoir, round which the Countess looked curiously.

"You have successfully concealed your medium, dear Marchesa!" she said.

"No! Lady Loreley, she is in full view! *I* am the medium!"

Her visitor started with surprise.

"*You!* Are you jesting with me, Marchesa? Is it possible that you can call back the spirits of the Dead?"

"Just as possible as anybody else! No one can *call* them back, Lady Loreley! But they come all the same, when they get the opportunity! Are you nervous? Shall you be afraid to sit in the dark with me?"

"O! no! I don't think so," replied the Countess, who was already shivering with fright.

Hannah lowered the blinds, closed the dark red silk curtains, locked the door and taking a seat on the sofa, invited Lady Loreley to sit beside her and hold her hand.

"But don't you require a table?" inquired the Countess.

"Not that I know of," replied Hannah. "No spirit that has ever come to me, has made any request of the sort! I don't even know if they use tables over there. Don't you see a bluish mist rising, close by the window curtains? Don't be frightened if I go to sleep. I generally do, but you will be quite safe. Nothing can hurt you."

And as she was in the midst of talking thus, the Marchesa went under control and knew nothing more. When she awoke, she found the Countess of Loreley on her knees before her, sobbing as if her heart would break.

"O! you dear Angel!" she cried, "I can never, *never* thank you enough, for what you have done for me to-day. You are a wonder! a miracle! You must have been sent on earth by God, expressly to give comfort to broken-hearted mothers like myself!"

"Why! have you seen anything?" demanded Hannah, rousing herself from her benumbing trance.

"Seen anything!" echoed Lady Loreley, "I have

seen that which has transformed me from a despairing woman to a happy one! I have seen my little Rose! You said you saw a bluish mist near the window. She walked straight out of that mist, and smiled at me! I spoke to her, and I thought her lips moved, but I could not hear any words, but she smiled at me—she stood there in her little white nightdress and bare feet, just as she was, dear darling! when I laid her in her coffin—and I know she lives, and I am happy once more—and O! dear Marchesa, what can I ever do to show my gratitude to you?"

"Only be quiet," said Hannah, holding up her hand, "and say nothing to anybody. Come and see me sometimes, Lady Loreley, and the more intimate you become with me, the more clearly you will see your little Rose, and the more confidently will she come back to you! Did no one else appear?"

"No one whom I recognised! An old man's face seemed hovering over your head, but it frightened me rather, and I did not look."

At those words "an old man's face", the Marchesa seemed to shiver slightly, and her next injunction was delivered rather hurriedly,

"Now, mind, Countess, you must not breathe a word of what has occurred this afternoon to any one, or it will never happen again. The Baron would be so angry he would forbid my sitting with you at all! You can see that I say this for *your* sake, more than for my own."

"O! yes, indeed," said Lady Loreley, "but, Marchesa—I was going to ask you such a great favour! My eldest daughter, the Duchess of Penywern, lost her baby last year—such a splendid boy, heir, of course, to the title and estates, and she would give her life, I verily believe, to see him again.

"And my aunt, Lady John Valerian, who is most interested in Spiritualism, would consider it such an inestimable favour, if you would let her accompany me, next time I have the pleasure of visiting you! They would be as silent as myself concerning our visits here, I can assure you, and I am certain you would like them both—my daughter especially, who is a most amiable young woman."

Hannah considered for a moment what she should reply. Here was the very thing which she had longed and striven for, dropping like a ripe plum into her mouth. A Countess—a Duchess—and the wife of a Lord! She must secure the lot, but not for séances in her private room—for exhibition at her public parties!

"You are asking a great deal, Lady Loreley," she replied, with a pursed-up mouth, as though she were considering the possibility of granting her request. "If it depended on myself, I should only be too pleased to accede to your wishes, but, as I have already told you, my husband would not approve of my sitting with ladies of whom I know, as yet, so little."

"O! but you must know more of us, dear Marchesa," cried Lady Loreley. "You must come to my house and let me introduce you to my daughter and my aunt! What day are you at liberty to dine with us? Would next Thursday suit you? I have no engagement for that day! Then if you and the Baron will give us the pleasure of your company at dinner, I will have the Duchess and Lady John to meet you!"

"I believe we are at liberty for Thursday," replied Hannah, with her air of *grande dame*, "but remember! Lady Loreley, the motive of your visit must be kept a dead secret, if you ever wish to see it renewed."

"You may depend on my discretion, Marchesa!" replied the Countess, as she grasped her hand; "I can never, never thank you sufficiently for what you have done for me to-day, and I hope we shall be the most excellent friends in the future!"

So Lady Loreley took her leave, and that was the beginning of the Marchesa di Sorrento counting dukes and duchesses amongst her visiting acquaintances.

Secretly, but surely, the news flew amongst the aristocratic crowd, that this mysterious Marchesa, the nationality of whom no one could determine, was the most wonderful woman on the face of the earth, and many were the little private séances held by her in her boudoir, unknown to all but the favoured few, whom she admitted there.

As time went on and one lady asked to be allowed to bring her brother, and another entreated that her husband might be initiated into the occult mysteries of the Marchesa's boudoir, gentlemen began to mingle with the lady sitters, and the séances became more general and more renowned.

Meanwhile Karl von Steinberg knew nothing of what went on during his absences from home, or that his wife ever sat for the amusement of the grandees who commenced to throng her receptions. He often wondered *where* she had picked them up, or how contrived to induce them to visit her, but he knew she was very clever, and admired her all the more for each fresh proof she gave him of it. He was not blind, however, to the kudos, which accrued to both of them, from the presence of the nobility in his wife's drawing-rooms, and he evinced it by the frequency with which he showed himself there. He constantly found the Marchesa the centre of an adoring group of ladies, and an admiring crowd of men, and the fact bound him closer to her. We always like others to approve of what we like ourselves—so long as they do not go too far!

There was one man, however—an Italian of the name of Gueglielmo, whom Karl von Steinberg began to view with aversion. He used to take his stand behind the Marchesa's sofa, and remain there the entire evening, whispering in her ear, or gazing at her face and figure. Once, Von Steinberg spoke to his wife about the too evident admiration of Signor Gueglielmo, and expressed his wish that she should discourage him a little, by directing her attention to the other gentlemen of the party.

"Discourage Gueglielmo!" she exclaimed tartly, "and why? Because he is the only one of my countrymen present! I shall do no such thing!"

Von Steinberg regarded her with surprise! She was beginning to use the same tone with him, that she had with his friend Ricardo.

"Your countryman!" he repeated; "what absurdity are you thinking of? Your being styled 'Marchesa' does not constitute you an Italian! He is neither your countryman nor mine, and I will not have him so much about the house. If you do not give him a hint on the subject, I shall!"

"Then you may do your dirty work yourself," retorted Hannah. "I like him and I shall not tell him otherwise. He is Italian! He soothes me!"

"You will have to obey me all the same," said the Baron, angrily. "If ever I catch him leaning over your sofa again in the open fashion he did last night, I'll——"

"Run me through with a dagger, I suppose!" interposed Hannah, with the sudden, cunning, evil look in her eyes, which he could never understand.

"What made you say that?" he asked, quickly.

She shrugged her shoulders, and commenced to whistle a popular air.

Von Steinberg left the room in a rage. There were times—many times—when he almost hated his wife! She had never shown any disposition for flirting—it was not her proclivity—she was too heavy and indolent and inert to take the trouble to lay herself out to fascinate any man. He could not suspect her of it. And yet, had she been the most desperate coquette in the world, she could not have been more determined to have her own way about this man Gueglielmo. And the look in her eyes, when she suggested he might stab her! whence did it come? The idea perplexed him! Sometimes he wondered if Hannah were always herself, or if evil spirits took possession of her and controlled her expression and her words.

When he met her next, at dinner, all trace of the unpleasant interview they had held together, had passed away. Hannah was Hannah once more—placid and obtuse as a well-fed cow grazing in a meadow, and without a care or an ambition in the world.

Before their meal was concluded, the footman brought a somewhat soiled envelope to the Marchesa, on a silver tray.

She took it up and looking at the address carelessly, inquired: "Who brought this?"

"A young man, my lady!—looks as if he came from the country," was the reply.

Hannah opened the letter and read it, then said in a loud voice,

"Tell this man I will not see him! I don't know who he is! Send him away."

"What is it, Hannah?" demanded Von Steinberg. She threw the envelope across the table to him.

"Only a begging petition! I receive them every day. It is no use answering these sort of people!"

The Baron glanced at the epistle, and frowned as he did so.

"My dear, you cannot have read this," he said, in a lowered voice, "it is from Joseph Brushwood! He has bad news for you."

"And who is Joseph Brushwood?" she asked; "I never heard the name before."

Von Steinberg ordered the servants in attendance to quit the room, until he rang for them, and to detain the messenger downstairs.

"Or stay!" he corrected himself, "put him in the library, and say I will be with him presently!"

"So the petition is for yourself, after all!" remarked his wife, as they found themselves alone.

"My dear Hannah! what are you talking about?" said the Baron. "You *cannot* have read this letter. It is signed Joseph Brushwood, and is to say that he has some bad news about your mother, and wants to speak to you by yourself!"

"And I repeat, who *is* Joseph Brushwood?" demanded Hannah, with genuinely astonished eyes.

"Why! surely you cannot have forgotten Joe Brushwood coming up to town with your mother, when we were at Mrs. Battleby's. Joe Brushwood, the young man to whom you were engaged, before you married dear old Ricardo! It is impossible that you can forget!"

"And he wishes to see me privately?" continued the Marchesa, with perfect calmness.

"Yes! I am afraid you must be prepared for a shock, Hannah, for he says he has come to town expressly to see you! Shall I accompany you?"

"No! I prefer to see him by myself!" replied Hannah, as she rose majestically from the table and proceeded to the library.

There she encountered Joe Brushwood, who had cast her off in the days gone-by, standing by the window and looking very sheepish. He was not altered in the least—a trifle stouter, perhaps, and a trifle coarser, but attired in his best velveteen coat and corduroy breeches, with a gaily flowered waistcoat. He started violently as he caught sight of Hannah.

He had heard that she had married a rich gentleman, but he had had no idea of encountering such magnificence as this. The Marchesa was arrayed in her ordinary dinner-dress, but it looked like a robe of state in the unsophisticated eyes of her former admirer.

"And what is it that you may want of me?"

she demanded, with her grandest air, as she advanced upon the astonished Brushwood.

"Lor! Hannah!" he exclaimed—but she quickly brought her foot down upon such insolent familiarity.

"Who are you? How *dare* you address me in such terms? I am the Marchesa di Sorrento! You will have the goodness to call me 'my Lady', if you speak to me at all."

"O! yes! certainly. I'm sure I begs your pardon," replied Joe, as he nervously twisted his bowler hat round in his hands, "but I came up from Settlefield a purpuss this mornin', and I've been walking round Lunnon for hours, trying to find out where you lived—"

"And what has all this to do with me?" demanded Hannah.

"O! I ain't done yet!" continued the young man. "Your pore mother, she's werry bad indeed, and she wants to see you terrible! I don't know what's the matter with her, but she's going fast, the Doctor says, and times 'ave been werry bad this season, and your father says 'e don't know 'ow 'e'll bury 'er, without some 'elp. And so—as we 'eard as you was married to a rich gentleman, we made so bold as to come up—leastways *I* did—to arsk if you could spare 'em a trifle, and go down and see your pore mother afore she dies!"

Hannah let the whole of this long-winded speech come to a finish, before she collected her forces and answered it.

"You have made a mistake, young man," she said at last, "I know nothing of Settlefield, or the people you are begging for. I am the Marchesa di Sorrento! Some one must have put you on the wrong scent for a joke! If your friends are in such want, you had better apply to their parish for relief! I have my own poor people to look after, and cannot afford to provide for strangers."

Joe Brushwood scratched his head, and opened his eyes wide.

"But you was Hannah Stubbs—sure-*ly*!" he ejaculated, "as lived at Settlefield and was my young woman! Everyone knows you down there, as well as the village pump! And sure-ly, you won't turn on your own mother now she's sick and dying and in want! A fiver would set 'em right, but the times 'as been 'ard, and they've several mouths to feed, and if you *are* a Mar-cheesa you might 'ave 'uman feelings!"

"You are an insolent impostor!" cried Hannah, indignantly. "How dare you speak to me in that way? Your young woman, indeed! I should like the Baron to hear you! I don't believe one word of your trumped-up story. I have no mother, nor father, and I never set eyes on you in my life before! If you presume to worry me again I shall give you into charge of the police."

"And you denies of them?" replied the young man, reproachfully. "I'm not so surprised at your saying as you don't know *me*, for I give you a nasty slap in the face larst time we met—but to deny the mother as bore you and she a'dying—and with hardly a rag to 'er back, or food to eat— well! I wouldn't 'ave your 'eart, for ever so! that I wouldn't!"

The Marchesa only replied by ringing the bell and summoning her footman.

"Show this man out," she said, "and take care that he is never admitted again. He is an impostor, and he has insulted me."

"Come! along with you!" cried the servant, as he hustled Joe from the room. "I'll take good care you never shows your nose inside of our 'ouse again!"

And so Joe Brushwood found himself upon the doorstep in shorter time than it takes to write the words.

The Marchesa joined her husband in the drawing-room, triumphant.

"Well! what had he to say to you?" demanded the Baron, as she entered.

"Nothing! It was all a hoax! No more Joseph Brushwood—whoever he may be—than you are! A fellow with a begging letter, and who became so insolent when I refused to give him money, that I was obliged to ring for Watson to show him the door!"

"You were quite right to refuse," said the Baron,

"I hate these begging letter writers. But how could he have got hold of the name of Joseph Brushwood?"

"Invented it, most likely!" replied Hannah, as she commenced to read the evening papers.

"But, my dear, that was the name of the young man you were engaged to," began Karl von Steinberg. "Surely, you must remember!"

"No! I don't, and I don't want to," persisted his wife, "I never think of that horrible time! It is past now! I wish nothing better than to blot out the memory that it ever existed."

She returned to the perusal of her paper, and her husband, after regarding her for a few moments as if she were some extraordinary animal whom he could not possibly understand—left the room quietly, and went to his club.

CHAPTER XVIII.

"WHY did Hannah pretend to have forgotten the fact that she had ever known Joseph Brushwood? What was her motive in refusing the prayer of her dying mother, to see her once again? Had her unexpected rise in life and position really made her oblivious of all that had gone before, or had her heart grown callous to the sufferings of her fellow-creatures?"

These were the questions that puzzled the brain of Karl von Steinberg, as he walked meditatively down to his club that night.

He had read the smeared epistle that Brushwood had sent in to his wife, from beginning to end. There was no mistaking its import. It stated plainly, that Mrs. Stubbs was in the last stage of disease—that the husband and children were in want—and that they only asked a little help from their rich daughter, to enable them to tide over the difficulty.

Why had not Hannah sent them money for their

need? She knew that she had but to ask him, to obtain any reasonable sum for the purpose.

Karl von Steinberg had an affectionate nature—rather weak indeed, but gentle and kind-hearted. He could not bear to think that his wife had been wilfully guilty of such negligence and indifference. When he reached his club, he drew four five-pound banknotes from his purse, and putting them into an envelope, addressed it to Mr. Stubbs, Settlefield and wrote the pardonable fiction inside, "With Hannah's love."

The reception of this munificent gift made a great revolution of feeling in the Stubbs' family, whither Joe Brushwood had preceded it, with an exaggerated account of his interview with Hannah.

"I sent in my note, quite respectful," he had told them on his return, "and thought if I didn't get a 'earty welcome, she'd at least talk friendly-like about 'er people! But not a bit of it! In she sails in a gownd like a peacock, trailing on the floor, and 'What may be your business with me, young man?' she says, as proud as a cat with a tin tail. 'Lor! Hannah!' I says, and she turns on me like a tiger, 'Oo are you a'speakin' to?' she says, 'and you'll please to say "my Lady" when you opens your mouth in my presence?' I did feel pretty well shut up, I can tell you!"

Mrs. Stubbs, who was sitting in an arm-chair, supported by pillows, looked incredulous at this account.

"Lor! Joe Brushwood," she said, "it couldn't never 'ave been our Hannah! You must 'ave gone to the wrong 'ouse!"

At this surmise, Joe himself turned pale.

"O! that's unpossible!" he exclaimed, "for 'twas Mrs. Battleby as give me the address. Baron von Stumbug, 2000 Portland Place. I writ it down in my pocket book. And I arsked for Lady von Stumbug, and the feller as answered the door, understood me quite well. Sich a grand 'ouse, Mrs. Stubbs, as you never see—all marble and picters and statties,—and Hannah in a yaller satin gownd, with black lace like cobwebs over it, and 'er 'air—well! you did ought to 'ave seen 'er 'air—'twas a transformation scene and no mistake!"

"I don't care nothing about 'er 'air," replied Mrs. Stubbs, "but I can't never believe as our Hannah, as was so meek and simple-like, would denige 'er own father and mother! You must 'ave mistook 'er words! I allers said as father ought to 'ave gone, instead of you."

"I didn't mistake nothing," said Joe, doggedly, "she's just as cold and 'eartless as they're made, and I'm werry glad as she never was my missus. She stood there, a'glaring at me, and she says, 'I ain't got no father nor mother,' she says, 'and you're a himpostor,' and she just rings the bell and orders the feller in green to put me out of the 'ouse, and mind I never enters it again. That's your Hannah, and that's gospel truth!"

"I can't never believe it!" repeated poor Mrs. Stubbs, "she was allays so humble, was our Hannah! I take blame to myself as I ever left 'er at Mrs. Battleby's, pore gal, and with all them devils about 'er too. I did ought to 'ave brought 'er 'ome, and exercised them out of 'er! But to speak in that rumptious manner! No! I can't never believe it! She was sich a simple one, was our Hannah—allays ready to cry if spoke to, almost a natural as you may say, but never 'aughty or proud. You went to the wrong 'ouse, Joe Brushwood! I'll maintain it to the last day of my life, which it won't be long!" she added, with a sigh.

"O! well! Missus," exclaimed Joe, rather nettled, "I 'opes as Mr. Stubbs will do 'is own work another time, for 'twasn't a pleasant job, I can tell ye. To 'ave to encounter a young 'ooman as you've rejected in marriage, and 'ear all the nasty things she may choose to say to you, ain't all jam, I'd rather meet the old gentleman myself any day."

"Well! you could 'ardly expect 'er to shake you by the 'and, and she a markiness and a baroness both in one, Joe Brushwood! You was a fool to reject 'er, that you was, and to lose the chance of being a baron yourself! Of course I know as 'er position and fortune 'ave set 'er above us, but I'll never believe but what my Hannah—as was so good 'earted and simple, though a bit slow—Lord! 'ow my arms 'ave ached trying to shake that gal up!—

remembers 'er pore father and mother, who never fell out with 'er, until she took up with the Devil and hall 'is imps!"

Joe Brushwood had left the cottage, grumbling at their incredulity and ingratitude, but the next day made him regret he had said so much. The postman brought Stubbs that wonderful letter, enclosing twenty pounds, with Hannah's love. The poor mother, who was really in the last stage of an internal disease, against which she had borne up bravely, until no longer able to stand, wept tears of thankfulness over her daughter's generosity, and quite forgot that she had been so sure that Joe had gone to the wrong house.

That young man was so beset with reproaches, when he next showed his face in their midst, that he fled incontinently from the cottage, and left the Stubbs' family to manage their own affairs for the future. And they—relieved from present necessity—sat down quite contented with spending their twenty pounds and talking of their daughter, the markiness, to any neighbour who might chance to look in.

Meanwhile, the Baron, puzzled and grieved as the days went on, to see no sign of repentance in Hannah, for the cruel part she had played with regard to her family, began to frequent his club more often than before. His wife had not yet quite lost her old fascination for him—it was misery to him to believe her cold-hearted and unfilial.

He never asked her to sit with him now—had almost given up talking of Spiritualism before her. Slight suspicions had crept into his mind of late, that the office of mediumship had not improved Hannah, in mind or manners—that she was more defiant and bold, and less grateful and submissive, than she used to be. Success in life could not alone have had the power to change her character thus, and he hoped by keeping her quiet and free from all these trances and controls, to see her one day return to the amiable and child-like disposition she had enjoyed.

His longing to see his old friend Ricardo was very keen, and if he could have found another medium through whom to communicate with him, he would have gladly availed himself of the opportunity. But he was unable to do so, and he would not urge Hannah to sit for him. Sometimes the longing was very great—sometimes he felt sure that Ricardo shared his anxiety and wished to speak to him.

More than once, as his wife slumbered by his side, he had fancied he heard a faint, gasping whisper on the air, in the tones of his old friend. But it had never culminated beyond that, and Hannah's objection to holding a séance with him was so palpably expressed, that he did not care to urge her to do that which was unpalatable to her.

Indeed, at this time, her arguments against the

practice of Spiritualism both in public and private, were so severe, that Von Steinberg honestly believed she had come to look upon it as something unlawful and forbidden. But his eyes were to be opened, and in a manner he little suspected.

On a certain afternoon, in summer, he was seated at his club in one of those deep arm-chairs with a high back, which, when turned from the company, entirely conceal their occupant. The day was warm, and the Baron had lunched and felt sleepy. He wheeled his chair into a corner of the club room, and turning its back to the centre of the apartment, prepared to indulge in a snooze. Men entered and left—the buzz of voices went on around him, but still he dozed—half awake and half asleep—too lazy to shake himself into complete consciousness.

By and by his first irresistible desire to slumber wore off, and he sat there, listening to what went on around him. Whilst in this condition he heard two men conversing together a few paces off, and soon recognised one voice as that of Major Maitland, who was a frequent visitor in Portland Place.

"I cannot understand what they see in her—a beastly, fat woman," he was saying, "and as vulgar as she can be! But she has got up this new fad of Spiritualism, and the women are all crazy about it—my wife amongst the rest. She professes to bring back their lovers and children and fathers and mothers, and there they all are, weeping and snivelling together, and swearing she is the grandest medium under the sun, and the most marvellous woman they have ever seen.

"I believe it is all humbug! She dresses up her housemaids and footmen to represent the dear departeds, and women are such hysterical creatures, they will declare they see anything which you may tell them is there! I have forbidden Mrs. Maitland visiting her, but it is of no use! I don't really know what has come to the women nowadays! They treat us, as if we were nobody! She's off this very afternoon to some big séance that this Marchesa is giving!"

"But who *is* she?" demanded the other speaker, "Marchesa—of what?"

"The Lord knows! *I* don't! She calls herself Marchesa di Sorrento, but who Sorrento was, she knows best. She is the wife—or is supposed to be—of a German, the Baron von Steinberg, who is really a very decent fellow, for a German—and he seems to let her do just as she likes! Finds it's of no use speaking to her, I suppose, poor devil! Where he picked her up I can't think! If you could only see her, Durant! She looks exactly like a cookmaid. A great, red, flat face with a turned-up nose, and a wide mouth! No more a lady than you are, but she is the women's new plaything, and they howl if you try to take her from them."

"It is all very strange," said Durant, "are you going to the séance this afternoon?"

"No! I'm black-balled, because I struck a match the last time I was there! I'm rather sorry. It was good fun, and really the most curious things happen. I've seen an old man appear there, looking just like one of Velasquez's portraits—with a pointed Venetian beard, and grizzled hair—not a bit like an Englishman—and, each time, he has asked for Von Steinberg—that's the husband, you know—but I suppose my lady doesn't let him hear of her little pranks, for I have never met him there!"

"Then I suppose you *do* believe something of this black art, Maitland. An Italian out of an old picture could hardly be impersonated by a footman, or a housemaid!" observed his companion.

"My dear fellow! to tell you the honest truth, I don't know *what* to believe! There may be something in it and there may not! All I know is, that women have grown so deuced clever in these days, that I think they are capable of anything—especially of deceit!"

Karl von Steinberg thought the same, as he lay back in his arm-chair, and listened to this conversation. Another man might have sprung up in a rage, and challenged the two gossips to prove what they asserted, but his was a phlegmatic temperament, which thought more than it said, and did more than it threatened. The day was over, when either Major Maitland or his wife would gain admittance to the house in Portland Place, but he did not tell them so.

On the contrary, he waited patiently until the two friends had adjourned to the billiard room, before he left his hiding-place, and hailing a cab, drove to his home.

His reflections on the way were not pleasant ones. Hannah, then, had deceived him! Whilst she had been denouncing Spiritualism, and declaring it was sinful and she would never have anything more to do with it, she had been giving séances to strangers, which she denied to himself.

He had no idea why this should be so, but he determined it should be so no more. He would demand to participate in that which she showered lavishly upon her acquaintances. Before he reached his house, he had determined on his action.

The séance would have commenced, doubtless, and the boudoir door would be locked. But he had a second key to the bedroom, which opened from the boudoir, and he could let himself into the house with his latchkey, without anyone being the wiser for it.

He used the greatest caution as he did so, and crept upstairs without meeting anyone on the way. As he entered the bedroom and turned the key behind him, he heard that the séance in the next apartment, which was in total darkness, had already commenced.

Murmurings of low voices—sundry questions from the sitters—and occasionally a half-stifled sob—told him that his anticipations were correct.

Cautiously approaching the intervening door, which was ajar, Von Steinberg joined the circle, without his entrance being perceived by any one. One lady asked another if she had moved from her seat, and being answered in the negative, declared that the spirits must be walking about the room, but no further notice was taken of his arrival. He stood aloof from the company, and observed all that was taking place.

Hannah had evidently had regular preparations made for this assembly, for a proper cabinet was erected in one corner, and the windows were covered with some black material to exclude every ray ot light.

"How unkind to take all this trouble for mere strangers, and to refuse my making one of the party," thought Karl von Steinberg, sadly, as he stood quietly in his corner. "How could my seeing dear old Ricardo again, do her any harm? If *she* did not love him, she knows that *I* did! This is the worst proof that Hannah has ever given me, of her ingratitude for all I have done for her."

But though his meditations were gloomy, the Baron was yet alive to all that was passing before him. He saw Lady Loreley's little daughter appear between the velvet curtains that formed the cabinet, and heard her mother's grateful thanks for having been accorded such a privilege—he watched Mrs. Maitland embrace the apparition of her brother, who had been lost at sea, and heard her comment on the fact that she could recognise the very clothes he wore.

Hannah's powers had evidently not decreased from want of practice. What a wonderful, marvellous medium she was! All his old astonishment at her powers—and all his old enthusiasm for the occult Sciences, came back to Von Steinberg, as he stood and watched and listened.

There appeared to be no end to the forms that peeped from between the cabinet curtains, or advanced, more bravely, into the centre of the room. Young men and young women—little children and hoary-headed fathers and mothers—even a negro boy, whom the sitters addressed by the name of Cicero, came, grinning from ear to ear, before them. What a gift she possessed! What a power to set her above the ordinary run of women! In that moment, Karl von Steinberg felt proud again to remember that she was his—that no one could take her from him—that Hannah was his wife, and his medium for ever more.

Presently his attention was arrested by a murmur amongst the sitters. A luminous mist appeared at the entrance of the cabinet, and some one whispered, "It is the old man again!"

Karl von Steinberg stretched his neck forward and strained his eyes to see the visitant from the other world. It was undoubtedly the form and face of Ricardo—his familiar features, shrunken and yellow, as they looked in death, appeared before him. Von Steinberg gave a start of surprise—an exclamation of pleasure—and went up to the curtains.

"Ricardo! Ricardo! my dear old friend," he exclaimed, "how delighted—how thankful—I am to see you again!"

"Can you see me? Do you recognise me? Am I like myself?" demanded the apparition.

"Just like! Exactly as I saw you last, dear old fellow!" replied the Baron, warmly. "I have longed to see you again—to hear if you entirely approve of what I have done, since you left us!"

The form held the curtains apart and beckoned to the Baron to accompany it inside the cabinet.

"Do you wish me to go inside there with you?" exclaimed Von Steinberg. "Why, of course I will, dear friend! I consider it an honour that you should ask me."

He passed within the velvet curtains as he spoke, and the sitters questioned each other who he was, and how he had got in there.

"I never saw him when we entered the room," said one lady to another, "I wonder if the Marchesa knows he is here!"

"O! she must! He would not have presumed to come without an invitation. I just caught a glimpse of his features as he entered the cabinet, by the old man's spirit light, and I fancied he was very much like the Baron himself!"

"But I thought the Baron never came to the Marchesa's séances. Does she not say that he disapproves of Spiritualism?"

"Well! I would not be sure—I may be mistaken—but he is a man of much the same build. Why! there is Cicero! But where can the gentleman be? I hope the spirits have not carried him away!"

They proceeded to amuse themselves with Cicero, who was one of those influences who seem sent on this earth simply to prove that they can come, and whilst they were pulling his woolly hair, and putting their fingers into his mouth, to see if he had any teeth, a hollow groan from the cabinet was succeeded by the sudden reappearance of the unknown gentleman, who, passing rapidly through their midst, vanished into the bedroom, and let himself out by the further door. His unaccountable exit left a sort of gloom and distrust behind it, which seemed to have a discouraging effect upon the spirits, for none else appeared that afternoon.

The sitters after waiting for half an hour in silence, resolved that they had better separate, and rising, created a little disturbance, which served to bring the medium to herself. She gave three or four extensive yawns—opened her eyes—closed them again —and finally, leaving her seat, walked out into the assembly, and asked,

"Well! have you had a good séance?"

Everybody was vehement in their assertions that nothing could have been more successful or delightful, until Lady Loreley said,

"Except for one poor gentleman, whom the spirits took into the cabinet, and what they said to him there we do not know, but as soon as he emerged again, he left the room, and has not returned since."

"But *what* gentleman?" asked the Marchesa, "I think all whom I invited are present!"

"We do not know! None of us have seen him before! It was dark when he joined the circle, or I should have said he was the Baron. He was very like him in shape and build!"

"And which Spirit took him into the cabinet?" demanded Hannah, breathlessly.

"O! the old man who has come so often, and asked for the Baron! We have told you about him, dear Marchesa! An old man with grey hair, and piercing eyes, and a pointed beard like Vandyke's. A nice face, he has, but very attenuated. He reminds me of that figure in Madame Tussaud's, of some old man who was starved to death in the Bastille!"

"But what does he say?" said the Marchesa, who seemed strangely agitated.

"O! he has never said anything until this afternoon—only looked round the circle as if in search of somebody, and called 'Karl' once or twice."

"Is the Baron's name, 'Karl', Marchesa? Anyway, the gentleman who joined our circle in the dark to-day, was evidently the person the Spirit was in search of, for directly he appeared, he beckoned to him to approach the cabinet. The stranger called the Spirit, 'Ricardo'—I heard him more than once —and said how glad he was to meet him again, and then the old man drew him into the cabinet and they were talking there for more than ten minutes. Not entirely on pleasant subjects either, I imagine, for we heard the gentleman groan several times, and as soon as he emerged, he went straight through your bedroom, and we have not seen him since. Could it have been the Baron, do you think, Marchesa?"

But the Marchesa stood before her, trembling.

"Yes! yes! no doubt," she contrived at last to utter; "who else could have passed through my bedroom? The Baron has a private key to my apartments. What a fool I was not to think of it!" she added to herself.

"And was 'Ricardo' an old friend of yours?" persisted the lady.

"He was a great friend of the Baron's," replied her hostess, whilst a pallid hue stole over her features; "they often talk together! I am surprised to hear that my husband seemed nervous! He is too well used to spiritualism for that, though, as a rule, he does not approve of it. What could Ricardo have said to him, to overcome him as you say?"

"Ah! that we cannot tell you, dear Marchesa, but if you had heard him groan! I only hope it was not the Baron. But you look quite tired—much more wearied than usual, so perhaps we had better leave you to rest! Good-bye! Such a delightful afternoon!"

Such a delightful afternoon! It looked like it, as Hannah stood in her bedroom free and alone, and reviewed the events of the day. Ricardo and Von Steinberg had met again at last. Notwithstanding her caution and her secrecy, they had met, face to face, and conversed with one another. What had they said?—what revealed?—what had her husband heard about her Past or Present? She stood there, sick with apprehension, until she heard a footstep approach her door, and felt that her hour had come.

CHAPTER XIX.

WHEN Karl von Steinberg rushed from the séance room, it was with the intention of seeking the open air. He felt as if he should be stifled in the atmosphere of his wife's boudoir—as if he could not breathe in that dark and airless chamber, so fraught with treachery, deceit, and crime.

He wanted to get out under God's pure Heaven, to walk miles and miles into the open country, and never go back to Portland Place again. But when he reached the hall door, he encountered a long line of carriages, drawn up in waiting for the aristocratic sitters, and he feared lest the traces of what he was undergoing might be visible on his features, and that he should betray himself before their servants. So he turned back and sought his private sitting-room instead, and sat down there, with his head buried in his hands, and tried to think.

What was this horrible thing that he had listened to?—could it possibly be true? or had he been made the sport of some devil, who had assumed the shape and features of his dear old friend?

But this idea, worthy only of such as have no knowledge of Spiritualism, was soon routed from his mind by reason. He *knew* that it was Ricardo himself, who had spoken to him—Ricardo, with his delicate aquiline features—his piercing eyes, overshadowed by bushy brows—his sensitive mouth, and pointed beard and moustaches.

If a devil could assume his every attribute in the séance chamber, then Von Steinberg might well doubt if the next acquaintance he met in the street were truly himself, or a devil in his guise.

This apparition of his best friend had come again and again (as he had heard on the testimony of strangers), and called his name, that he might confide to him the awful story which was stirring his being to its depths. He had told it to him—not for his own sake, the wrong was over, for him—but lest Von Steinberg should fall into the same net in which he had been caught. But could it—could it—*could it be true?*

Von Steinberg glanced round at the evidences of luxury which surrounded him—the soft Persian carpet—the carved furniture—the valuable paintings—the Venetian glass—and wondered what *more* he could have bestowed upon this woman, whom he first thought of befriending for Ricardo's sake—Ricardo, who she had sent into Eternity!

It was not so much the horror of his friend's

death that oppressed him—those who are convinced that the dead still live, come to look very calmly on the separation, which more ignorant mortals regard with fear—but the contemplated horror of living on with the woman who had betrayed him! *That* he felt to be impossible!

He could never again take Hannah in his arms and call her "wife", whilst the spirit of Ricardo stood between them and hurled another name at her. What should he do? What was to be his next step? How were matters to be arranged for the future? He wished at that moment that he were a medium himself, and had the power to call back the spirit of Ricardo, and ask his advice about it all.

After he had brooded over the terrible affair for some time, Von Steinberg began to question whether, after all, he might not be mistaken, or that Ricardo might have been so! He knew that spirits on their first appearance after death, were often confused and but half conscious—could not remember names or dates—nor recognise those to whom they had been dear! But yet he had never heard of anyone making a mistake on so important a subject as this.

Then, for his own doubts concerning it. He threw his thoughts back to that time, just before Ricardo's death, when Hannah had begun to coquet with him, and he had been foolish and dishonourable enough to meet her advances half-way—to the quarrels she had with her husband—to Ricardo's assurance to him that she made his life a hell, and he could stand it no longer—to his hints about taking his life—to his (Von Steinberg's) cautions to Hannah on the same subject—and then, to his friend's sudden demise, to that awful night when he was called to the Cottage and found the Professor, dead—by his own hand as he then fully thought—and the subsequent decision he had arrived at, partly because he believed it to be a duty on his part.

But now, in a moment, the truth seemed to flash upon him, and he wondered that he had been so blind as not to see it from the beginning. Hannah had been discontented and repining from the time he had come into his uncle's property—she had coveted it—his own folly had encouraged her to think she could gain it—Ricardo was the obstacle, and so——Von Steinberg groaned within himself as he thought these things, and that his dearest friend had paid the forfeit of his own good fortune.

But it must be put an end to at once—his suspicions must be allayed, or turned into certainties—he would not sleep one night under the same roof as Ricardo's murderess—there must be a separation between them, now and for ever.

The house was again quiet, the guests had all departed, and Von Steinberg took his way up to his wife's room. He thought that Hannah knew nothing of what had occurred, so he resolved not to be too violent, but to extract the truth from her by degrees. He found her standing by the side of her sumptuous bed, with its hangings of rich brocade, looking rather white and weary, but with a sparkle of determination in her eye, as if she guessed what was coming and had her weapons ready. Von Steinberg for his part appeared completely crushed—the revelation of the last hour had knocked all his manhood out of him.

"Well!" began Hannah, abruptly, "and what may you want here?"

"I have come expressly to see you, Hannah! I wish to speak to you! Why did you not tell me that you were giving these séances?"

"Because I do not acknowledge that it is any business of yours," she answered carelessly, "they are my own concern altogether!"

"Perhaps! but as I have asked you frequently to give me a sitting, and you have systematically refused, it is strange that you should leave me to hear that you are constantly holding these meetings, from a stranger at my club."

"Yes?" said Hannah, nonchalantly.

"Yes! and I know the reason of your reticence now, into the bargain," replied the Baron angrily. "Are you aware *who* came back through you this afternoon, and held converse with me?—*who* told the story of his death and why he had left this world so suddenly—*who* has asked for me again and again, in order to tell me the truth, but whom you have kept away because you were afraid of what revelations he might make?"

"Not in the least," said Hannah, insolently, though her face had become very fixed during her husband's questions.

"You are lying to me—you *do!*" exclaimed the Baron, "I should have gone on for the rest of my life, poor fool that I am! fancying that you had come to regard the practice of Spiritualism as wrong and harmful, and refraining from asking you to act contrary to your principles, had it not been for the idle tongues of two men in the club this afternoon, who were discussing these séances of yours without knowing that I was within hearing. Though I could hardly believe my ears, I returned home to find they were correct in what they had said—and when I joined your circle, Ricardo came back to me—Ricardo, your late husband and my dearest friend—Ricardo, whom you——"

"Be careful what you say," interposed his wife, "if you make accusations against me, which you have no means of proving, I will have satisfaction from you in a court of law. Professor Ricardo died from the effects of poison, administered by his own hand —that was the certificate of death I believe, written by yourself. What will people say, if you deny it now?"

The Baron was staggered by her coolness and

perspicuity! It was true; he had no proofs to bring forward of his assertion.

"I would believe the word of my dead friend before the evidence of my own senses," he replied, less vehemently. "Ricardo was too good to you during his lifetime to bring a false and unnecessary accusation against you now! I may never be able to prove it, but I am as convinced of the truth as if I had seen it done, and I will never live with you again—so help me God!"

Still Hannah was perfectly unmoved.

"That is of little consequence to me," she answered; "so long as you make me a suitable allowance. But you will be forced to do that! I will not consent to a separation, unless it is legally settled by law!"

Karl von Steinberg gazed at her in silent amazement. Was she bewitched?

"What has come to you in the last few months?" he said, "you are not the same woman that you used to be!"

"How do you know what sort of woman I used to be?" she asked him, quickly.

"I mean, when we first met you—poor Ricardo and I—at Mrs. Battleby's. You were modest and humble then—shy and retiring—you were an amiable, good-humoured girl, only anxious to please and oblige! Now—my God! what a difference!—I should never have known you for Hannah Stubbs!"

"Who is Hannah Stubbs?" demanded the Marchesa.

"Enough of this folly," exclaimed Von Steinberg, angrily, "don't pretend to misunderstand me! You have altered in every respect! I have raised you to a position above that to which you were born, and your head has been unable to stand the elevation. You have become vain, haughty, arrogant, and insolent! Yet I could have borne all that and only cursed my own folly for it, but this crime—no! no! I can never live under the same roof with you again. We part to-night!"

"That is as you please!" cried the Marchesa, shrilly, "it will leave me freer and more independent! I shall have more opportunities of seeing Signor Gueglielmo, and my other friends!"

"No! by my faith you won't!" exclaimed the Baron. "If the man ever enters this house after I am gone, I will drag you and him into the Divorce Court, and let my misery end there!"

"That is to be seen," remarked the Marchesa.

"You defy me!" cried Von Steinberg, "*you*—who murdered my best friend! Yes! we need not mince words here, Madame la Marchesa, the time is past for that! Ricardo told me all—how you purchased the arsenic (which I was fool enough to believe the poor fellow had procured himself)—at the Hampstead chemist's, under the pretence you wanted it for vermin—and how you mixed it with the whiskey and water which you persuaded him to drink because you said *I* had ordered it! You think you are so secure that you can defy and insult me! What if I looked up that chemist and examined his books, and proved the date you bought the poison from him to be that of your husband's death? What then, Madame la Marchesa?"

He had sprung forward as he spoke, and approached her so nearly that the woman felt alarmed, but still her native insolence upheld her.

"What then?" she echoed. "Why! I would force you to declare that you gained your information through Spiritualism, and make you the laughing-stock of London. How would Spiritualistic detectives accord with the English law, Baron von Steinberg, eh?"

"But you would leave the Court with an indelible stain upon your character, and where would your friends be then?"

"I should go to Signor Gueglielmo, and in his beautiful Italy I should soon forget that I had ever inhabited such a cold, gloomy, unsociable country as this!"

"Signor Gueglielmo! You acknowledge he is your lover then?"

"*One* of them!" she replied, shrugging her shoulders.

"Good Heavens! That I should have lived to hear you accuse yourself of such baseness! Are you a woman, or a devil? Are you yourself, Hannah, or does some evil spirit possess you, and obscure the humble virtues you once had?"

"Do you think women are all fools?" she retorted, turning on him fiercely, "are you men to take your pleasures as you will, and we to be debarred from any? Why should I not have lovers. I am young and beautiful."

In saying these words, the Marchesa assumed such a coquettish air, that solemn though the occasion was, Von Steinberg almost laughed.

"And the men admire me! Is all my youth to be wasted in prudery and pretending I do not enjoy that which is the breath of my life—the admiration of the other sex? O! you needn't glare at me like that! You need not attempt to strike me! I am well provided against your assaults! And you are not the only one who has suffered through my being *femme galante!* Sorrento writhed under the knowledge more than you do, and he tried to avenge himself on me, but you see it was useless! He believed me to be a model of all the virtues, to the day of his death—perhaps even now he does the same. But you men are all alike. Fools where you should be wise, and blind where you ought to see! Sorrento smiled when he should have been weeping, and struck when there was no cause. Do you remember the story of Centi?"

"The man for whose sake Leonora deceived poor

Ricardo! Yes! I see now, he was right! You women are all alike! Born to lie and to deceive those who trust in you! He did well to send her out of a world which she disgraced."

At this assertion, Hannah laughed jeeringly.

"O! she was none the worse for it, you may depend! When earthly lives are cut shorter than the Creator intended, either by our own hands, or those of others, they are not ended, though mortals may think so! We all live on this earth just as long as was originally meant for us—neither more nor less—in the flesh or out of it—but still here,— sometimes for our own punishment, sometimes for that of others, but still here,—*here*—where you and I stand to-day. Don't waste your pity on Leonora, for she does not need it!"

"You defend her action—doubtless you sympathise with her crime," said the Baron, sarcastically. "Perhaps you would wish to copy her example, that is, if you have not already done so!"

"You are right," replied the Marchesa, "I sympathise with her deeply. She was young and beautiful and admired, and she loved life, and she hadn't fair play. You think with me, surely, that Sorrento did her a grievous and irreparable wrong, in sending her so abruptly and cruelly from a world she loved!"

"I do not! I think that she was rightly served for her infidelity, and that she paid too little for her crimes. Her husband only took his just revenge.

Such women are better out of the world than in it!"

"So that is your opinion," said the Marchesa, looking him straight in the eyes, "what then of the way he met his own death? Was *that* not a just revenge also? a righteous retribution for the way he treated Leonora? Was I not justified (who met my death at his hands) in sending him also into another world, when it suited my convenience, and he interfered with my plans?"

"You—*you*?" stammered the Baron, falling back a pace or two. A light broke in upon him—a light which seemed to make both the Past and Present clear—which absolved the innocent and condemned the guilty.

"You are *not* Hannah Stubbs!" he exclaimed vehemently, as he sprang towards her, "I see it all now! You are a devil in human form, who has been traducing by your actions, one of the most simple and humble of God's creatures! You are not *Hannah Stubbs*—it is but her carcase that you inhabit! You are Leonora d'Asissi! the false wife of the Marchese di Sorrento!"

The face of the Marchesa seemed to change to that of a fiend as he thus accused her—she drew herself up to her full height—her eyes blazed fury—her arm was raised as if to strike. But she braved the accusation out, returning it in full force upon herself.

"Go on! go on!" she cried, "you cannot say too

much, nor yet enough to harm me! I am all you say, Leonora d'Asissi, the false wife of your dear friend—false to him, not with Centi only, but with everyone who caught my wandering fancy. He believed every word I chose to tell him, poor craven fool! who had the courage to avenge his wrongs, but not to rest satisfied with his victory.

"Yes! I am Leonora d'Asissi, in the ugly, uncouth form of Hannah Stubbs, but I have made her mine, and I will use her to the end—until it pleases me to give her up of my own free will! You may claim this rough body if you choose, but you must take my spirit with it. I will possess it and animate it with my words and graces, and make it copy my faults, and hate as I hated and love as I loved, until it ceases to exist. Have I not shown my power over it already? Who but *I* prompted her to poison Sorrento? to coquette with Gueglielmo? to defy you? to trick? to lie? to deceive? Who but I—I—I? and I will continue to make her follow my will, until she ceases to breathe!"

"You shall not! I defy you in my turn," exclaimed Von Steinberg, "this country girl, uncouth and plain as she may be, is worth a thousand such as you, with all your wit and beauty, and devilish fascinations. She is my wife—I have promised to defend and protect her, and I will drive your hateful spirit from her body, if I have to set hers free, in order to accomplish it? By what right do you cling to a creature, who is so much your superior? In the name of the Holy Trinity, I command you to depart!"

Leonora laughed scornfully.

"And who gave me possession but yourself—you, and your dear friend Ricardo? How could I have obtained such powerful hold of her if you had not used this girl as an instrument to satisfy your curiosity concerning the mysteries of Spiritualism?— if you had not made her sit, night after night, to minister to your pleasure, until her brain and body were both so wearied, that it was an easy matter for me, or any other who had chosen, to oust her spirit and take its place. I obtained first possession and have kept it ever since."

"But to what end? What pleasure could it give you, wretched woman, to add to your list of crimes, all of which you will have to expiate, when you might have been advancing in grace and penitence? What object had you in controlling this unfortunate child, who had never done you a wrong, and making her odious by the execution of your unholy wishes?"

"Because I am no longer able to commit crimes for myself—because the execution gives me a reflected satisfaction—because, above all, my thirst for revenge was ungratified, and I longed to make Sorrento feel the same misery he had inflicted upon me! That is why I returned, not to earth, for I have never left it, but to a human body, and if you wish to know who helped me to it, it was *yourself.* Now! do you understand?"

"Yes! but, by God, you shall persecute my poor wife no longer!" exclaimed Von Steinberg. "She is stupid and ignorant, but she shall not suffer for your crimes. I suspected her of murdering Ricardo—he thinks so even himself—but I will clear her from the imputation. You shall inhabit her body no more, from this time henceforward! It is uncouth, as you said, but it is too pure for such as you. Depart at once, I command you, and come here no more!"

"Command away!" cried Leonora, "it would take more than you to turn me out of my lodging-house! I have got too firm a hold upon your pure and unsophisticated wife! She didn't seem so very pure, whilst she was holding her secret assignations, unknown to you, with Gueglielmo, did she? nor so unsophisticated when she gave séances to attract the aristocracy to her house, and bound them to secrecy because *you* so highly disapproved of such doings. She is a lovely tool, but I wish myself that she were a little more refined. It is so difficult to train her large, flat tongue to lisp the soft Italian syllables, or to play the coquette with those enormous hands of hers and those splay-feet. I have almost made myself a laughing stock sometimes, by forgetting they were not my own, and putting them forth for public admiration.

"But still she is useful, poor Hannah—very useful at times—and I have not the least intention of parting with her—not, at all events, my friend, until you desert her for another woman! Are you not surprised to hear me talk English so well? I learned most of that from you, when you used to come to the Cottage at Hampstead to give me lessons in etiquette, and sometimes in something else, eh, Baron? I don't think your very dear friend Ricardo would have trusted you alone with his adored Leonora, had he known what a dangerous man you were!"

Karl von Steinberg was almost frothing at the mouth with rage that he knew no fit means of expressing. He felt like those unfortunates of whom we have read, who were tied hand and foot, whilst those they loved best were tortured before their eyes, and they had no power to redress their wrongs. He longed to shake Leonora out of Hannah's body, but what force could he use against air? He covered his face with his hands and gave vent to a groan, which seemed to rend his heart-strings. The vicious Spirit reviled his discomfiture with a mocking laugh of confidence.

"That's right! Groan away! That's what all you mortals do, when you have committed the error and there is no remedy for it! Why didn't you think of the consequences, when you made Hannah sit for you and the Professor, till she lost her spirits and her strength and her power to resist? And now you have had enough of me, and would like to send me flying! But you won't! I'm in the body of your lawful wife, and if you don't choose to live with me, you must make me a suitable allowance. I shan't weep, I assure you. I shall much prefer it to your company! Bad taste in me, is it not? but the truth all the same!"

"Allowance! I would give my whole fortune to ensure this poor child being set free from your evil influence. My God! the injury I have done her! How can I know the extent of it, or if it will ever cease? Poor ignorant Hannah! Heaven forgive us for bringing you within the toils of such a devil as this!"

Leonora flaunted by him, and essayed to pass through the open door. But Von Steinberg prevented her. "No! by Heaven!" he cried, "if you will not quit her body, I can at least prevent your dishonouring it! If you *will* stay, you must, but you will remain a prisoner in one room, and no eye shall witness your infamy and my disgrace."

He put forth his hand to detain her, but she rushed past him, to the landing.

CHAPTER XX.

THE landing upon which their sleeping chamber opened, was a spacious platform, covered with a carpet of the softest dyes. It held a couple of settees—a towering palm in a majolica vase—a bronze statue, bearing a lamp—and a stand of flowering plants. Full, rich curtains drawn at the head of the staircase, partially concealed it from the public view, beyond which the marble stairs, supported by carved oak banisters, led down to the hall. It was a nook, fitted to form a boudoir in the warm weather, and was always heated in winter, like the rest of the house, by hot water pipes.

As the Marchesa rushed out upon this landing, the Baron, unable to deter her action, followed as quickly as he could. He was fearful of what she might do, or say. In her state of excitement, which bordered on insanity, she might inform the entire household that she was not the woman she appeared to be, and make them think she was a lunatic.

It was with the best intentions, therefore, that he pursued her.

"Leonora! Leonora!" he cried, "be careful! Come back, I entreat you, and let us argue this matter together."

But the Marchesa ran to the head of the staircase, and defied him.

"What do I care?" she cried, "let them all hear! Let them all come, and I will tell them who *I* am, and what *you* are!"

She gave a kind of shrill cry, half of triumph and half of despair, as she concluded, and Von Steinberg already heard a bustle below stairs, as if the servants had been attracted by the noise and were hastening to the rescue. He advanced to her side and essayed to place his hand upon her mouth. She drew a knife at once from her pocket—he could see the flash of the blade as she grasped it in her hand. The instinct of self-preservation made him push her from him—she retreated towards the stairs and slipped on the yielding carpet, and before he could do anything to save her, the great unwieldy body, unable to recover itself, had rolled with a scream of terror, down to the very hall, where it lay inert and unconscious, crushed into a mass of senseless clay.

As the Baron realised the accident that had occurred, all his resentment was merged in compassion. He forgot the mocking evil spirit that had so lately defied and insulted him, and remembered only that here lay a suffering fellow-creature—a patient to be relieved.

His medical skill rose paramount to every other consideration, and he was at the foot of the stairs almost as soon as she was. Three or four servants appeared upon the scene—all had heard the heavy fall and the scream which had accompanied it. Karl von Steinberg turned the body gently over—it was totally unconscious and the limbs fell limply from it. He could not tell how much or how little she was injured—the first thing to do was to carry her upstairs again to her room—the next to dispatch a servant for the best surgeon in Town, to render his professional assistance.

Meanwhile the body of Hannah lay crumpled up upon the bed, and had not given a single sign of life. She was not dead, so far Von Steinberg was able to ascertain, but if she would ever regain her consciousness, he was unable to say. In a short time, he was joined by the famous surgeon who had fortunately been disengaged, and between them they undressed the poor mangled carcase, and ascertained the amount of injury done to it. It was fearful. One thigh had to be set—two ribs—the left arm—and an ankle. When the operations were completed, Hannah lay like a swathed mummy in her bed, with her body broken in all directions, and still unconscious.

"Will she recover?" demanded her husband, "will she ever speak, or open her eyes again? What is your opinion?"

"It is hard to say, Baron! *You* should know the lady's constitution better than I can. She appears to have a powerful frame, if her physical strength corresponds with it, I should think it probable that she will regain her consciousness by and by—but as to recovery, I really should not like to express an opinion. You see for yourself the maimed condition she is in—all I can say is, that a cure is possible, but not at all probable. How did this sad event occur?"

"We were laughing and playing together on the landing," replied Von Steinberg, unwilling to disclose the real cause of the accident to a stranger, " and the Marchesa went back towards the staircase and overbalanced herself. I made a rush, with the hope of catching her, but I was too late to prevent her falling. It is a terrible height, and she lighted on the marble floor at the bottom, with her head under her. I made sure at first, that she had broken her neck. I was going to add, 'Thank God, it is not so,' but I really do not know which would be worse!"

"No! no! you must not be so despairing as all that!" replied the other, "your wife may recover sufficiently to enjoy her life yet, and if not—at all events you would like to say a few words to her before she leaves you! Now, I will send you a good hospital nurse at once—one quite experienced in these cases—and I shall look in again before nightfall. You are, of course, perfectly competent to look after the case yourself, but we all like to take counsel with our friends on such occasions. For the present then, good-bye!"

He left Von Steinberg sitting by the side of their patient, and he did not stir thence until the nurse arrived. What strange thoughts coursed through his mind, as he held that silent, solitary vigil!

He looked at poor Hannah, bandaged from head to foot, with the deepest compassion. Was this to be the end of it? Was she to pay for the indulgence of other people's curiosity, with her life?

The poor girl looked twice as distasteful in her mutilated condition than heretofore. Her dull, flat face had resumed its normal vacuous expression, whilst the rosy colour had fled from her cheeks, to be replaced by a livid, purplish hue. Her large, coarse hands lay outside the coverlet, and were discoloured and bruised, whilst her beautiful eyes—her sole point of attraction—were closed, and left her rugged features without expression.

Yet in Von Steinberg's sight, she appeared more interesting now than she had done for a long time past. He gently raised her swollen hand and held it between his warm palms. How cold and heavy and sodden it felt, almost as if she were already a corpse. The livid face did not repulse him, as it had done when Leonora's evil spirit animated it! It awoke no feeling in his breast but pity for a young life so spoilt and mis-used for the sake of others. He resolved that if she recovered he would take her away to some place far from London, and the inquisitiveness of strangers, and see if he could not contrive to let her pass the remainder of her life in peace and quietness, as Hannah Stubbs, ignorant and uncouth perhaps, but refreshingly simple and pure, after the experience he had lately had with her.

The time passed on, but the Baron still kept his place by the bedside. The servants came up to announce that his dinner was ready, but he declined to partake of it—the housekeeper begged her master to let her take his place if only for a few minutes, but he shook his head and told her to leave him to himself. The dusk deepened and they offered him lights—he said he preferred to sit in the dark till the nurse arrived. So the door was closed and he remained there by himself, musing sadly on the events of the day.

Suddenly, when he had spent some fifteen or twenty minutes in these reflections, not knowing how time went, he mechanically raised his eyes, and perceived, standing at the foot of the bed, the most beautiful woman he had ever seen. Her unbound hair, black as the raven's wing, fell in thick masses below her waist—her large luminous eyes glowed like two fires—her white arms and hands were stretched towards him—whilst her gaze was wistful and melancholy. He stared at her in return, wondering who she could be, and whence she had come. Gradually, as he was looking at her, and just about to speak, he saw the melancholy look on her face change to a bewitching smile, the eyes sparkled like diamonds, the features assumed an arch expression—she changed from an angel to a devil—*it was Leonora!* Von Steinberg felt murderous—had she been mortal, he would have killed her!

"What are you here for?" he exclaimed. "Have you come to gloat over your cruel work? Get out of my sight, I command you, and never dare to trouble her or me again!"

Leonora gave her mocking smile as answer. The Baron felt in despair. "God Almighty!" he cried, clasping his hands and looking upwards, "deliver me and mine from the power of this mocking devil!"

As he pronounced the words, with all the fervour of which his soul was capable, the Spirit gave a shriek, and flew like lightning down the stairs. The sound was heard all over the house, and the housekeeper appeared again to inquire if her ladyship had stirred.

"No! Mrs. Marston," replied the Baron, sorrowfully, "she lies in exactly the same state. I am beginning to give up all hope!"

"O! don't say that, Baron! Whilst there's life, you know, there's always hope! But who was it, then, that screamed just now?"

"Screamed!" he echoed, "did you hear a scream?"

"Dear me, yes! we all heard it! I quite thought it was her ladyship coming to!"

"And did you meet anybody on the stairs?" asked Von Steinberg, with interest.

"*Meet anybody!* why, no! Baron! they're all of them below, and I have given particular orders that they don't stir, without my permission, lest they should disturb her ladyship. But there's the bell. I shouldn't wonder if that was the nurse! I'll go and see!"

It proved to be the nurse, and Mrs. Marston returned with her to the bedroom. The new-comer regarded her patient in silence. It was not her business to pass an opinion of any kind, but an acute observer might have read from the expression of her eyes, that she had not much hope of a favourable ending to the case. As soon as she had taken over charge, Von Steinberg retired to his own room, leaving strict orders that he was to be called, if there was the slightest change.

His head was confused and dizzy—his heart alternately burning with indignation and sorrow—

he felt as if he was the greatest sinner that had ever breathed.

He could not rest, but spent the evening pacing up and down the room, trying to think of some compensation for the unintentional wrong he had done. The surgeon came at midnight, and pronounced that there was no change in the Marchesa's condition—gave a few directions to the nurse—and promised to visit his patient again on the morrow. Von Steinberg gave another look at the pale, uninteresting face that had almost become dear to him—pressed the lifeless hand—and cautioned the attendant to be sure and call him if necessary.

At about four in the morning, she tapped at his door.

"If you please, Baron, the lady has spoken, and seems to be looking for some one, but I'm afraid she is not yet in her right mind—a little lightheaded, I mean, but you'd better come and see her."

Von Steinberg hurried on his clothes and hastened to Hannah's bedside.

Her eyes were open, and roving round the room in a strange, mystified manner, but when she caught sight of the Baron, she recognised him at once and gave a pitiful smile for welcome.

"Lor! Doctor, 'ave they sent for you? I'm sure I dunno what 'ave come to me, but I feels so bad—as if I was broke all over. Why did you bring me 'ere? Be it a horspital? And do the Professor know? I should like to see the Professor, Doctor, for I feel *that* bad, and 'e was very good to me!"

"Hush, Hannah! Hush! my dear!" said Von Steinberg, quickly, noting the bewildered look of the nurse at hearing a Marchioness talk in so uneducated a manner, "you shall hear everything when you are a little stronger! Yes! you have met with a bad accident, my dear, and I am afraid you will have to remain quiet for a few days, but you will get all right, if you will be patient. Here is your nurse, who will pay you every attention, and make you well as soon as she can, and I am here, too, to look after you!"

Hannah regarded him with the limp, stolid expression which he remembered so well of old, as if she were trying to follow the sense of what he said to her, without the capability of doing so.

"But where's the Professor—my 'usband. you know! I wants to see 'im, 'e may be vexed 'cos I said I would get 'im a nice little supper—tasty, what he likes—and if I don't get back in time, he won't 'ave none."

"Hannah! Ricardo cannot come to you just now! You must believe what I tell you! Nurse! have you any beef-tea ready? Give her a teaspoonful with a little brandy in it. She is growing faint."

"O! I haches all hover!" groaned poor Hannah,

as the weak tears oozed from her eyes with the pain she was enduring, "I shan't be able to get the Professor's meals, not for days and days, and 'e *will* be sorry when 'e ears I'm in the horspital. Was I run over, Doctor? I feels like it! just as if a great cart wheel 'ad gone right hover me, and crushed all my bones! O! it's hagony!"

"I know it must be, poor child, but we are doing all we can to relieve you! Here! drink this!" said Von Steinberg, as he held the broth, into which he had dropped some sedative, to her lips, and stood by her, until she had dropped off into a moaning slumber.

In the morning, after the surgeon's examination, the Baron anticipated his dictum.

"You need not attempt to buoy me up with false hopes," he said, "for I can see the truth for myself. She will not get over it!"

"I fear not! She has a wonderful constitution—the strength of a lion—but there are internal injuries, and mortification has commenced, and a few hours (say twenty-four), must see it terminated. I cannot give you any hope!"

"Thank you for being candid! It is best to know the worst at once! I suppose we may give her anything she can take!"

"Just so, but I should advise the use of soporifics if great pain comes on, as it must, I fear, do!"

The men shook hands, and the Baron returned to

Hannah's side. At all events, he thought, she should not accuse him of inattention now. He found her again awake and restless, with bright feverish eyes and an anxious look on her features.

"Doctor!" she gasped, as soon as he appeared, "I shan't get over this—I feel it! There's a great fire inside of me, and my 'ead keeps going round. I've got my death some'ow, I know. And I must see my pore mother afore I dies!"

"Your *mother*, Hannah!" cried Von Steinberg, aghast.

"O! yes, Doctor, please!" replied the girl, weakly sobbing, "'cos she was very good to me, afore I took up with devils and things. She couldn't abide woices nor shadders, couldn't mother, and I was a bad gal, I feels it now, to go agen 'er! It cut me to the 'eart, when we parted so cruel, and if the Professor 'adn't stood my friend, I dunno what I *should* 'ave done! And Joe too—my young man as was—he turned me off along of the same thing, and I dessay 'e was right, but I loved 'im true, Doctor—I told the Sig-nor so—and I should like to say good-bye to 'im also since I'm a'going!"

"But, Hannah, you must not talk like that! You're in great pain, I know, but we will pull you through yet—see if we don't!"

"No! you won't," replied the girl, shaking her head; "there's a summat in my stummick, as tells me I shan't never walk out of this 'ere bed. And so, if I could see my pore mother once more, Doctor, and—and—my young man, if so be 'e ain't married another yet—it would make me easier than anythink else!"

"Then you shall see them, if it is in my power," said Von Steinberg, as he rose to leave her.

"And the Professor, too, Doctor—my pore old 'usband," added Hannah. "'E'll miss me a bit, won't 'e, cos we was always sich good friends—'e and I,—always sich good friends!" murmured the dying girl, in a faint voice.

Commending her to the care of the nurse, the Baron did what he considered was the last and kindest duty he could perform towards her, and that was to go down with all haste to Settlefield, and if possible bring her people up to London to see her once more.

He used the utmost expedition in accomplishing his errand, but it was some hours before he reached the village, and then it was to find the little cottage in darkness and mourning—Mrs. Stubbs having died the day before.

When the widower heard the errand on which Von Steinberg had come, he expressed a sort of rough regret at his daughter's hopeless condition, but he did not volunteer to accompany him back to Town.

"You see, Sir, it's loike this," he argued, "the missus she would 'ave been very glad to see our Hannah afore she died, but it was not to be, and she lays dead in that theer room, and 'ave lef' me with hall these childer on my 'ands, which I can't leave 'em, not for Hannah, nor no one. You must please to tell 'er with my dooty as it is so, and p'r'aps when she's strong and 'earty agen, she'll remember her pore father and 'ow 'e 'as to work to maintain 'er brothers and sisters, and she rolling in riches, as you may say."

"But she will *never* be strong and hearty again," exclaimed Von Steinberg, impatiently. "I tell you that my poor wife is dying. She cannot last more than four-and-twenty hours!"

"Well! I couldn't go so soon, if I wanted ever so," replied the man. "Theer's my lawful wife a'laying dead in that theer room, and I wouldn't leave the 'ouse whilst she's in it, not for a 'undred darters, be they whom they may!"

"Very well, then, it is of no use my staying here," said the Baron, "but I thought you would have had a little more heart!"

"Our Hannah haven't been sich a perticular good darter to us, Sir, arter all, you know! She wouldn't give up them devils and things, as near broke 'er pore mother's 'eart, and when she was married to rale gentlemen like Mr. Ricardo and yerself, she never come anigh us, nor sent us a word for years—not till she sent them twenty pounds, which I'm sure another little sum like that larst, would come in very convenient just now!"

Karl von Steinberg was too much irritated by his refusal to visit his dying child, to feel very liberally inclined towards the cold-hearted old grumbler just then.

"I cannot stay to hear any more of your troubles now," he said, "for I must return to the side of my poor wife. By and by, perhaps, when I have time to think, I may help you a little, for her sake!"

He tore back to London as quickly as he could, half expecting to find that Hannah had left *him* also, without a last good-bye. But she was still alive, and in less pain—the cruel mortification had done its work—her spirit was holding on to earth by a single thread.

As he entered her room, he found both the nurse and housekeeper there, whilst Hannah was sitting up in bed, notwithstanding her splints and bandages, with a bright look of expectation on her face. He was just about to try and soothe her last moments with some pleasing fiction of her mother coming to her soon, when he was startled by hearing her exclaim, as she stretched out her arms towards the foot of the bed,

"O! mother! mother! I know'd as you'd forgive me at the larst! Ah! it *is* good to see you, mother, arter all these years! But don'tee cry! I shall soon be well again, now you've come to fetch me, and forgive me for them devils and things, and take me 'ome to live along of you!"

The plain face glowed with delighted anticipation—the swollen hands were stretched out with rapture—the eyes, lovely to the last, beamed upon the apparition that stood before her, and the spirit of Hannah Stubbs, with the most gratifying result of all her mediumship, flew into the arms of her waiting mother, whilst her body fell back lifeless on the pillows. She had passed away in total ignorance of all that had befallen her since she had left her mother's care for that of Ricardo—she did not know that she had ever been obsessed by Leonora, or that her hand had committed a murder, or that she had been unfaithful, or insolent, or overbearing! Poor ignorant, innocent Hannah Stubbs! Stupid, plain and uninteresting, as she came from His hand, she returned to her Creator, to be beautified and refined and enlightened, under the process of her Father's love!

THE END.

34, PATERNOSTER ROW,
September 1895.

HUTCHINSON & CO.'S
ANNOUNCEMENTS
FOR THE AUTUMN OF 1895.

A FINE ART WORK.

THE BOOK OF BEAUTY. Late Victorian Era. Containing 40 full-page Photogravure Portraits and many smaller Portraits, by celebrated Artists; also numerous Original Drawings, Sketches, and Writings by talented people. With Autograph Signatures to portraits and contributions.

The PORTRAITS *include—*

The Princess of Wales.	The Duchess of York.
The Duchess of Portland.	The Duchess of Leinster.
The Duchess of Montrose.	Princess Henry of Pless.
The Marchioness of Ormonde.	The Duchess of Sutherland.
The Marchioness of Londonderry.	Georgina, Countess of Dudley.
The Countess of Powis.	The Countess of Yarborough.
Lady Helen Vincent.	Lady Cynthia Graham.

Lady Eden, and others.

Among the ARTISTS *are—*

Sir Frederick Leighton.	Sir J. E. Millais.
Sir E. Burne Jones.	Luke Fildes.
W. B. Richmond.	J. McNeill Whistler.
G. F. Watts.	H. Herkomer.
J. S. Sargent.	Ellis Roberts.

And others.

Original Writings and Sketches by

Rudyard Kipling.	The Marchioness of Granby.
Viscountess Hood.	The Countess of Dundonald.
Princess Henry of Pless.	Lady Ileene Campbell.
Hall Caine.	Lord Houghton.
The Hon. Mrs. Henniker.	Lord Alington.
Sir William Eden.	The Hon. Oliver Northcote.
George Moore.	Mrs. W. H. Grenfell.
Lady Margaret Sackville.	Eric Mackay.
Helen, Lady Forbes.	Mrs. Beerbohm Tree.
Frankfort Moore.	Mr. George Curzon, M.P.

And others.

TO BE PUBLISHED BY SUBSCRIPTION.

In one large Handsome Volume, the portraits printed on India paper and mounted. Edition limited to 200 copies, each copy numbered and signed. Price £5 5s. per copy.

Hutchinson's New Books

MASTER WILBERFORCE. The Story of a Boy. By "RITA." With 30 Illustrations by G. H. EDWARDS.

In crown 8vo, cloth gilt, 5s.

A COMEDY IN SPASMS. Being a New Volume of the Zeit-Geist Library. By the Author of "A Yellow Aster," etc. With Frontispiece and Title-page in colours. The first edition of 10,000 copies was over-subscribed; a second edition immediately sold, and a third edition is nearly exhausted.

In cloth gilt, 2s.; in artistic paper, 1s. 6d.

> "It is a work of art, abounding in brilliant and delicate characterisation, and sparkling with flashes of keen insight into the recesses of the human heart."—DAILY CHRONICLE.

A MAN AND HIS WOMANKIND. Being a New Volume of the Zeit-Geist Library. By NORA VYNNE, Author of "The Blind Artist's Pictures," "Honey of Aloes," etc. With Frontispiece and Title-page in colours. The first edition immediately sold; a second edition now ready.

In cloth gilt, 2s.; in artistic paper, 1s. 6d.

> "This is a brightly-written and clever story; the main idea of it is decidedly out of the common; the conversations are remarkably well managed; the various characters are admirably drawn."—GLASGOW HERALD.

> "The story is refreshingly robust."—SCOTSMAN

for the Autumn, 1895.

THE MIGHTY ATOM. By MARIE CORELLI, Author of "Barabbas," "A Romance of Two Worlds," "Thelma," "Ardath," etc. Being a New Volume of the Zeit-Geist Library. With Frontispiece and Title-page in colours.

In cloth gilt, 2s. ; in artistic paper, 1s. 6d.

THE WALLYPUG OF WHY. By G. E. FARROW. With 18 Full-page Illustrations by HARRY FURNISS and many Illustrations by DOROTHY FURNISS.

In crown 4to, handsomely bound in cloth gilt and gilt edges, 5s.

THE ONE WHO LOOKED ON. A New Story. By F. F. MONTRÉSOR, Author of "Into the Highways and Hedges."

In crown 8vo, cloth gilt, 3s. 6d.

AFTER SEDGEMOOR. Being the History and Adventures of Clement Noel in the days of King James the Second. By EDGAR PICKERING, Author of "In Press-Gang Days," "An Old Time Yarn," etc. With Full-page Illustrations by SIMON HARMON VEDDER.

In crown 8vo, cloth, richly gilt, 3s. 6d.

A DANGEROUS BRUTE. A Sporting Sketch. Being the Story of a Horse. By Mrs. ROBERT JOCELYN, Author of "Run to Ground," "Drawn Blank," etc.

In crown 8vo, cloth gilt, 3s. 6d.

Hutchinson's New Books

WHEN GREEK MEETS GREEK.
A New Novel. By JOSEPH HATTON. With Frontispiece and Cover Design by W. H. MARGETSON.

In crown 8vo, cloth gilt, 6s.

THE CAVALIERS.
A New Historical Romance. By S. R. KEIGHTLEY, LL.D., Author of "The Crimson Sign." With Illustrations by SIMON HARMON VEDDER.

In crown 8vo, cloth gilt, 6s.

THE SILVER FAIRY BOOK.
Fairy Tales of other Lands. By SARAH BERNHARDT, E. P. LARKEN, HORACE MURREIGH, HÉGÉSIPPE MOREAU, QUATRELLES, EMILE DE GIRARDIN, WILHELM HAUF, XAVIER MARMIER, LOUIS DE GRAMONT, etc. With 84 Illustrations by H. R. MILLAR. Uniform with "The Golden Fairy Book."

In crown 4to, silvered cloth and silvered edges, 6s.

A VICTORY WON.
A New Story. By ANNIE S. SWAN. With 12 Full-page Illustrations by RICHARD TOD.

In crown 8vo, cloth gilt, 5s.

THE CALICO PRINTER.
A Novel. By CHARLOTTE FENNELL, a new writer.

In crown 8vo, cloth gilt, 6s.

for the Autumn, 1895.

ARROWS OF SONG. A Volume of up-to-date Poems. By a well-known writer who desires for the present to preserve a strict incognito.

In crown 8vo, cloth gilt, 5s.

LADY LOVAN. A New Novel. By AGNES FARRELL.

In crown 8vo, cloth gilt, 6s.

"*A novel of high literary quality and constructive merit; a true work of genius, rife alike with artistic beauty and with human interest. An unquestionably forcible and fascinating book.*"—DAILY TELEGRAPH.

BARDOSSI'S DAUGHTER. A Florentine Romance. By MARIE HUTCHESON, Author of "Bruno the Conscript," etc.

In crown 8vo, art linen gilt, 6s.

"*The novel is one of the brightest and best of the year. The interests are wholly natural, the situations admirably conceived and skilfully treated, the descriptive passages numerous and beautiful, the character-painting simple and effective.*"—DUNDEE ADVERTISER.

RELIGIOUS & DIDACTIC POETRY. A New Volume of "The Poets and the Poetry of the Century." Edited by ALFRED H. MILES. Containing selections from the poetry of John Keble, J. H. Newman, Stopford Brooke, E. H. Plumptre, S. Baring Gould, S. J. Stone, W. H. How, Richard Wilton, Dr. Alexander, and others, with Biographical and Critical Notices by leading critics.

⁎⁎⁎ This new volume completes the work in 10 volumes.

In fcap. 8vo, cloth gilt, and gilt top, 4s.
In buckram gilt (limited Edition), 6s.
In parchment gilt, complete sets of 10 vols. only (Edition limited to 100 sets), 75s.

Hutchinson's New Books

PHYLLIS OF PHILISTIA. A New Novel. By F. FRANKFORT MOORE, Author of "I Forbid the Banns," "A Gray Eye or So," "They call it Love," etc.

In crown 8vo, cloth gilt, 6s.

THE SCRIPTURE READER OF ST. MARK'S. A Novel. By K. DOUGLAS KING, a new writer.

In crown 8vo, cloth gilt, 3s. 6d.

COURTSHIP BY COMMAND. A Story of Napoleon at Play. By M. M. BLAKE, Author of "The Siege of Norwich Castle," etc., with 6 Full-page Illustrations, Vignette Title-page and Cover Design by the Author.

In crown 8vo, art linen, silver gilt, 3s. 6d.

THE REVOLUTION OF 1848. By IMBERT DE SAINT AMAND, the Author of the "Famous Women of the French Court" Series. Translated by ELIZABETH GILBERT MARTIN. With four Portraits.

In crown 8vo, cloth gilt, and gilt top, 6s.

THE LADIES' PARADISE. By EMILE ZOLA. With a Preface by ERNEST A. VIZETELLY, and Frontispiece by G. H. EDWARDS.

In crown 8vo, richly silvered and gilt cloth, 3s. 6d.

for the Autumn, 1895.

A WOMAN IN IT. A New Novel. By "RITA," Author of "Peg the Rake," etc.

In crown 8vo, cloth gilt, 3s. 6d.

NATURAL HISTORY IN ANECDOTE. Illustrating the Nature, Habits, Manners and Customs of Animals, Birds, Fishes, Reptiles, etc. Arranged and Edited by ALFRED H. MILES, Editor of "One Thousand and One Anecdotes," "The New Standard Elocutionist," etc.

In crown 8vo, cloth gilt, 400 pages, 3s. 6d.

A DEADLY FOE. A Romance of the Northern Seas. By ADELINE SERGEANT, Author of "The Story of a Penitent Soul," etc.

In crown 8vo, cloth gilt, 3s. 6d.

THE DOOMSWOMAN. A Romance of Old California. By GERTRUDE ATHERTON, Author of "A Whirl Asunder," etc.

In crown 8vo, cloth gilt, 3s. 6d.

A PITIFUL PASSION. A New Novel. By ELLA MACMAHON, Author of "A New Note," "A Modern Man," etc.

In crown 8vo, cloth gilt, 6s.

Hutchinson's New Books

THE VILLAGE OF YOUTH. Fairy Tales. By BESSIE HATTON, Author of "Enid Lyle," etc. With about 30 Full-page and other Illustrations and Cover Design, by W. H. MARGETSON.

In crown 4to, cloth gilt, 3s. 6d.

FIFTY-TWO STORIES OF LIFE AND ADVENTURE FOR BOYS. By G. A. HENTY, G. MANVILLE FENN, DAVID KER, and other well-known writers. Being a New Volume of "The Fifty-two Library." Edited by ALFRED H. MILES. With Illustrations.

In large crown 8vo, cloth, richly gilt and gilt edges, 5s.

FIFTY-TWO STORIES OF LIFE AND ADVENTURE FOR GIRLS. By SARAH DOUDNEY and other well-known Writers. Being a New Volume of "The Fifty-two Library." Edited by ALFRED H. MILES. With Illustrations.

In large crown 8vo, cloth, richly gilt and gilt edges, 5s.

FIFTY-TWO STORIES OF THE INDIAN MUTINY AND THE MEN WHO SAVED INDIA. By well-known Writers on India and Indian Life. Edited by ALFRED H. MILES and ARTHUR JOHN PATTLE. Being a New Volume of "The Fifty-two Library." With Illustrations.

In large crown 8vo, cloth, richly gilt and gilt edges. 5s

for the Autumn, 1895.

Hutchinson's Select Novels.
Each in crown 8vo, handsome cloth gilt, 3s. 6d.

NEW VOLUMES.

A SECOND LIFE. By Mrs. ALEXANDER, Author of "The Wooin' o't," "The Heritage of Langdale," etc.

THE MISTRESS OF QUEST. By ADELINE SERGEANT, Author of "The Story of a Penitent Soul," etc.
[*In preparation.*

FIDELIS. By ADA CAMBRIDGE, Author of "A Marriage Ceremony," etc.
[*In preparation.*

OTHER VOLUMES IN THE SERIES.

THE STORY OF AN AFRICAN FARM. By OLIVE SCHREINER. New edition, completing the 83rd Thousand.

THE CUCKOO IN THE NEST. By Mrs. OLIPHANT.

A MARRIAGE CEREMONY. By ADA CAMBRIDGE.

A HOUSE IN BLOOMSBURY. By Mrs. OLIPHANT.

THE TRAGEDY OF IDA NOBLE. By W. CLARK RUSSELL.

THE HERITAGE OF LANGDALE. By Mrs. ALEXANDER.

Hutchinson's New Books

A QUESTION OF FAITH. By L. DOUGALL, Author of "The Zeit-Geist," "Beggars All," etc., with Illustrations by GORDON BROWNE.

In crown 8vo, cloth gilt, 3s. 6d.

A STEPMOTHER'S STRATEGY. A New Story. By EVELYN EVERETT-GREEN. With Full-page Illustrations. By SIMON HARMON VEDDER. Being a New Volume of "The Girls' Golden Library."

In crown 8vo, cloth gilt and gilt edges, 3s. 6d.

A YELLOW ASTER. By "IOTA," Author of "Children of Circumstance," "A Comedy in Spasms," etc. Sixteenth and Cheaper Edition.

In crown 8vo, cloth gilt, 3s. 6d.

"*A Saul has arisen among the fictional prophets. 'A Yellow Aster' is distinctly a work of genius —one of those rare novels of superb quality which compel the iciest criticism to thaw and resolve itself into warm admiration and unqualified praise.*"—DAILY TELEGRAPH.

TEMPEST-TORN. By Lieut.-Colonel ANDREW C. P. HAGGARD, D.S.O., Author of "Dodo and I," "Ada Triscott," etc. Third and cheaper edition.

In crown 8vo, fancy cloth, 3s. 6d.

"*Let me advise you to buy Colonel Haggard's 'Tempest-Torn.' It is a weird and original story, and I feel sure you will like it.*"—TRUTH.

for the Autumn, 1895.

A DAUGHTER OF THE KING. By "ALIEN," Author of "The Majesty of Man," etc. Third and cheaper edition.

In crown 8vo, cloth gilt, 3s. 6d.

"*A fascinating and powerful story, as interesting as it is well-written.*"—CHRISTIAN WORLD.

SIR JULIAN'S WIFE; Or, Hopes and Misgivings. By EMMA JANE WORBOISE. Being a fourteenth and cheap edition of this most popular story, printed from entirely new type.

In crown 8vo, artistic paper, 320 pages, 1s.

A NEW NOTE. A Novel. By ELLA MACMAHON, Author of "A Modern Man," etc. A sixth and cheap edition of this successful novel, forming a New Volume of "Hutchinson's Popular Novels."

In crown 8vo, cloth richly gilt, 2s. 6d.

"*Its merits are far above the average—the characters are admirably drawn, they are living people; the authoress has knowledge of the human heart . . . there is much power in the book.*"—MANCHESTER GUARDIAN.

A STUDY IN PREJUDICES. A Novel. By GEORGE PASTON, Author of "A Modern Amazon," etc. A second and cheaper edition.

In crown 8vo, art linen, gilt, 3s. 6d.

"*The story, naturally conceived, worked out with restraint, and conveying even more by suggestion than is put into words, is of value both as a work of art and as a sane contribution to one of the problems of the hour. It embodies an interesting narrative unfolded to its legitimate conclusion with a good deal of literary skill.*"—THE GLOBE.

Hutchinson's New Books

THE LAND OF THE SPHINX. By G. MONTBARD, Author of "Among the Moors." With 186 Illustrations by the Author. New and cheaper edition.

In demy 4to, richly gilt cloth, 7s. 6d.

DAVID PANNELL. A Novel. By Mrs. ALFRED MARKS, Author of "Masters of the World," "A Great Treason," etc. A Second and Cheaper Edition.

In crown 8vo, art linen, gilt, 3s. 6d.

"*Mrs. Alfred Marks may be congratulated on having given an unusually clever contribution to the novels of the day. Her delineation of character and motive, and the charming setting which she has chosen for them, make 'David Pannell' an eminently readable as well as enjoyable book.*"—GUARDIAN.

PASSION'S PUPPETS. A Third and Cheaper Edition of this successful Novel.

In crown 8vo, cloth gilt, 3s. 6d.

"'*Passion's Puppets,' that singularly forcible and fascinating story. The book is one of which any of our ablest living romancists might be justly and even exultantly proud.*"—DAILY TELEGRAPH.

THE GREEN BAY-TREE. A Tale of To-Day. By W. H. WILKINS and HERBERT VIVIAN. Fourth and cheaper edition of this popular novel.

In crown 8vo, cloth gilt, 3s. 6d.

"*An unusually successful piece of collaboration. It is a brilliant and most amusing book.*"—ATHENÆUM.

for the Autumn, 1895.

New Series of Books of Adventure.

Each volume in crown 8vo, handsome cloth gilt, 3s. 6d. With Illustrations. The Illustrations by STANLEY L. WOOD, HUME NISBET, SIMON HARMON VEDDER, and G. H. EDWARDS.

EUGÉNE VIDOCQ. A Complete New Story. By DICK DONOVAN, Author of "From Clue to Capture," "Found and Fettered," etc.

THE WEB OF THE SPIDER. By H. B. MARRIOTT WATSON, Author of "Marahuna," "Lady Faintheart," etc.

VALDMER THE VIKING. A Romance of the Eleventh Century by Sea and Land. By HUME NISBET, Author of "Bail up," "The Divers," etc.

THE CRIMSON SIGN. A Narrative of the Adventures of Mr. Gervase Orme, sometime Lieutenant in Mountjoy's Regiment of Foot. By S. R. KEIGHTLEY, LL.D., Author of "The Cavaliers," etc.

THE TEMPLE OF DEATH. By WILLIAM MITCHELL.

Hutchinson's New Books

New Series of Books for Boys.

Each in crown 8vo, handsome cloth gilt, bevelled boards and gilt edges, with full-page Illustrations printed on plate paper. Price 5s. each

FROM MIDDY TO ADMIRAL OF THE FLEET. Being the Story of Commodore Anson. By Dr. MACAULAY, Author of "All True," "Stirring Stories of Peace and War," etc.

THE DESERT SHIP. A Story of Adventure by Sea and Land. By J. BLOUNDELLE-BURTON, Author of "The Hispaniola Plate," etc.

FROM POVERTY TO THE PRESIDENCY. Being the Story of General Andrew Jackson. By OLIVER DYER, Author of "Great Senators of the United States," etc.

THE ADVENTURES OF LEONARD VANE. An African Story. By E. J. BOWEN, Author of "An Inca Queen," etc.

FROM PRIVATE TO COLONEL. By WILLIAM MITCHELL, Author of "Harry Brunton," "Wenning Moordyke," etc.

for the Autumn, 1895.

New Series of Books for Girls.

Each in crown 8vo, handsome cloth gilt, bevelled boards and gilt edges, with full-page Illustrations printed on plate paper. Price 5s. each.

GOLDEN GWENDOLYN. By EVELYN EVERETT-GREEN, Author of "My Cousin from Australia," "A Stepmother's Strategy," etc.

THROUGH PAIN TO PEACE. By SARAH DOUDNEY, Author of "Where Two Ways Meet," "A Family Difficulty," etc.

NAMESAKES. By EVELYN EVERETT-GREEN, Author of "Golden Gwendolyn," etc.

FAITH, HOPE, AND CHARITY. By ANNA E. LISLE, Author of "Self and Self-Sacrifice," etc.

GODIVA DURLEIGH. By SARAH DOUDNEY, Author of "A Child of the Precinct," etc.

DARE LORIMER'S HERITAGE. By EVELYN EVERETT-GREEN, Author of "Namesakes," etc.

HOOKS OF STEEL. By HELEN PROTHERO-LEWIS, Author of "A Lady of My Own," "Her Heart's Desire," etc.

Hutchinson's New Books.

AN AIDE-DE-CAMP to NAPOLEON I.
By COUNT PHILIPPE DE SÉGUR. Translated by H. A. PATCHETT MARTIN. New and cheaper edition. With photogravure Portrait.

In demy 8vo, 464 pages, cloth gilt, 6s.

"*The historical interest is undoubtedly great.*"—TIMES.

"*The Count's personal story of adventure is so thrilling, and his opportunities of watching Napoleon so constant and so ably utilised, that this work deserves honourable mention among works which show us history in the making, and the realities as well as the romance of war.*"—DAILY TELEGRAPH.

MILES'S NEW STANDARD ELOCUTIONIST.
Comprising a Treatise on the Vocal Organs by LENNOX BROWNE, F.R.C.S.; a Chapter on Musical Accompaniments by CLIFFORD HARRISON; an Essay on Elocution and a Selection of upwards of 500 pieces from the best Authors by ALFRED H. MILES. Second large edition now ready.

In large crown 8vo, half-bound leather gilt, 640 pages, 3s. 6d.

"*The best all-round book that we have yet seen placed at the service of Elocutionists.*"—SCHOOL BOARD CHRONICLE.

"*In all respects a great advance on any other book of its kind.*"—ALEX. WATSON.

LONDON:
HUTCHINSON & CO.,
34, PATERNOSTER ROW.

CPSIA information can be obtained at www.ICGtesting.com
Printed in the USA
BVOW061606220112

281063BV00005B/1/P